CW01022359

Palgrave Politics of Identity and Citizenship Series

Series Editors: **Varun Uberoi**, Brunel University, UK; **Nasar Meer**, University of Strathclyde, UK; and **Tariq Modood**, University of Bristol, UK

The politics of identity and citizenship has assumed increasing importance as our polities have become significantly more culturally, ethnically and religiously diverse. Different types of scholars, including philosophers, sociologists, political scientists and historians make contributions to this field and this series showcases a variety of innovative contributions to it. Focusing on a range of different countries, and utilizing the insights of different disciplines, the series helps to illuminate an increasingly controversial area of research and titles in it will be of interest to a number of audiences including scholars, students and other interested individuals.

Titles include:

Parveen Akhtar
BRITISH MUSLIM POLITICS
Examining Pakistani Biraderi Networks

Heidi Armbruster and Ulrike Hanna Meinhof (*editors*)
NEGOTIATING MULTICULTURAL EUROPE
Borders, Networks, Neighbourhoods

Peter Balint and Sophie Guérard de Latour
LIBERAL MULTICULTURALISM AND THE FAIR TERMS OF INTEGRATION

Fazila Bhimji
BRITISH ASIAN MUSLIM WOMEN, MULTIPLE SPATIALITIES AND COSMOPOLITANISM

Rosi Braidotti, Bolette Blaagard, Tobijn de Graauw and Eva Midden
TRANSFORMATIONS OF RELIGION AND THE PUBLIC SPHERE
Postsecular Publics

Bridget Byrne
MAKING CITIZENS
Public Rituals, Celebrations and Contestations of Citizenship

Jan Dobbernack
THE POLITICS OF SOCIAL COHESION IN GERMANY, FRANCE
AND THE UNITED KINGDOM

Jan Dobbernack, Tariq Modood (*editors*)
TOLERANCE, INTOLERANCE AND RESPECT
Hard to Accept?

Romain Garbaye and Pauline Schnapper (*editors*)
THE POLITICS OF ETHNIC DIVERSITY IN THE BRITISH ISLES

Nisha Kapoor, Virinder Kalra and James Rhodes (*editors*)
THE STATE OF RACE

Peter Kivisto and Östen Wahlbeck (*editors*)
DEBATING MULTICULTURALISM IN THE NORDIC WELFARE STATES

Dina Kiwan (*editor*)
NATURALIZATION POLICIES, EDUCATION AND CITIZENSHIP
Multicultural and Multi-Nation Societies in International Perspective

---

Palgrave Politics of Identity and Citizenship Series
Series Standing Order ISBN 978–0–230–24901–1 (hardback)
(*outside North America only*)

You can receive future titles in this series as they are published by placing a standing order. Please contact your bookseller or, in case of difficulty, write to us at the address below with your name and address, the title of the series and the ISBN quoted above.

Customer Services Department, Macmillan Distribution Ltd, Houndmills, Basingstoke, Hampshire RG21 6XS, England

Identity and Political Participation Among Young British Muslims

Believing and Belonging

Asma Mustafa

Senior Research Fellow in the Study of Muslims in Britain, Oxford Centre for Islamic Studies and Linacre College, University of Oxford, UK

Foreword by

Anthony Heath

CBE, FBA, University of Oxford, UK

© Asma Mustafa 2015
Foreword © Anthony Heath 2015

All rights reserved. No reproduction, copy or transmission of this publication may be made without written permission.

No portion of this publication may be reproduced, copied or transmitted save with written permission or in accordance with the provisions of the Copyright, Designs and Patents Act 1988, or under the terms of any licence permitting limited copying issued by the Copyright Licensing Agency, Saffron House, 6–10 Kirby Street, London EC1N 8TS.

Any person who does any unauthorized act in relation to this publication may be liable to criminal prosecution and civil claims for damages.

The author has asserted her right to be identified as the author of this work in accordance with the Copyright, Designs and Patents Act 1988.

First published 2015 by
PALGRAVE MACMILLAN

Palgrave Macmillan in the UK is an imprint of Macmillan Publishers Limited, registered in England, company number 785998, of Houndmills, Basingstoke, Hampshire RG21 6XS.

Palgrave Macmillan in the US is a division of St Martin's Press LLC, 175 Fifth Avenue, New York, NY 10010.

Palgrave Macmillan is the global academic imprint of the above companies and has companies and representatives throughout the world.

Palgrave® and Macmillan® are registered trademarks in the United States, the United Kingdom, Europe and other countries.

ISBN 978–1–137–30252–6

This book is printed on paper suitable for recycling and made from fully managed and sustained forest sources. Logging, pulping and manufacturing processes are expected to conform to the environmental regulations of the country of origin.

A catalogue record for this book is available from the British Library.

Library of Congress Cataloging-in-Publication Data
Mustafa, Asma, 1980–
    Identity and political participation among young British Muslims : believing and belonging / Asma Mustafa, Research Fellow in the Study of Muslims in Britain and Senior Tutor and Senior Research Fellow, Oxford Centre for Islamic Studies and Linacre College, University of Oxford, UK ; foreword by Anthony Heath, CBE, FBA, University of Oxford, UK.
    pages cm
    ISBN 978–1–137–30252–6
    1. Muslim youth—Political activity—Great Britain. 2. Identity (Psychology)—Great Britain—Religious aspects—Islam. 3. Muslims—Political activity—Great Britain. 4. Muslims—Great Britain—Social conditions. 5. Multiculturalism—Great Britain. I. Title.
    HQ799.G7M873 2015
    305.6′970941—dc23   2014030379

Dedicated to my children, with love

Contents

Illustrations

Figures

Table

Foreword

The integration of migrants and their children is one of the most top-ical and contentious concerns in contemporary Western society and is likely to remain so for some years as demographic change will inevitably lead to an even more diverse society. However much some politicians (and their supporters) talk about reducing immigration, we cannot turn the clock back even if we wanted to. There is a growing proportion of young British-born citizens from diverse ethnic and religious back-grounds (although by no means as high a proportion as in some other Western countries), especially in our major metropolitan areas. Their futures will form a major part of the continuing story of Britain.

We have a moral responsibility towards the future of these young people – many are here because the British government and employers actively wanted their parents or grandparents to come and work in the expanding post-war economy, or had recruited their forebears for service in the British military. Others came as refugees, often following the tur-moil of British withdrawal from its imperial possessions and the conflicts in the newly independent countries of South Asia and East Africa where Britain had not perhaps managed the transition to self-government as well as it might have done. More recently our interventions, however well intentioned, in the Middle East and Afghanistan have led to new waves of refugees.

Apart from the powerful moral case for working for the successful inte-gration of Britain's minority populations, I would argue that diversity is a potential source of creativity and social progress, bringing bene-fits to the wider society as well as to the migrants and their children. The world's most diverse societies such as Australia, Canada and the USA are also some of the most impressive for their dynamism and social cohesion. While we cannot be sure of cause and effect, levels of diver-sity much higher than the current British level appear to be entirely compatible with maintaining a rich and stable society.

But it would be foolish to deny that rapid social change – whether it is demographic change resulting from immigration or the collapse of mining and manufacturing industries during the de-industrialisation of the 1980s – brings challenges for society. There will be economic losers as well as winners. And it takes time, both for the migrants and for established members of the British majority group, to adjust to the new conditions and character of British society. So there will inevitably be some frictions or tensions, just as there were at the time of earlier migrations of Jewish refugees or Irish workers escaping economic hardship.

A great deal of the quantitative survey-based work that has been carried out on minority and majority populations suggests that adaptation and integration follows either a life-course or generational pattern. (See for example the articles in the special issue of *Ethnic and Racial Studies* (2014) on generational change.) In particular we find that younger generations of white British citizens, who have grown up in a multicultural society, feel less prejudiced or xenophobic than older generations, who grew up and developed their attitudes and expectations about life in Britain at a time when migration from Commonwealth or European countries (other than Ireland) was still relatively rare. Similarly we find that recent arrivals from abroad, whether from Africa or Asia, are less likely to speak English, to have British friends, to have British citizenship or to think of themselves as British than migrants or their children who have lived in Britain for longer. It can hardly be surprising if recent arrivals are not especially 'integrated' in the sense of speaking English, having a British identity or engaging in British civic and political life. Much more concerning, from a policy point of view, would be a failure of integration on the part of the 'second generation' – that is, of the children of the migrants.

In this important book Dr Mustafa focuses on the identities, experiences and political repertoire and engagement of young second-generation British Muslims. As we have argued elsewhere (Heath and Demireva, 2014), a focus on the second generation is critical for a proper understanding of the dynamics of integration and possible future scenarios. And a focus on Muslims is timely since they have become one of the largest faith communities in Britain and are often seen, rightly or wrongly, by some Western commentators as having values and interests which may be unusually difficult to accommodate within a Western European and notionally Christian context.

Dr Mustafa's work complements the usual quantitative survey-based research that my colleagues and I have conducted with in-depth qualitative work which allows young people to speak for themselves, in their own words. This kind of research adds a more fine-grained and more dynamic analysis than the snapshot which our typical survey provides. Perhaps most importantly it brings out the diversity of Muslims' experiences, views and reactions to life in Britain. The typical move in survey research is to show that, on average, British Muslims are more likely to practise their faith and to have a strong religious identity than do British Christians. But a focus on average differences between Muslims and Christians runs the risk of 'essentialising' both Muslims and Christians, treating them as immutable and homogeneous communities. As Dr Mustafa skilfully brings out, however, young British Muslims are far from a homogeneous group and there are crucial variations in their strengths of religious and national identities, their orientations towards British society and their modes of political engagement. A key emphasis in her research is on the differences between four different sorts of young Muslim – those who downplay their Muslim identification and retain simply a symbolic ethno-religious identity; those with a cosmopolitan, internationalist and multicultural identity; those with a dual identity, thinking of themselves as British Muslims (the largest single group); and finally a small group who prioritise their Muslim identity and for whom a British identity is at best secondary and purely pragmatic, with little emotional attachment to Britain.

I would add that similar distinctions could almost certainly be found within other faith communities such as Jewish, Sikh and Christian communities. We need to recognise that there is diversity within the overall religious diversity of British society. Understanding this diversity within the broad Muslim community is central for informed policy-making, just as understanding the diversity within Christian and agnostic populations of Britain is also crucial for understanding that there is not one single set of British values or British way of life to which Muslims or other faith communities might wish or be expected to adapt. Simple stereotypes about either Muslims or about Britain are not a helpful way of thinking or policy-making.

Once one has understood the diversity within all our faith communities, it is a natural second step to attempt to understand the variety of processes which are implicated. The varied experiences people have in their encounters with other members of society, and the messages they hear from politicians or the media, will be important in influencing whether some of these four groups increase or shrink in size. (And similarly, encounters and experiences of other British citizens with their Muslim compatriots will have reciprocal consequences too for patterns and profiles of sympathy and social distance.)

Their experiences of life in Britain will also shape the patterns of political engagement of these young British Muslims. Feelings of frustration, anger and discontent, often about the way in which one's identity group is unfairly treated or marginalised, are powerful stimuli for engaging in a range of political activities, broadly defined – consumer boycotts or non-violent demonstrations, for example, although also conventional electoral participation and campaigning for mainstream political parties. This is, I suspect, the same kind of political repertoire as we would find among other young British citizens, but what may be more distinctive among young Muslims is the feeling that they belong to groups who are at one and the same time unfairly treated and have little chance of securing effective redress through conventional channels. These are by no means always complaints about political opportunities in Britain: the situation of Palestinians in the Middle East and their perceived inability to make progress through conventional diplomacy worries young Muslims too as members of the world-wide ummah of the faithful. What comes out particularly strongly from Dr Mustafa's interviews is the sense that young Muslims' concerns are not narrowly selfish 'pocket-book' concerns but instead derive from subjective identification with a wider community and are in that sense altruistic. Similarly, much of their political action has to be seen as expressive rather than instrumental; it is intended to signal their concerns to political authorities who too often seem not to be listening.

It is also important to understand, as Dr Mustafa again clearly demonstrates, the dynamic nature of these processes. Whether we like it or not, British communities of all faiths or none are experiencing processes of continual change, sometimes faster, sometimes slower (though we probably wrongly tend to see current changes as proceeding faster and past changes as proceeding slower). As Tancredi says in *The Leopard*, 'If we want things to stay as they are, things will have to change.'

The challenge, however, is to work out what aspects of British society one wants to stay as they are, and what things will have to be changed in order to achieve this. British traditions of tolerance, open-mindedness and a pragmatic willingness to compromise are some of the things I would wish to preserve, while the 'othering' and negative stereotyping of Muslims (and of other non-Christian faith groups) will need to be changed. Readers of Dr Mustafa's book will find a rich and suggestive account, which I trust will lead us to think more deeply about how best to overcome the challenges and take advantage of the opportunities which increasing diversity is bound to entail.

Professor Anthony Heath CBE, FBA
Department of Sociology, University of Oxford
Emeritus Professor of Sociology, Emeritus Fellow of Nuffield College

Acknowledgements

Over the years, I have received generous support which made possible the preparation of this book. I am grateful to the Oxford Centre for Islamic Studies (OCIS) for offering me my first academic post as Research Fellow, which gave me the opportunity to complete this book.

I am deeply indebted to Professor Anthony Heath, CBE, whose unwavering support and guidance have been invaluable. His patience and commitment were reassuring throughout the many years of academic development and achievement. I also owe a debt of gratitude to Dr Mohammed Talib from the Department of Anthropology at the University of Oxford, and OCIS, for his auspices and advice over the years.

The development of this book has been aided by numerous people. Special thanks to Professor Tariq Modood for engaging with this proposal from the start, and for his enduring academic support. I would also like to thank the illustrator Arub Saqib who took my thoughts and words and turned them into such beautiful images for this book.

This research would not have been possible without the help of the many friends and well-wishers who assisted in approaching respondents. To the interviewees themselves (who, though remaining anonymous, know who they are) I am inordinately appreciative. I hope the material you have provided will shed a wondrous light upon being young, British and Muslim for years to come.

I must dedicate this book to the people in my life who have been with me from the start, during the late nights, fieldwork away from home and numerous meetings. To those who have financially, emotionally and academically supported me throughout, without whom this book would be but a dream. To my dearest parents, Basil and Najwa; to my loving siblings Bara, Maysa and Rashed; and to my treasured husband, Mohanned, whose guidance and support has been invaluable – and with whom this long path was steadily walked.

Abbreviations and Acronyms

Engage	Campaign group for Muslim political participation (since become MEND)
FOSIS	Federation of Student Islamic Societies
Himmat	Himmat project, more information: http://www.himmat.org/
HMC	Halal Monitoring Committee
HT	Hizb ut Tahrir
ISB	Islamic Society of Britain
MAB	Muslim Association of Britain
MCB	Muslim Council of Britain
MPac	Muslim Public Affairs Committee
MYH	Muslim Youth Helpline
OCIS	Oxford Centre for Islamic Studies
PET	Preventing Extremism Together
PRC	Palestinian Return Centre
UKIM	UK Islamic Mission

Glossary

Abaya	Ankle-length cloak or dress, usually black and single piece.
Abid	Servant or worshipper.
Allah	God.
Ayah	Sign or miracle. Verse of the Quran.
Deobandi	Individual who follows the Deoband Islamic movement.
Eid	Islamic festival.
Fast	Abstaining from food, liquids usually during Ramadan.
Fatwa	Islamic religious ruling or legal opinion by an Islamic scholar.
Fiqh	Knowledge and explanation of Islam through its laws.
Hadith	Traditions of the Prophet Muhammad.
Hajj	Pilgrimage to Mecca in Saudi Arabia (Pillar of Islam).
Halal	Permitted/sanctioned in Islam.
Hanafi	One of the four schools of Islamic law, founded by Abu Hanifa.
Haram	Prohibited or unlawful within Islam.
Hijab	Headscarf.
Hijabi	Female who wears a headscarf.
Hokum	Religious juristic ruling.
Imam	Religious leader, leads prayer in mosque.
Inshallah	God willing.
Jihad	Struggle.
Jilbab	Long ankle-length cloak or dress.
Jummuah	Friday. Usually referring to Friday prayers.
Khalifa	Successor. Leader of Muslim ummah.
Khilafah	The caliphate system – leadership system of Muslim nation (ummah).
Masjid	Mosque.
Mosque	Muslim place of worship.
Mujahid	Fighter for Islam.
Munkar	Wrongdoing.
Nafs	Soul or self.
Nasheed	Religious songs or music.
Niqab	Female veil usually covering the face (or partly covering).

PBUH	'Peace be upon him', said after 'Prophet Muhammad'.
Quran	Islam's holy book.
Ramadan	Muslim month of fasting (Pillar of Islam).
Salah	Prayer (Pillar of Islam).
Salwar kameez	Ethnic long shirt and trousers.
Sharia	Islamic law.
Shaytan	Devil.
Sufi	Muslim mystical order.
Sunnah	The practice and example of the Prophet Muhammad.
Sura	Chapter in Quran.
SWT	Subhanahu Wa Ta'ala ('Pure is He and He is exalted').
Tablighi Jamaat	Religious movement for spreading Islam, founded in India.
Ummah	Global Muslim community.
Zakat	Alms-giving (Pillar of Islam).

Introduction

There are international events that have such a resounding impact on people's lives that imagining a world in which they had not occurred would be difficult. For many Muslims, that 'moment' was the 9/11 terrorist attacks. There has been considerable pressure placed on Muslims since then – through media coverage, local and national government policies, regulations regarding security and laws preventing extremism.

The young Muslims in this book have experienced constant scrutiny of their identity. The focus on 'belonging', citizenship and identity has intensified as a result of actions such as the 7/7 London bombings, wars and conflicts (Iraq, Afghanistan and Israel/Palestine among others), and the attention given to the issue by policy-makers, think tanks and government initiatives (e.g. CONTEST strategy and PET – Preventing Extremism Together). This pressure on young Muslims is exacerbated by the results of opinion polls and surveys, the banning and burning of religious clothing and other symbols (hijabs, face coverings, mosques and Qurans) and the experiences of discrimination, Islamophobia and prejudice. These incidents, events and actions have been ongoing for over a decade, and have shaped the mindset of young Muslims who have lived through these experiences.

The critical focus on Islam and Muslim identity is perceived as a threat to one's deepest identity and to one's belief. When people feel pressured, inspected, judged and targeted, it potentially breeds dissatisfaction, frustration, perceived inequality and double standards. When it is asked why young second-, third- or further-generation Muslims identify so strongly with their religion, it could be argued that their perceived alienation from being 'British', 'European' or 'American' is pushing them further towards the only group identity they are familiar and comfortable with – their religious one.

Identity is a delicate, fluctuating and fluid concept. If we want to understand what makes religion a salient 'political' identity for these

1

young Muslims (over any other identity), then we must explore and understand how they identify themselves and how they perceive their surroundings. Muslim identities are not unified and singular; there is richness in the narratives of difference and diversity, even among the young. If identity is actively moulded and redefined, then the experiences, thoughts and feelings of these young Muslims must be understood in essence before exploring how and why this identity impacts their political world.

While race, ethnicity and political participation have been heavily linked in literature on migrant communities (Dawson, 1995; Saggar, 2000; Hechter, 2005), religion has until recently been given less attention. So it is vital that questions are posed – does the identity of young Muslims impact on political issues, concerns and action? Does a global identification with ummah (a worldwide religious community) manifest itself in global transnational political activity?

> Not only have British ethnic minorities not united under a single identity capable of mobilising them all, but the number of identities that generate intensity of commitment and community mobilisation grows all the time . . . These identities are pragmatic moves, and they all define the field in which the moves are made. And yet all this leaves unanswered the question, why is it that ethnic (i.e. regional and national origins) and religious identities have come to be politically prominent among south Asians in Britain instead of other group identities, most notably, a colour-based identity?
>
> (Modood, 2005: 158)

Through exploring concepts of identity(ies) and their relationship to the political sphere, one can eventually gain an insight into integration. Political engagement is a significant method of gauging integration and belonging; it is a key means for minority ethnic and religious groups to express their preferred choices and to attempt to lobby to achieve them. Political participation is also important to religious minority groups because of government authority over legal frameworks. These laws may infringe on the right to practise one's chosen religion or culture, as has been seen in France owing to the ban on religious insignia.

This book tackles unanswered questions about British Muslims and political participation: Can blogging be considered as a political activity and how is music related to political engagement? Do young Muslims advocate political violence as depicted by the media? Do those who do not vote fail to do so because they feel less British, or because they are doubtful of the electoral system? Do British Muslims donate to political parties? Do they canvass for political campaigns? Does anyone view political graffiti favourably? Can flag burning ever be justified? These are some of the varied questions which are answered in the following chapters, providing a fascinating insight into the political participation of young British Muslims.

It is important to highlight at this point that the political engagement referred to during this book is not limited to the electoral field, as electoral activities alone do not define political engagement. Quantitative large-scale studies that confine their participatory definition to electoral activities are ignoring a large part of the social picture. Other forms of political participation should not be undervalued, since the conventional methods of participation may be inefficient, ineffective or inappropriate for certain citizens. It may also be that new forms of political activity go undetected if only conventional and traditional formats of political action are analysed, thus affecting participation rates (White et al., 2000; O'Toole, 2003).

Aside from discussions relating to political participation, this book also delves into questions of citizenship. Citizenship and civic engagement are terms that are difficult to concisely define owing to their breadth. In brief, civic engagement is the estimated needs of the political community and one's active participation within it to fulfil those needs. Because it is linked to the political arena and citizenship, the premise of this book is highly relevant to the debates that recurrently flare up across Europe and North America about multiculturalism, integration and belonging and/or difference. Debates over assimilation versus integration are ongoing both in academic literature as well as in the policy arena. Some argue that ethnicity and religious identity weaken through the generations; but other research has highlighted that this is not necessarily the case. If we take a look at North American examples, the future of Muslim group identity could follow a 'symbolic' route as described in the work of Waters (1990). For young Muslims in the West, religious practice and identity may become 'optional' – some practices are retained and cherished, while others are allowed to wither away – as in the example of American white second- and third-generation migrants, who assimilated through the generations.

Similar to the experience of African Americans, where politics and race are inextricably linked (Dawson, 1995), Muslims may choose religious group identity over other identity facets – cutting across ethnic and class divisions. Just as race was regarded as the uniting factor for African American politics before the 1960s, and is significant in African

American politics today, religion may potentially play an influencing role in the political participation of British Muslims.

> [the Fourth National Survey] found that minority ethnic individuals, including those born and raised in Britain, strongly associated with their ethnic and family origins; there was very little erosion of group identification down the generations.
>
> (Modood, 2005: 194)

Statistically, Muslims belong to the second largest faith group in Britain, numbering 2.7 million according to the 2011 census. Muslims have the youngest age structure – over 50 per cent are under the age of 24. Nearly 45 per cent of British Muslims are born in the UK and thus constitute the second or third generation. Research on Muslims has been conducted on such diverse aspects of life as housing, employment and education (Sarwar, 1991; Modood et al., 1997; Sellick, 2004; Abbas, 2005). However, little research exists regarding Muslims and the wider political sphere, especially concerning the role that identity and belonging play in influencing political engagement.

It is important to study the second generation because they can relay much more to us about integration and cultural transmission than the first generation. It is with research based on the second generation that we can understand and prepare targeted social and public policies for the coming minority ethnic and religious generations. Research on the second generation is also vital in understanding cultural transmission. This is because members of the second generation gain a sense of cultural identity from their parents, as well as being socialised in the wider context (through schools, social media, sports clubs, etc.). The second generation explore and respond to both their context and their socialisation, and make choices based on their perceptions and experiences.

This book is concerned with hearing the voices of young British Muslims, discussing the intricacies of identity, local community and their place in society. It explores how these individuals understand their place in both British society and the wider world; it examines the debates on the nature of citizenship and belonging, on what engaging politically means to them, and asks how young British Muslims are politically engaged and to what degree their engagement is focused on ethnic, national or religious issues.

The research and fieldwork contained in this book are based on doctoral research conducted at the University of Oxford, using qualitative methods. Qualitative methodology was chosen because the research objectives required vivid descriptions of individual attitudes, values and motivations, and most importantly the accounts given by actors of their actions and motivations. A key concern during the fieldwork was how to elicit responses from participants discussing intricate and intimate issues, especially when articulating views relating to identity and discussing methods of political engagement. During these engaging semi-structured interviews, a variety of creative sub-methods were incorporated in order to gather credible material. These innovative methods included auto-photography and word sorts to elicit concepts of identity, and photographic vignettes to capture concepts of political action.

During this research, auto-photography (Ziller and Lewis, 1981) was a tool used to assist respondents in discussing their self-identity. Auto-photography allowed respondents to take photographs which they then used during the interview to explain their identity (see Figure 2.1 for examples). The procedure of generating images in response to the question 'who am I?' means that respondents may highlight a number of topics or material items in their surrounding environment and then discuss them, something they may not otherwise have considered during static time-frame and a verbal conversation. Some respondents refused the offer and came to the interview without photographs. The respondents who accepted the offer were asked to take photographs relating to their identity, and after processing, these were used at the start of the interview to examine their self-perception and to explore the respondent's reaction. Twelve participants took part in the auto-photography and four took digital photographs. Aside from those 12, four other participants 'forgot' to take photographs though cameras were posted and received (16 respondents could potentially have participated in the auto-photography method). Most of the photographic images were very personal to the respondents, and at times they felt passionate about the subject matter. Some participants loved a musical instrument and felt it explained who they were, while some felt impassioned about a geographical location such as Sparkbrook or East London. The creativity of the exercise also made them feel like part of the proceedings: they took an active rather than a secondary role in the interview.

In the scenario that occurred, some participants would not or could not take part in the auto-photography method described above. This left them exploring and expressing issues regarding their identity without an aid – and some participants found it challenging to express verbally how they felt. As the interviewer, it was difficult to ask questions without leading participant answers. This problem needed a solution, which was found in the word sorts. Word sorts are small rectangular laminated cards with words on them that may or may not relate to identity (such as 'Britain', 'foreigner', 'gender', 'eyes'). They included words that have little relation to ethnic, national and religious identity. The words chosen by no means covered all that could possible relate to national, ethnic and religious identity, but they at least assisted in eliciting identity-based respondent descriptions. Respondents were also given the opportunity to discuss as many other ideas regarding identity as they wished that they felt had not touched upon during the segment of the interview.

Vignettes are short scenarios in either written or pictorial form, which are concrete examples of people or their behaviours, on which participants can offer comment or an opinion. Vignettes allow participants to define the situation in their own terms and explore how they would react, or have reacted, and why. Pictorial vignettes were used in this research in the form of photographs in order to explore political actions, with the intention of extracting a response from the participants regarding that action. Respondents were asked whether they considered the act in the photograph to be a 'political action', why, and whether they have participated in a similar action. The reason behind the use of this method was essentially that verbal questioning was loaded and could be dangerously leading. In asking a participant, 'Have you participated in flag burning' or 'What are your opinions on flag burning', I felt that the question in itself caused the respondent to be on guard, on the offensive; whereas a photograph of a group of men burning a flag presented a more neutral setting in which to express a viewpoint: the opinion regarding the action is aimed at the group in the photograph. Participants were able to express opinions such as 'that's criminal' or 'I can see why they would do that', which was then followed up with further questioning and probing, easing the way for follow-up questions.

The empirical research on young British Muslims was conducted across Britain. The main method of conducting the research was via semi-structured interviews with 67 young British Muslims aged between 16 and 35. The participants came from a variety of ethnic backgrounds. The sample was collected via snowball and then purposive sampling methods. The fieldwork took approximately 24 months to complete, in varying stages (January 2006–October 2007; June–July 2009).

Measuring the religiousness of young Muslims was not the intention of this research. Variation in the sample regarding religiosity was, however, a key consideration. Some respondents practised the five tenets or pillars of Islam (belief in one God; prayer five times daily; fasting during Ramadan; performing hajj once in a lifetime; giving *zakat* [alms]), while others stated that though they consider themselves 'Muslim', they follow little of the religious laws, doctrines and practices. I used a broad definition of 'Muslim', allowing respondents to fill in the gaps (see Figure 0.1).

In an effort to place the British material in an international context, the later chapters subtly compare similar research conducted on Muslims living elsewhere in the West. The political participation of American Muslims as well as those living in Europe will be explored throughout the political participation analysis in order to understand the similarities and differences.

This book begins with a background chapter on British Muslims. It describes the context in which second-generation British Muslims have been socialised and in which their identities have developed. The aim is to provide an introduction to the political environment within which Muslims are being brought up today. The chapter covers the demographic profile of British Muslims, both electoral and non-electoral patterns of engagement, as well as descriptions of transnational political participation. This sets the scene for the research.

Chapter 2 provides a theoretical foundation regarding identity, which can be reflected upon and reviewed in light of the fieldwork data. Chapter 3 illuminates how identity features in the lives of the young second-generation British Muslim respondents, presenting a four-group typology. This four-group typology assists in setting a framework within which the political motivations of the respondents can be explored.

Chapter 4 uses the typology-based identity framework to understand motivations for political participation. It explores how the respondents make certain decisions regarding political action, and uncovers the relationship between identity facets and political motivation.

Chapter 5 explores the theoretical and factual background of political engagement, drawing a comparison for the succeeding chapters (6–8) that follows the political engagement of the respondents – the extent to which they are participating in a form of political activity. These chapters also underline what the respondents consider to be political in nature, why, and whether these actions are effective or ineffective; which activities are considered borderline or contextual political activities; and finally, which political actions are deemed unpopular from their perspective, and why.

Finally, the conclusion wraps up the findings from the previous chapters. It argues that the focus on religion and religious identity from policy-makers and media outlets means that being Muslim is never far from the respondents' minds, and identifies many of these youths, whether because they wear hijab, sport beards or because their names are Mohammed or Aisha.

8

Noora

Non practicing Muslim female. She drinks alcohol and has boyfriends. Describes her views as liberal, though comes from a practicing Muslim family.

Iman & Leyan

*Iman comes from a non-practicing Muslim family and became 'Muslim aware' during her Master's degree.
Leyan is an English convert. She wears a headscarf and is fully covered in modern non-ethnic clothing.*

Tuqa

Parents expect Tuqa to wear the shalwar kameez at home, cook ethnic food and speak in their local dialect. In public, she works as a professional, speaks English and wear non-ethnic clothes.

Mekki

Grew up studying in a British Madrasah, studies A-Levels and GCSEs at the same time as Islamic subjects and memorizing Quran.

Tahir

Taxi driver from a Tabligh-i-Jamaat background.

Sameer

University student, also a member of the Territorial Army and Young Labour Party.

Dalal

Female of mixed ethnic background. Teenager who recently questioned her identity due to media focus.

Sana

Hijab wearing female who campaigns on behalf of the Respect Party.

Hassan

Member of the Green Party socialises with non-Muslims more than Muslims. He is interested in local issues and goes to the pub with friends.

Figure 0.1   Illustrated respondent capsules

1
Setting the Scene

The years following the tragic events of the 9/11 attacks have been tremulous ones for Western Muslims. The political discourse among the political right, the frenzied tabloid media craving a new 'threat' and the general misunderstanding of Muslims has created a negative environment that has since escalated to permeate social opinion. Doug Saunders has succinctly described this fear and misconception as:

> These Muslim immigrants, and their children and grandchildren, are not like earlier groups. They are reproducing at an unusually rapid pace, with fertility rates far higher than those of exhausted Western populations, and at some point soon – perhaps by mid-century – Muslims will become a majority in European countries and North American cities. This is a danger because, unlike other immigrants, they are loyal to Islam, not to their host society. They do not regard their religion as a private source of inspiration, but as a political ideology they intend to act upon. A line of shared belief connects the moderate Muslim believer to the radical Islamist and makes the majority of Muslims impossible to assimilate. They will permanently alter the West and promote a political agenda that will destroy our traditions and freedoms...
>
> (Saunders, 2012: 5)

Saunders goes on to refute the above allegations, but the persistence of these attitudes towards Muslims continues nonetheless. The purpose of this book is, in essence, to explore how a second generation of British Muslims has grown up surrounded by these negative experiences, suspicions, veiled threats, while the majority of British Muslims identify with being British, both as a homeland and as an identity. The book explores the effect that their faith and identity has on their politics and the reasons behind the trend. This chapter draws on the significant events, occurrences, government policies, social surveys, and media output to illustrate the impact these have had on the outlook of young British Muslims, setting the scene for the remaining analysis.

Muslims make the second largest religious group in England and Wales, with 2.7 million members (4.8 per cent of the population) according to the latest 2011 census (ONS, 2013b). Among religious groups, Muslims continue to have the youngest age profile, with nearly half of Muslims (48 per cent) aged under 25 (1.3 million) and 88 per cent aged under 50 (2.4 million). The gender divide is very slight, with marginally more men than women (52–48 per cent) (ONS, 2013b).

Though Muslims are ethnically diverse worldwide, British Muslims are more ethnically concentrated – 68 per cent were from an Asian background, including Pakistani (38 per cent) and Bangladeshi (15 per cent). In the 2011 Census, 11 per cent of Muslims (including Arabs, Turks, Persians and other ethnic groups) identified themselves as belonging to the 'other' ethnic category, while Black/African/Caribbean/Black British made up 10 per cent. Nearly half of all British Muslims were born in the UK (ONS, 2013b). The concentration of Muslims living in London continues to rise (12.4 per cent), with Tower Hamlets having the highest proportion of Muslims (34.5 per cent) and Newham having 32 per cent (ONS, 2013b). Elsewhere, Blackburn has 27 per cent Muslim population, and Bradford, Luton, Slough and Birmingham have over 20 per cent each. In comparison with the 2001 census, London's Muslim population has increased by 3.9 per cent (ONS, 2013a).

Muslims in Britain are very heterogeneous. They are diverse in ethnicity, language and class. They vary in their migratory patterns, geographical settlement and economic propensity. However, the key issues that affect young British Muslims are high unemployment and poor housing. This dangerous combination faces a large cohort of young British Muslims.

Evidence for high unemployment and lower economic activity rates for Muslims comes from several sources. The 2011 census results highlight that Muslims have the lowest levels of economic activity (55 per cent). The main reasons were because they were students (30 per cent) or because they were looking after the home or family (31 per cent), compared with 17 per cent of those with no religion and 8 per cent of Christians. This matches the younger age structure found among Muslim minorities.

However, for those who are economically active (i.e. those in or seeking employment, excluding individuals who are retired, looking after family/home or long-term sick/disabled), Muslims have the highest levels of unemployment: 17 per cent of economically active Muslims were unemployed compared with around 6 per cent of Christians and 9 per cent of people with no religion. In a continued exploration of employment penalties (in the labour market outcome literature this is a term used to refer to the poorer labour market outcomes observed, even where factors such as educational attainment and age are taken into account), researchers have recently begun comparing religious groups. The results have shown that religion is more important than ethnicity in explaining employment penalties for British Muslims (Lindley, 2002; Simpson et al., 2006; Berthoud and Blekesaune, 2007; Heath and Martin, 2012), especially among Bangladeshi and Pakistani women. The penalty faced by Pakistani and Bangladeshi women takes into consideration their family positions, and so having children does not explain why they face such employment penalties (Berthoud and Blekesaune, 2007; Heath and Martin, 2012). In the most recent study, Heath and Martin (2012) used pooled data from the 2005 and 2006 Annual Population Surveys and found a strong 'Muslim penalty' in unemployment and economic activity rates for both men and women from different ethnic groups. The penalties are greatest for women's economic activity and smallest in men's unemployment, but still significant enough to warrant attention.

Though British Muslims are mainly of South Asian descent, South Asian culture is not representative of Islam itself. In essentialising Islam this way, or to assume ethnic culture characterises the religion, we would be ignoring the wide variety of cultural, linguistic, historical and religious variations found among Muslims worldwide. In summary, the next chapter will highlight the influence that this global world has on the identities of these young British Muslims; these move beyond the ethno-religious dichotomies and labels used for generations past – the fluidity of identification has indeed created mosaics of identities.

In 2011, the ethnic group that ranked highest (71 per cent) in terms of association with the British only identity was the Asian/Asian British: Bangladeshi group. This was followed by the Asian/Asian British: Pakistani group and Asian/Asian British: Indian, with 63 and 58 per cent of these ethnic groups associating with the British only national identity respectively, rather than the British only; English and British; Welsh only/Welsh and British; Other UK identities; Irish only and Other only categories. This could highlight the fact that many British Muslims identify English/Scottish/Welsh and so on as 'White' racial categories, rather than a national identification.

There are numerous pieces of research that highlight the importance that Islam plays in people's lives, as found in the 1994 Fourth Policy Studies Institute survey, in which 74 per cent of Muslims acknowledged that Islam plays a very important role in their daily lives, whereas only 43 per cent of Hindus and 46 per cent of Sikhs said the same of their religion (Modood and Berthoud, 1997: 301):

> Islam serves as a frame of reference – a pattern of thought and com-
> munication – and gives meaning to their condition and behaviour.
> These Muslims may also have very diverse attitudes towards Islam
> and its practice. But what they do have in common is knowledge of
> Islam, on which they draw while engaging in a discourse so that they
> can communicate meaningfully and with relevance.
>
> (Ansari, 2004: 13)

It is also the case that younger people are more likely than older people to identify themselves as Muslim. It seems that the spheres of influence that used to be accepted, such as parents, elders and cultural dictates, have been swept aside by young Muslims in favour of religious decrees and spiritual guidance: 'Indeed, in the context of Islam, it has been claimed that increasing numbers of young Muslims in Britain are using the Qur'an and hadiths directly as a resource, rather than accepting the traditional views passed on to them from their parents...' (Spalek, 2007: 196).

Research also underlines that, as well as religion playing a role in the behavioural decisions of young Muslims, the views of youths are becoming more conservative in comparison with the views of their parents and grandparents. In a survey of 1,000 Muslims by Populus on behalf of Policy Exchange (between July 2006 and January 2007). It was found that 86 per cent of the respondents surveyed felt that their religion was the 'most important thing' in their life. Populus believed that the results indicated a growing religiosity amongst the younger generation of Muslims (Mirza et al., 2007). It seems that for young British Muslims, identity and religiousness are still important markers:

> It is argued that, although secularisation has occurred at a societal
> level in Britain (as in other parts of Western Europe), it has not nec-
> essarily occurred at the level of individual consciousness, such that

people continue to seek out religious and/or spiritual frameworks of understanding to help make sense of their lives....

(Spalek, 2007: 193)

However, material and research on the influence of identity on political decisions is limited. Little is known regarding the political views and actions of young British Muslims. Considering the effects of 9/11, 7/7 bombings, conflicts in Iraq and Afghanistan, bans on minarets, headscarves and face veils across Europe, the recent murder of Drummer Lee Rigby and many more topical events, it is surprising that few have explored the possible influences of these occurrences on young Muslims. The Preventing Extremism Together Working Group set up by the government after the 7 July 2005 London bombings attempted to engage young British Muslims via grass-root activities.

The social context

In order to understand the identification and political participation of young British Muslims, an acknowledgement of the social context in which they live and have previously experienced is crucial. What is the social context and how is it defined? It generally refers to the social environment of wider society:

Social context refers to the patterns of human relationships and interactions that characterize social life...social organizations provide the context that largely determines what a person does in life...your behaviour is largely determined by the social context of which you are part. As your social context changes, so does your behaviour.

(Zusman et al., 2009: 5)

The range of arenas that have affected the environment in which British Muslims have lived are areas that are the focus of much sociological research – including official political discourse, and media propaganda and stereotyping, all of which have a crucial influence on the social context to which British Muslims are reacting and in which they are living. This book will at times refer to theorists, mainly from the social interactionist school of thought, because symbolic interactionists believe that as humans we react to the context around us, while also contributing to it and affecting others. Humans perceive the symbols, communication and evidence around them, then 'interact' or react and respond to it.

Later in this book the explanations for the way in which young British Muslims act and make decisions use this theoretical framework.

One's socialisation in this social context has a strong influence on the way in which one perceives oneself and the decisions one takes. It is imperative to appreciate these details in order to manage the forthcoming narrative about identification of nationality, ethnicity and religion. In exploring the political activities of these young British Muslims, researchers must appreciate how their decisions are made and in what context, as they do not exist in a historical vacuum: this cohort has been affected by a wider political narrative, a media mania and a wider social discourse over which it has little control.

This chapter explores the historically important events that have influenced this cohort of young British Muslims, these events mainly taking place before and even during the fieldwork phases (January 2006–October 2007; June 2009–July 2009). These occurrences are highly relevant in situating the data collection, as well as in helping to understand the respondents' attitudes. Although historical events that occurred before the World Trade Center attacks are important, 9/11 is highly relevant to understanding the mindset and attitudes of some young Muslims – though it is difficult to pinpoint a starting point for such analysis: are historical events as far back as the Bosnia genocide (1993–1996) and the first Gulf War (1990–1991) relevant, or should we go further back into colonial and imperial history to the carving up of the Middle East after the First World War? Although elements of this history will be brought up later in the book, the emphasis on a historical background to this research is to illustrate the impact that these events have on the social context, and more specifically on the socialisation of individuals. The continued fear of terrorist threats continued with the Madrid bombings in 2004 and the London bombings in 2005. The shock that these were perpetuated by second generation British Muslims has reverberated for years afterwards.

The social climate during the last decade in Britain has seen the development of a subtle panic or hysteria that exists around Muslims. There is a 'fear' of Islam and Muslims are perceived as a threat; whether this is real or imagined, people react to these negative feelings. In this chapter, four main factors are discussed as influential in perpetuating this fear: 'propaganda' orchestrated by the media; governmental statements, political policies and legislation; counter-terrorism measures; and the creation of an 'othering' of Muslims, maintained by rumours, misunderstanding and misinformation. These factors have spawned a prejudicial and discriminatory environment surrounding

British Muslims, channelling disparaging images and symbols, building stereotypes and attaching negative labels that reflect adversely on British Muslims, including terrorist, outsider, extremist, oppressor and violent.

Many high-profile events occurred before and during the two field-work stages that affected access to respondents. These events included the July 2005 London bombings; the printing of cartoons of the Prophet Muhammad in September 2005 by the Danish *Jyllands-Posten* newspaper, which caused controversy; the June 2006 Forest Gate raid scandal; the government's attempted blacklisting of the group Hizb ut Tahrir in 2007; several negative newspaper reports and documentaries about Muslim groups and organisations, including Tablighi Jamaat in 2006, and a *Dispatches* programme about 'undercover mosques' in 2007; and the public courtroom murder of Marwa Ali El-Sherbini by a xenophobic man in 2009, which created shockwaves across Europe. The list could go on and on.

Media

The negative typecasting of Muslims in various forms of media, including popular fiction, tabloid press, documentaries and film, is fairly well documented (Poole, 2002; Shaheen, 2003; Ameli and Merali, 2004; Richardson, 2004; Poole and Richardson, 2006; Moore et al., 2008; Morey and Yaqin, 2011). There are several fearmongering publications that follow the 'Eurabia' thesis, arguing that Muslims intend to and will take over the West, imposing their law, values and lifestyles on their host nations (Phillips, 2006; Bawer, 2007; Caldwell, 2010).

Christopher Caldwell's (2010) *Reflections on the revolution in Europe: Immigration, Islam, and the West* also illustrates the deeply held fear of European Islamification. His book warns European politicians from being lax, and ultimately states that the European public is well aware of the cultural threat that Islam poses and is willing to fight against it. Popular writers and bloggers clamour to outshine each other in their abusive comments about Islam and Muslims. This negative representation is joined by popular fiction and novelists who demonise Muslims. The maligning of Islam and Muslims is no longer a private matter, and famous people with mass followings feel at liberty to express their distaste of Muslims without question:

> Here is Martin Amis, one of Britain best-known novelists, on Muslims. What he has to say is extraordinarily shocking. His words, if used about any other minority, might have been seen as inciting

hatred, if not violence. 'There is a definite urge – don't you have it?', Amis told Ginny Dougary of *The Times*: 'The Muslim community will have to suffer until it gets his house in order. Not letting them travel. Deportation – further down the road. Curtailing of freedoms. Strip-searching people who look like they're from the Middle East or from Pakistan. Discriminatory stuff, until it hurts the whole community and they start getting tough with their children.' Amis has since defended his remarks by asserting that he was engaged in a 'thought experiment'. Here Martin Amis is doing much more than insulting Muslims. He is using the foul and barbarous language of fascism.

(Oborne and Jones, 2008: 15)

The globalisation of news also has an impact on the familiarity of localised or national issues, which become sensationalised through international media. The uproar in New York over the 'Mosque at Ground Zero' is a case in point. American incidents tend to take precedence owing to the volume and popularity of anti-Muslim incidents, including 'Burn a Koran day' in Florida initiated by Pastor Terry Jones of Gainesville and more recently the anti-Islam video 'The innocence of Muslims' in 2012.

Several publications catalogue the fabrication, falsification and exaggeration of news stories by both the mainstream and tabloid press in the UK (Poole, 2002; Poole and Richardson, 2006; Moore et al., 2008; Oborne and Jones, 2008). Evidence of negative headlines and stories focused on Muslims is plentiful: some of these stories have no evidence (such as Muslims demanding Christmas be banned – Osborne and Jones, 2008: 20), and some are stories that occurred, though not necessarily with any Muslim involvement (such as the banning of piggy banks – Osborne and Jones, 2008: 20). The common feature is the desire to sell newspapers, based on a negative image and portrayal of the Muslim 'other'. Any subsequent 'corrections' that are made by these papers fall short of the apology that any other maligned person would expect for defamation of character.

There is also evidence that the public opinion polls designed, commissioned and analysed by media outlets reflect their own agenda and preferred narrative in order to garner attention and sell stories: 'Commissioning of polls is, therefore, in addition to reporting, a tool with which media impose their own coherent narrative and shape the public's understanding of Muslim integration, terrorist threat and other aspects of Muslim public opinion' (Sobolewska and Ali, 2012: 6). The media consider the outcome of public opinion polls as representative of the group surveyed – in this context Muslims (Lewis et al., 2011). In an analysis of public opinion polls conducted in the 18 months following the London bombings, Sobolewska and Ali (2012) found that poll commissioners and the reporting of these polls that resulted, significantly linked a lack of integration and terrorism. Sobolewska and Ali highlight that despite any independent empirical evidence, the media connected a lack of integration and terrorism in an attempt to pursue their personal agenda.

Islamophobia and anti-Muslim hate crime: A London case study by the European Muslim Research Centre (EMRC), based at Exeter University (Githens-Mazer and Lambert, 2010), finds a contributory relationship between religiously motivated hate crimes and the anti-Muslim rhetoric found in wider society.

> In this report we introduce empirical evidence that demonstrates tangible links between Islamophobia or anti-Muslim bigotry in both (i) mainstream political and media discourse and (ii) extremist nationalist discourse and anti-Muslim hate crimes. That is to say the report provides prima facie and empirical evidence to demonstrate that assailants of Muslims are invariably motivated by a negative view of Muslims they have acquired from either mainstream or extremist nationalist reports or commentaries in the media. Moreover, the evidence is clear that the major motivating factor for violence against Muslims is a negative and false belief that Muslims pose a security or terrorist threat. The evidence arises from compelling and original primary data: interviews with victims, perpetrators and witnesses of hate crimes in London.
>
> (Githens-Mazer and Lambert, 2010: 11)

Pervasive anti-Islam rhetoric is heavily entrenched in the media. The demonisation of Muslims has become normalised in the minds of readers, viewers and listeners.

> We think we should all feel a little bit ashamed about the way we treat Muslims in the media, in our politics, and on our streets. They are our fellow citizens, yet often we barely acknowledge them. We misrepresent them and in certain cases we persecute them. We do not treat Muslims with the tolerance, decency and fairness that we so

often like to boast is the British way. We urgently need to change our public culture.

(Oborne and Jones, 2008: 30)

The media concentration on seeing Muslims either as a national threat or as culturally inferior is problematic and has a long-lasting impact, on young generations of British Muslims and more importantly on the perceptions of the general population. The negative discourse and language used to refer to Muslims not only becomes firmly imbedded in the minds and language of wider society, but is also detrimental in the long-term future, when this discourse is used both privately and publicly to socialise a new generation of young people to see Muslims as alien, a threat and too radical to belong (Moore et al., 2008: 3):

> Our findings suggest that the coverage of British Muslims has increased significantly since 2000, peaking in 2006, and remaining at high levels in 2007 and 2008. This rise is partly explained by the increase in coverage devoted to terrorism and terrorism related stories – 36 per cent of stories about British Muslims overall are about terrorism. This is especially notable after the terrorist attacks in the US and the UK in 2001 and 2005. In recent years, however, we have seen the increasing importance of stories focusing on religious and cultural differences between Islam and British culture or the West in general (22 per cent of stories overall) or Islamic extremism (11 per cent overall). Indeed, 2008 was the first year in which the volume of stories about religious and cultural differences (32 per cent of stories by 2008) overtook terrorism related stories (27 per cent by 2008).
>
> (Moore et al., 2008: 3)

Having said this, other research does emphasise that though news coverage of Muslims is overly negative, Muslims are not being targeted as a 'suspect community' (Nickels et al., 2010). The impact of negative media representations of Muslims in the long term is difficult to gauge, but such attitudes do become ingrained in the social and psychological perspectives of the general population. It is clear that this coverage provides the media with an 'other' group that encourages attitudes of value superiority. It fuels the desire for hostility, threat and fear in the readership.

The negativity towards Islam and Muslims attached to the (usually) exaggerated, salacious and popularity hungry media formats filtered through to the potential respondents, and made it more difficult to access suitable respondents in key geographical locations. There was a distinct air of scepticism about the collation of information, with fears of undercover journalistic reporting and anxiety that interview material would be manipulated. Here is a quote from an email written by an acquaintance who was attempting to recruit his stepfather as a gatekeeper (the stepfather lives in Beeston, Leeds, where some of the 7/7 London bombers were based):

> I spoke to my step-dad [social worker] and apparently he didn't prove to be too helpful for you – sorry about that. He said he spoke to a few people and groups, but they were unwilling/apprehensive about being involved with this kind of stuff because of all the attention Beeston's received from the press, so they're a bit untrusting.

The Dispatches documentary *Undercover Mosque* that was aired in January 2007 showed footage of mosque leaders, imams and speakers who were critical of British integration, prohibited democracy and praised violence. The documentary caused an outcry in the UK amongst some Muslims, and was followed by *Undercover Mosque: The return* in 2008. The undercover nature of such documentary work (though useful in collating and highlighting such questionable opinions) proves difficult to distinguish from researchers conducting openly honest research. The fear of being recorded discussing sensitive topics such as identity, jihad and political integration (as this research did) was exacerbated by these sensational and opportunistic media programmes.

Politics

The presence of Muslims in the British government is by no means representative[1] of the statistical numbers of British Muslims, but the last decade has seen a strong rise in the numbers of elected and unelected officials at all levels of government. Since 1997, when Mohammad Sarwar was elected as the first British Muslim MP, the House of Commons has seen eight more MPs elected,[2] including three female MPs. The trend continues in local councils, the civil service and the House of Lords (including Baroness Warsi and Lord Ahmed).

The positive increase in Muslim representatives has also been supported by legislation protecting British Muslims. The enactment of the Racial and Religious Hatred Act in 2006 ensured that it is an offence to intentionally aggravate hatred against people on religious grounds, protects Muslims from hate crimes, and enforces dress-code sensitivity in public service/sector jobs such as the police and armed forces, and has been openly welcomed by British Muslims as providing the inclusivity they desire.

Unfortunately, the security and counter-terrorism debate of the previous decade (see further details below) has also repeatedly been supported by political statements from MPs and officials emphasising British Muslims as the 'other' (Spalek and Mcdonald, 2010). Tony Blair's press conference comments in 2006 on the face veil, referring to it as a 'mark of separation' in support of Jack Straw's (at the time Leader of the Commons) controversial request that Muslim women remove their face veils when attending his constituency surgeries in Blackburn, cannot but be seen by Muslims as corrupting a sense of British belonging and impinging on the assimilationist policies endorsed by other European states.

These earlier debates have recently been followed by political debates surrounding the perceived failure of multiculturalism. Prime Minister David Cameron's speech on 5 February 2011 stating that multicultural state policies have failed came at the end of a string of world leaders echoing similar sentiments (German Chancellor Angela Merkel in October 2010, former Australian Prime Minister John Howard in 2010 and former French Prime Minister Nicolas Sarkozy in 2011), most of whom were referring to Muslims within their respective countries:

> Under the doctrine of state multiculturalism, we have encouraged different cultures to live separate lives, apart from each other and apart from the mainstream. We've failed to provide a vision of society to which they feel they want to belong. We've even tolerated these segregated communities behaving in ways that run completely counter to our values ... This hands-off tolerance has only served to reinforce the sense that not enough is shared. And this all leaves some young Muslims feeling rootless. And the search for something to belong to and something to believe in can lead them to this extremist ideology. Now for sure, they don't turn into terrorists overnight, but what we see – and what we see in so many European countries – is a process of radicalisation.
>
> (Cameron, 2011)

The central supposition of many critics of multiculturalism is that it specifically refers to Muslims – and that the 7 July London bombings are an example of this failure. Critics argue that multicultural policies, such as exemptions for the wearing of religious/ethnic symbols, laws allowing halal and kosher meat, and the provision of state-funded religious schools, nurture separate communities that pervade the generational divide, preserving ethnic norms and values that are counter to that of wider society, encouraging hostility and hindering national identification. The argument that this then leads to radicalisation is unproven and problematic. Academic research exploring the extent to which ethno-religious groups lead parallel lives, including the analysis of patterns of co-ethnic partnerships, friendships, civic engagement, worship, residential segregation and work segregation, have rejected the above descriptions of the failure of multiculturalism. Using the latest 2010 Ethnic Minority British Election Survey data (EMBES), Professor Anthony Heath and Dr Neli Demireva found:

> On the one hand, it is true that some south Asian groups, particularly those of Pakistani and Bangladeshi background, do exhibit high levels of in-group marriage and friendship, but they do not lead parallel lives since residential and workplace segregation is actually rather low. We also find that people of Pakistani and Bangladeshi background are the most likely to feel bothered about intermarriage but on the other hand they are no more inclined to reject integration into British society, to reject a British identity, or to contemplate violent protest than are other ethno-religious groups. Indeed, it is the black groups who are the most likely to reject a British identity, while there are no significant ethnic differences in the propensity to contemplate violent protest. In short, high levels of ingroup marriage and friendship are compatible with the adoption of a British identity and a positive orientation towards British society...A third lesson is that perceived discrimination (both individual and group) has some of the strongest effects on negative outcomes. Discrimination is at least as plausible an explanation as multiculturalism for lack of integration. In this respect our results are consistent with those found by Maxwell (2006), who has shown (using a quite different data set) the importance of perceived discrimination for lack of British identification.
>
> (Heath and Demireva, 2013: 17)

This political debate regarding British Muslim integration or lack thereof is indicative of an 'othering' of Muslims, creating a strong sense of 'us Brits' and 'them Muslims'. This 'othering' has significant repercussions on the perception of British Muslims with regard to their identity, belonging and who they perceive as belonging to 'their' group. The impact that the Far Right political discourse has had on the perception of Muslims is incalculable. The BNP turned to target Islam in an attempt to garner support, a cynical strategy to feed off the ignorance of Islam, and it inevitably gets them media attention. Their political campaigns are run on heavily malicious anti-Muslim platforms (Oborne and Jones, 2008: 25). As a result, Muslims have attempted to organise themselves into campaigning bodies and to be represented as a unified core, starting with the success and then waning influence of the Muslim Council of Britain (MCB). The influence of the MCB during the last decade has declined as varied governments have attempted to liaise with alternative groups to varying success. The growth of alternative organisations, and those not under the umbrella of the MCB, included the British Muslims for Secular Democracy (BMSD), while Preventing Extremist Terrorism (PET) funding helped to create and allowed investment in organisations and networks such as Quilliam (a counter-extremism think tank), the Young Muslims Advisory Group (YMAG), the Sufi Muslim Council and MINAB (Mosques and Imams National Advisory Board).

One of the MCB's key outreach actions involved Muslim electoral engagement. Electoral engagement is important for ethnic minorities because it is a way of encouraging wider involvement in society (Saggar, 2000). If large groups follow patterns of non-participation or indifference then this will harm the longer-term sustenance of our liberal democracy – and a more detailed analysis of electoral politics will be found later in the book. Most of the research that has been conducted regarding Muslims and British politics has concentrated on electoral politics (Anwar, 1998; Saggar, 1998) in terms of voting and turnout. However, some research has focused on the views and attitudes of local councillors and politicians within the electoral system (Purdam, 1996; Adolino, 1998), but this is of less relevance to this research. Saggar's (2000) objective was to compare the voting behaviour of ethnic minorities using 1997 data from the Ethnic Minority Election Study. He found that Pakistanis' and Bangladeshis' turnout rate was close to that of whites for the 1997 election. Saggar argues that social class seems to underpin white and black votes, but not Asian voting patterns (Saggar, 2000); other circumstantial factors seem to play a role in their turnout/abstention:

> for Asians, the implication appears to be that other collective forms of political calculation and mobilisation lie behind both their overall high levels of turnout as well as the inability of social class to have much bearing on turnout... [which] serves to reinforce the

idea that collective group based political identity and engagement strategies underpin the position of Asians in the British democratic process.

(Saggar, 2000: 117)

Since then, research has highlighted that in terms of electoral voting, Muslim participation rates are similar to those found among the wider British electorate (Fieldhouse and Cutts, 2007). Registration rates are 93 per cent; and for those who are registered, turnout is 58.5 per cent, only 3 per cent higher than the overall mean. Similarly, results from the 2010 General Election provide further insight into ethnic minority trends via 'The British Election Study Ethnic Minority Survey', which again emphasised that though registration is slightly lower than the white majority, turnout rates are very similar to British White ones (Heath et al., 2013). Evidence on trust in democratic institutions follows a similar pattern, with the 2008–2009 Citizenship survey (CLG, 2010: 50) finding that Muslims trusted Parliament more than the general population (60 and 35 per cent, respectively). They were also more likely to say they trusted their local council than was the general population (71 and 60 per cent, respectively).

The limited research on Muslims and electoral political involvement (mainly because there is little difference from the wider population to discern) is in sharp contrast to the amount of research on transnational politics. Many researchers note the dynamic interrelationship between first- and second-generation immigrants and home country politics (Foner, 1997; Vertovec and Cohen, 1999). This was true of Italian, Polish and Irish immigrants in the US, and remains true of Asian and Caribbean immigrants in the UK. Ethnic minorities show political interest in international issues, especially in the politics of their home country or country of parental origin. Ethnic groups have long been involved in the political activities of their home states – the British Irish, Italian Americans and the Jews are all testaments to such trends (Foner, 1997).

Most research on Muslims in Britain before the 1990s discussed Muslims in their ethnic categories, because ethnicity was seen as the most important aspect of identity. Much of what was discussed relating to identity is crucial because though an issue such as the controversy centred on Salman Rushdie's *The Satanic Verses* (from 1988) may be identity connected but not inherently political, it becomes a political issue when it is symbolised as such by the community actors (Eickelman and Piscatori, 1996; Mandaville, 2001; Werbner, 2002). In the past few decades, it has been mainly international issues such as Kashmir, Iraq, Afghanistan and recently the political uprisings in the Middle East that have been considered transnational (and mainly ethnic) political issues. However, recent cases within Europe have caught the attention of religious groups and have caused an overlap between religious identification and international political decisions. For Muslims, this involvement in transnational political issues evolves from the religious emphasis of the 'ummah' (worldwide religious community):

> The assertion of an Islamicate political identity means that being Muslim begins to mean something other than observing the rituals and practices of Islam. It means that one tries to read from being a Muslim, one's social and political obligations. Being a Muslim requires an engagement with the rest of the ummah; it would be difficult to imagine how one could be a Muslim without regard to the rest of the ummah. This ummatic component of Muslim identity is precisely where Muslims come into contact with authorities of the Westphalian state – since a Muslim identity transcends the boundaries of the nation – state. Hence, the figure of the Muslim has become symptomatic of the crisis of the nation state. It is not mere coincidence that the emergence of Islamophobia in Europe seems to go hand in hand with the articulation of a pan European identity.
>
> (Sayyid, 2003: 89)

Research suggests that it was the Rushdie Affair of 1988 and 1989 that spurred British Muslims to develop and fight for attainable local agendas through campaigns and projects (Nielsen, 1988; Werbner, 2002; Hussain, 2003). The Rushdie Affair protests were not originally a political stance, but a religious protest. However, what began based on religious protest was taken to symbolise the rights of religious minorities in a secular society (Modood, 1990; McLoughlin, 1996), especially when it was illuminated on the international scene by the involvement of the Iranian fatwa on Rushdie. Over time, it has been said that the Rushdie Affair was a turning point for Muslims in Britain. It was an opportunity to organise and orchestrate systematic protest and develop future political agendas, while it united or strengthened the concept of a 'Muslim' identity especially among the second and third generation, and was a religious mobilisation of a deeply conscious group (Samad, 1996; Werbner, 2002). 'The "Rushdie Affair" is not about the life of Salman Rushdie nor freedom of expression, let alone Islamic fundamentalism or book burning or Iranian interference in British affairs. The issue is of the rights of non European religious and cultural minorities in the context of a secular hegemony' (Modood, 1990: 151).

However, it is not only international cases that shift from the religious sphere to the political when symbolised as such. Shaw's (1988) four year anthropological study of an Oxford Pakistani community saw Pakistani political mobilisation easily encouraged if religious values were used (Shaw, 1988). The Pakistani community had a strong sense of religious identity which was used for political action, as seen when the local council wanted to close a girls' school and make it mixed. For most parents, the quality of their children's education was of foremost importance, but when the case was presented 'in terms of a threat to Islamic values, many of these parents sided with those campaigning to maintain the all girls' school' (Shaw, 1988: 141).

The connection with the ummah is also influenced by the perceived marginalisation and disadvantage of Muslims. The international political context that young Muslims of this cohort have experienced leads to a strengthening of these ties and a stronger connection with their religious group and their perceived obligations. A feeling of alienation, together with feelings of discrimination, inequality in political representation and a feeling that their grievances are not being addressed, builds group resentment:

> Foreign policy is, without doubt, one of the most significant sources of anger within the Muslim community in the UK and is contributing to the community's growing sense of alienation. Its ability to provide a connection between personal grievances, conditions in countries of origin and the situation for the rest of the Islamic world make it a particularly potent catalyst for mobilisation.
>
> (Briggs et al., 2006: 47)

Ethnographic studies have shown that among young generations of Muslims, a new revivalist movement is developing in reaction to the cultural alienation and political disenfranchisement they feel in the West (Kibria, 2008). These young Muslims identify politically with a more global community or ummah, owing to the marginalisation they are experiencing.

There are no longer clear-cut lines between what religious and political issues. The blurring of these lines has led to the politicisation of religious matters. The question is whether this political involvement is followed up by second- and third-generation British Muslims, who might be expected to feel less attached to their parents' homeland. Unless we understand what is considered as politically important by the British Muslim youth and why, we are unlikely to be able to explain their attachment to certain political issues.

Counter-terrorism measures

The counter-terrorism measures have varied during the previous decade or so, as has their impact on human rights, equality, community cohesion and policing. Counter-terrorism measures include gathering intelligence, covert surveillance, stop and search, arrests, lengthy periods in detention and security checks at airports (including body scanners). CONTEST was the name allocated to the governments overarching counter-terrorism strategy. The Labour government announced its Prevent strategy (2007–2010), developed in the wake of the 7/7 London bombings. The schemes enshrined in this strategy encouraged local authorities to fund groups and organisations in order to tackle violent and extremist 'Islamic' attitudes and recruitment to Al-Qaeda-style organisations, using the £60 million offered by government. The Preventing Extremism Together taskforce (PET) met in 2005 in order to develop policy[3] suggestions which could be rolled out across the country and to counter the extremist attitudes the government believed was prevalent among British Muslims. CONTEST 2 was outlined in 2009 (Home Office, 2009), of which the Preventing Violent Extremism (PVE) agenda was one strategy of four suggested; it became the prioritised agenda.

The Prevent schemes were scrapped in 2011 after acknowledgement from the Home Office that there was not enough separation between counter-terrorism tactics and tackling social exclusion in Muslim communities, so the schemes were becoming counterproductive. This ambiguity in policy led to the widespread belief among British Muslims that they were being monitored, and that such policies (including underhand tactics) were gathering intelligence on innocent British citizens (Briggs et al., 2006; Spalek and Lambert, 2007; Mythen et al., 2009; Spalek, 2010; Spalek and McDonald, 2010). The monitoring of British Muslims was aggravated by government guidelines in 2006 (Department for Education and skills, 2006), aimed at tackling the promotion of 'extremism in the name of Islam' in universities, as well as reports over the years of British Muslims being 'blackmailed' into turning 'informant' (see Verkaik, 2009). The Prevent policies also ignored far-right extremism, focusing completely on British Muslims as the problem.

There is no monolithic Muslim experience of counter-terrorism policing (Choudhury and Fenwick, 2011), as it seems certain geographical
regions and age categories experience these measures differently:

> The lack of contact between most Muslims and extremists is high-
> lighted in the response by Muslims to a YouGov poll in 2005.
> Forty-seven per cent of Muslims in the poll believed that radicalis-
> ing imams existed. At the same time, 69 per cent had never come
> across one, whereas 22 per cent had heard one once or twice and
> only 5 per cent reported coming across them frequently. A counter-
> terrorism officer interviewed for this report found there was little
> pressure from communities to take action as 'so much of the activity
> appears to be unknown to the community'. Interviewees who worked
> with young Muslims also argued that claims that Muslim communi-
> ties were in denial about violent extremism and radicalisation needed
> to be placed in the broader context of the disconnection between
> young Muslims and their parents across a range of social and cultural
> issues.
>
> (Choudhury and Fenwick, 2011: 154)

It is not only measures in our own country that spread distrust and
fear among Muslims. As recently as 2011, the FBI acknowledged that
their counter-terrorism courses were heavily focused on Muslims. The
NYPD became the focus of new reports the following year, when it was
revealed that the Police Department showed new police recruits a highly
inflammatory and anti-Muslim film, *The Third Jihad*, and media frenzy
followed revelations of NYPD surveillance programmes focused on New
Jersey Muslim residents (Holpuch, 2012). The relationship between
British Muslims and the police force does not seem to be problematic,
the 2008–2009 Citizenship survey (CLG, 2010) finding that Muslims
trusted the police almost as much as the general population (79 and
81 per cent, respectively).

However, the debate surrounding Muslims as a 'suspect' community continues (Kundnani, 2009; Pantazis and Pemberton, 2009; Greer,
2010; Hickman et al., 2010; Choudhury and Fenwick, 2011; Pantazis
and Pemberton, 2011). For Pantazis and Pemberton (2009), the state's
focus of anti-terrorist legislation on Muslims has the effect of turning
this minority into a 'suspect community'. This proposal was critiqued
by Steven Greer (2010), who argued that while individual Muslims or
certain organisations and networks have been under official suspicion,
there is little evidence that this is a nationwide witch-hunt against all

British Muslims. His argument is that if some Muslims feel alienated and victimised, it is not necessarily because of the anti-terrorism laws, but rather the Islamophobia caused by terrorist incidents themselves (Greer, 2010: 1187). He offers that expressing solidarity with state repression and restriction of human rights of British Muslims is vastly different from evidence that being Muslim alone is sufficient to arouse systematic suspicion. Pantazis and Pemberton (2011) responded by re-emphasising their arguments that 'suspect' communities vary depending on one's definition of the term, but ultimately they propose a series of policies that would challenge the construction of British Muslims as a 'suspect' community:

> a commitment to an equalities and human-rights agenda; limiting the use of exceptional powers for terror suspects and their incorporation within the 'Ordinary' criminal justice; and disentangling the 'securitization' agenda from social cohesion programmes. It should ensure that the various constituents of the 'suspect community' are involved in the policy process to better inform policy makers and practitioners of their experiences, grievances and needs. Moreover, these policy principles need to be situated within a broader discursive field that does not seek to 'other' Muslims. Specifically, this should involve an informed and inclusive dialogue that no longer constructs the problem of violence as the exclusive responsibility of the Muslim community.
>
> (Pantazis and Pemberton, 2011: 1060)

Although these counter-terrorism measures do not directly affect many Muslim youths, they do contribute to a wider sense of targeting, and this builds resentment and a sense of injustice (Choudhury and Fenwick, 2011). Fear of security services monitoring was one reason for Muslim participant caution; research is received with scepticism, guardedness and doubt because of a social context that includes a cohort who have lived through the varied counter-terrorism measures and their continued aftermath.

The fieldwork phase inevitably meant dealing with distrust and scepticism among potential respondents, and at times people close to them. A young respondent (Dalal) explained after we met that her father did not want her to take part in the research, and had repeatedly tried to persuade her not to participate because of his views on politics, security services and the police. Parents worry that the security services are watching, noting and holding information on people, and that any recorded information can be used against them.

An othering identity?

The complex identification of second-generation British Muslims has long been studied. Reflections on the push-pull relationship between the cultural first generation of their parents and the expectations of British culture is very simplistic, but in essence is the start of the contested nature of their self-identification. British Muslims generally identify strongly with their 'British' identity. The 2009 Gallup survey found that British Muslims are more likely than all populations to identify strongly with their national identity and express stronger confidence in its democratic institutions (Gallup, 2009: 21–4.). Similarly 83 per cent of Muslim said they were 'proud to be a British citizen' higher than for Britons generally (79 per cent) (Wind-Cowie and Gregory, 2011: 39–40). The 2008–2009 Citizenship survey (CLG, 2010) found that 93 per cent of Muslims (same number as wider society) felt they were a part of British society (CLG, 2010: 40) and interestingly they were less likely than the general population in England to choose English as one of their national identities (12 per cent compared to 60 per cent of the general population) and more likely to choose British national identity (65 per cent) compared to the general population (44 per cent) – suggesting that English is seen as an ethnic identity rather than a national one (CLG, 2010: 42). A similar finding came from the 2011 census (ONS, 2013b).

The impact that the social context since 2001 has had on the lives of young British Muslims is immense. Negative media portrayals are supported by policy reports, public opinion surveys and political discourse that are also indicative of the damaging focus on British Muslims (Allen, 2010a; Allen, 2010b; Amnesty International, 2012; Pew Report, 2012; Goodwin, 2013). This social context has also seen the rise in Islamophobia, prejudice and harassment – the 2008–2009 Citizenship survey found one in five (7 per cent) of Muslim-reported harassment was a very or fairly big problem in their local area (CLG, 2010: 35). Anti-Muslim prejudice has been highlighted by initiatives such as Tell MAMA (Measuring Anti-Muslim Attacks) run by Fair Matters. The first data released by Tell MAMA in March 2013 indicated 632 cases of anti-Muslim hate recorded in the first year, 74 per cent of which occurred on social media sites; 58 per cent of the victims were female, whereas the perpetrators were mostly male (75 per cent) (Tell Mama, http://tellmamauk.org/).

As discussed earlier, the role that negative media portrayal, the emphasis of counter-terrorism measures and the harmful political discourse centred on Muslims has led to feelings of 'othering' among British Muslims – a sense that no matter how attached a Muslim is to their national identity, he or she is always seen as an outsider, a foreigner. The Open Society Institute report highlighted this, finding that 49 per cent of Muslim respondents expressed cultural identification with the state (saw themselves as British, French, etc.). However, only 24 per cent felt that others saw them as nationals:

> The two English cities, London and Leicester, had the largest proportion of Muslim respondents who saw themselves as nationals (82 per cent in Leicester and 72 per cent in London) as well as the highest proportion of Muslim respondents (40 per cent) who felt that they were likely to be seen as nationals by others in their country. However, these are also the cities where difference between how respondents perceived themselves and how they felt others perceived them was greatest.
>
> (Open Society Institute, 2009: 73)

After years of facing negative commentary on your ethnic identity, your culture, your parents and how they live their private lives; after being singled out as 'terrorist', 'insurgent' and 'insider'; and being told repeatedly that you will never belong unless you change your whole life, culture and belief, the only response to such a struggle is to become proud of the group identity that will accept you, where you can be proud of the identification:

> When you no longer see any pride or value in being Senegalese, African, black or immigrant, but the people around you still won't accept you as Belgian, British or European, almost the only welcoming cultural identity that remains – at least for one prominent group of second generation kids – is religious.
>
> (Saunders, 2012: 143)

New generations of young Muslims are finding novel strategies for managing their varied identities in order to counter the resentment they hold regarding the stereotyping of their identities and the broad and deeply insulting generalisations about Muslims. Recently we have seen the hijacking of the #MuslimRage hashtag, instrumentally set up by *Newsweek*, which instructed readers to discuss the magazine's inflammatory cover story about Islam on 17 September 2013; instead it was hijacked by Muslim and non-Muslim Twitter users alike who have mimicked and mocked *Newsweek*'s cover story and its stereotypical perception of Islam and Muslims. This has since been followed by the amusing takeover of #creepingshariaa in 2012 and #askTommyRobinson in 2013.

British comic films that have attempted to highlight the renegotiation of identities (Macdonald, 2011) include Damien O'Donnell's *East Is East* (1999), Chris Morris's *Four Lions* (2010) and Josh Appignanesi's *The Infidel* (2010), each drama resonating with young Muslims who are negotiating with the identities, traditional religious and cultural attitudes as well as expectations of the first generation, while juxtaposing them against their modern lifestyles, newer religious perspectives and challenging the extreme views that are perceived as their own.

This is where this chapter leads us – to questions that explore loyalty and belonging. To what extent are these second generation youth religiously observant? Where do their loyalties lie? Where are the sources of their self-identity? This will provide a sounding board to help analyse the political attitudes and engagement of this cohort.

2
Theorising Identity

The way one identifies oneself is a multifaceted mirror of the way one sees oneself. This identity may affect certain behaviour, practices and decisions: does this identity have an impact on the political choices young Muslims make and if so, how? By exploring the role that ethnic, national and religious identity play in the lives of the second generation, one can attempt to unravel the links. This book captures second-generation young British Muslims' motivations for political engagement or disengagement and whether identity is a source of motivation – it explores the reasons that the participants provide to account for their behaviour. This chapter does not offer a set of formal hypotheses, but provides a basic theoretical foundation which can consistently be reflected upon and reviewed in light of the fieldwork data.

> Social scientists have tended to look at culture as a result or a dependent variable. Sociologists have used these more or less easily measured aspects of culture (such as language preferences) to assess acculturation (Gordon, 1964; Alba and Nee, 2003). They have been examined as a function of generation or time in the United States. The main question is how immigrants become more like Americans, in terms of language use, food eaten, music listened to, visits home, and holidays celebrated, as time passes. But culture can also be an independent variable, as we ask how a system of values and meanings influences individual choices. The different ways in which groups see the world influence their trajectory into the American mainstream.
>
> (Kasinitz et al., 2008: 84–5)

Theories of identity are very popular and many exist in areas of psychology, politics, sociology, anthropology and cultural studies. It is impossible to review all the research on this topic, which is highly multifaceted and complicated, but possible to provide a brief overview of a few influential theories about identity that are relevant to this research. There are numerous starting points for exploring identity. The most popular and useful sociological understanding of identity emphasises the role that social groups play in shaping how individuals perceive and view themselves.

Social identity is how we recognise ourselves, especially in comparison to others, it is how we place people into categories and associate with people and groups who are like ourselves. The process of identification is negotiable, fluid and does not consist of one but multiple identities.

Identity in part is a psychological question about the self, but it is also a social status, as we may choose to identify with a group – be it football team, ethnic group or philosophical association. It is based on one's perceived similarities with the social group, and its differences and distinctiveness from others. Social identity is a combination of how one sees oneself, and also how others perceive and categorise you.

Socialisation is also crucial in the development of identities. Through intergenerational transmission, parents teach children about relations and kinship, creating familial identity; and educational institutions develop career identities, teaching children about achieving the 'roles' of lawyer, policemen or mechanic. Our peers impart knowledge and shape our social identities as 'sporty', 'geek' or 'fashionable'. These labels mould how humans interact, and can be negative, including 'bully', 'terrorist' or 'stupid'. This indicates that self-identifying may not be successful if the wider audience refuses to accept a person as such, and negative labelling and stereotyping of children and adolescents such as 'criminal', 'chav' and 'stupid' can shape an individual's self-perception and identity when emphasised over periods of time. At times, people are not free to choose their identity; we are born into certain identities such as gender and race groups.

The most recent influential work conducted on concepts of social identity comes from Social Identity Theorists[1] and Identity Theorists.[2] The two theories are by no means incompatible, but attempt to explain identity from different points: whereas Social Identity Theory explains identity from the perspective of who one is, in light of group differences, Identity Theory perceives identity from individual 'roles' and what they 'do' for the identity. Some researchers argue that Social Identity Theory and Identity Theory are conceptually different and better studied separately (Hogg et al., 1995: 266), while others argue that the similarities outweigh the differences and the two theories can be merged (Stets and Burke, 2000). Without over-complicating the matter at hand, let us explore these two theories further.

Social Identity Theory stems from Henri Tajfel's theory of social identity. It explores the importance that social groups play in influencing the self-identification and categorisation that individuals place on themselves and those around them. Henri Tajfel defined social identity as 'that part of an individual's self-concept which derives from his knowledge of his membership in a social group ... together with the value and emotional significance attached to that membership' (Tajfel, 1981: 255). Tajfel argued that identifying with a group leads individuals to 'buy into' three distinct aspects of identity group attachment. The first is the cognitive knowledge that one belongs to the group; the second is the evaluative knowledge regarding negative and positive associations relating to the group; and the third is acknowledging and accepting emotional ties to the group and to those who are not members. This means that the social identity of the individual is the information he or she has, as well as the principles and beliefs held in relation to the group. Tajfel argues that human social conduct is fundamentally rule-governed. People aim to act properly in comparison with the social norms and values of their own group as well as wider society.

> Each of these memberships is represented in the individual member's mind as a social identity that both describes and prescribes one's attributes as a member of that group – that is, what one should think and feel, and how one should behave.
>
> (Hogg et al., 1995: 269)

Similar views can be found among symbolic interactionists and the Social Identity theorists, who believe that the construction of identity is based on how an individual is perceived and defined by wider society and how the individual responds to that categorisation (Herbert Blumer, 1969). George Herbert Mead (1934) began by highlighting the consciousness that humans have of their wider perception as individuals. We use clothing, gestures (e.g. the way we walk, talk and so on) and language as indicators for others to identify, label and judge us. This process is subjective – and it may or may not be effective (an individual may want to be perceived as a punk or an intellectual, but the symbols may fail to signify this identification, or the social group might reject the efforts that are made).

Goffman's work (1959) emphasised that signs, signals and symbols of human behaviour impact on individuals' perception of themselves, as well as their perception of their surroundings. Individuals attempt to control the image they present to wider society through signals and symbols of behaviour. Humans try to project an image, and to convince wider society of their identity and their belonging to particular categories.

Individuals learn from the group they identify with; they pick up norms, values and attitudes that assist in their further belonging to and recognition as part of the group. The advantages of social group membership include self-enhancement, a sense of belongingness and the nurturing of individual self-worth (Burke and Stets, 2009: 121). The concept of identity is no longer a clear-cut monolithic term; people have fragmented, fluid and constantly changing identities. Our social identities stem from social groups, members of which identify themselves in a similar way (Hogg and Abrams, 1988). A social group's members identify with others who hold similar values, language, symbols, physical attributes and so on. Those who are considered different are an 'out-group'. When individuals embody a group-based identity, they are becoming 'like' the other members – there is a sense of uniformity, acceptability and understanding. There is also an 'othering' of the out-group. Experiments on social identity have found that just by labelling individuals as belonging to certain social categories, they begin to associate with and emulate that category (Turner et al., 1987). Thus, labelling youngsters as criminal or 'loose' could further push individuals to enact and embody those categories, without questioning whether the label is deserved.

Ultimately, individual perspectives and social structures interact back and forth. People act within the boundaries constructed – they perceive, reflect and then act. Their actions and symbols are interpreted and responded to by groups and wider society.

Most individuals have multiple identities, for example as mother, banker and environmentalist. However, many people choose to identify with one social identity more strongly than with their other identities, although some may hold more than one identity equally, and thus will attempt to negotiate and balance their multiple identities. This interaction of identities is not problematic if they share similarities; for example, if being a mother in the banking industry is normal.

> If more than one identity is activated in a situation, we expect that the identity with the higher level of prominence or the identity with the higher level of commitment, will guide behaviour more than an identity with a lower level of prominence or commitment.
>
> (Burke and Stets, 2009: 133)

The question is, what occurs when a person has multiple competing identities – when conflicting roles may clash? Again, the most prominent identity will surface, with the lesser taking a secondary role. The shifting of identities is constant, and in most cases is completed unawares. We shift our identities when we interact with different people, and some identities remain dormant, or are awakened in specific circumstances or by special events.

Ethnic group identity

Race, ethnicity, religion and nationalism have become highly contested and politicised identities in modern societies. They have been used to mobilise civic unrest, to compete for resources and to fight for rights within nations. Fredrik Barth's influential work *Ethnic Groups and Boundaries* (1969) attempted to understand the relationships between such varied identity groups. He posits the idea that groups can and do make choices in their own interest, especially in relation to other groups. This 'boundary maintenance' is how ethnic minority groups interact and deal with the social distance that separates them from the mainstream population. Barth's argument is that ethnic identities are interdependent, and though they are continuously adapting, groups are still maintained through boundaries of inclusion and exclusion: 'The critical focus of this investigation from this point of view becomes the ethnic boundary that defines the group, not the cultural stuff which encloses it' (Barth, 1969: 15).

Following on from the work of Barth, Alba (2005) focuses not on the boundaries that are maintained by the minority group, but on the boundaries that are institutionally created and held by nation-states in regard to minority groups. He distinguishes between 'bright' boundaries and 'blurred' boundaries. Blurred boundaries are inclusive policies that assist in the assimilation of most minority ethnic groups, whereas 'bright' boundaries are state policies that are geared to be more exclusive which limit the ability for assimilation by some people or groups. His case studies include second-generation Turks in Germany and Maghrebins in France: he highlights the fact that 'bright' boundaries exist for the Turks and Maghrebins – the only option for assimilation of these groups into their nation-states is complete boundary crossing and assimilation into the mainstream – possible only for secularised members of both groups. In these cases, citizenship, relationship between state and religion, race and language are key factors in state-based 'bright' boundary maintenance:

One case is that the boundary is bright and thus that there is no ambiguity in the location of individuals with respect to it. In this case, assimilation is likely to take the form of boundary crossing and will generally be experienced by the individual as something akin to a conversion, i.e. a departure from one group and a discarding of signs of membership in it, linked to an attempt to enter into another ... growing distance from peers, feelings of disloyalty, and anxieties about acceptance.

(Alba, 2005: 24)

The counterpoint to a bright boundary is one that is or can become blurred ... This could mean that individuals are seen as simultaneously members of the groups on both sides of the boundary or that sometimes they appear to be members of one and at other times members of the other. Under these circumstances, assimilation may be eased insofar as the individuals undergoing it do not sense a rupture between participation in mainstream institutions and familiar social and cultural practices and identities; and they are not forced to choose between the mainstream and their group of origin. Assimilation of this type involves intermediate or hyphenated stages that allow individuals to feel simultaneously as members of an ethnic minority and of the mainstream.

(Alba, 2005: 25)

In the 1920s, theorists of the Chicago School (Park et al., 1925; Wirth, 1928, 1941) led an assimilationist line of analysis, which argued that the longer immigrants resided in the USA, the less influential their ethnic group identity became. In order for immigrants to gain employability and a good standard of living, they assimilated themselves into the mainstream culture, and their ethnic identity was weakened. This interest-driven attitude would eventually sideline their ethnic culture:

A process of interpretation and fusion in which person and groups acquire the memories, sentiments and attitudes of other persons or groups, and, by sharing their experience and history, are incorporated with them in a common cultural life.

(Park and Burgess, 1921: 735)

They point out that the structural forces that maintain ethnic group solidarity and cohesiveness have been waning. The declining residential segregation of white ethnic groups, declining occupational specialization, increasing intermarriage, social mobility, and distance in time and generations from the original immigrants all decrease the isolation of the ethnic group that has maintained its cohesiveness. As the descendants of the original immigrants leave the ethnically homogeneous ghettos of urban areas, it is argued, their social world is increasingly ethnically mixed and their ties to the original ethnic culture are reduced.

(Waters, 1990: 4)

The most important factor for assimilationist theorists such as Gordon (1964) is structural assimilation – that is, if the primary relationships of marriage, friendships, neighbourhoods and so on are not ethnically concentrated, then assimilating to the 'core' culture will occur, thus weakening the ethnic group identity. While neighbourhoods stay ethnically concentrated, marriages are maintained within the ethnic group and friendships are focused on cultural similarity, then assimilation will occur only on a shallow level. A major critique of the theory has questioned which 'core' culture the theory refers to, as well as questioning the likelihood that the ethnic culture in itself would disappear altogether.

During the 1960s and 1970s, the pluralist perspective (Greeley, 1971; Novak, 1978) developed and debated whether cultural assimilation will unavoidably occur, even if important relationships are ethnically mixed. It was argued that ethnic group identity is still maintained however 'mixed' ethnic groups become, citing the fact that in the third and fourth generations, ethnic group identification in some cases is strong, as is inter-ethnic intermarriage, evidence that ethnic identification is not declining but adapting.

A slightly different theory about ethnic behaviour is that of 'symbolic' identification. Since the concept of 'symbolic identity' was coined by Gans (1979), much discussion has ensued regarding the strength of ethnic identity. Gans highlighted that generations after the migration of white immigrant American groups (such as the Irish, Italians and Polish), ethnicity is now used symbolically on specific occasions to express group belonging (e.g. the Irish celebration of St Patrick's Day). The symbolic usage of ethnic identity becomes a voluntary choice (Gans, 1979; Alba, 1981; Waters, 1990), and people participate in 'a nostalgic allegiance...a love for and pride in a tradition that can be felt without having to be incorporated in everyday behaviour' (Gans, 1979: 9).

In *Ethnic Options* (1990), Mary Waters follows Gans's argument by highlighting the role that symbolic ethnicity[3] plays in the life of many white second- and third-generation people. She highlights aspects of identity that can be turned on and off according to convenience or cultural trends. As ethnic groups assimilate through the generations owing to changing social networks, culture and economic status, the ethnicity of the forefathers becomes 'optional'. Symbolic identity becomes peripheral; it is not relinquished, but is adapted – some elements are retained, others are sidelined. The voluntary nature of symbolic identity is a key element in its popularity.

> In contrast, conventional accounts of ethnic identity shifts among the descendants of white European immigrants, conceived as part of a larger, linear process of assimilation, have pointed to the 'thinning' of their ethnic self-identities in the United States. For their descendants, at least, one outcome of widespread acculturation, social mobility, and intermarriage with the native population was that ethnic identity became an optional form of 'symbolic ethnicity'....
>
> (Rumbaut, 2008: 110)

Recent attempts have begun to connect the assimilationist and pluralist perspectives. Segmented assimilation theory[4] is a structure for comprehending second-generation integration into the host society and for developing an analysis to understand the different ways integration occurs. The theory focuses on differing patterns of adaptation[5] and how these patterns lead to varying paths of integration – mainly that the mode of incorporation of the first generation gives the second generation access to different types of opportunities and social networks. Migrants who are integrated into groups with strong ethnic networks, access to social capital and fewer ties to negative American minority cultures are better off. Ethnic groups which create networks of social ties and provide access to job opportunities while reinforcing parental authority tend to have the more successful second generation.

'Reactive' ethnicity, 'resistance model' and 'oppositional culture' on the other hand are theories that describe the rejection of mainstream values and norms through subcultural movements of the second generation. Those socially closest to American minorities may adopt an 'oppositional'[6] or 'reactive' ethnicity (Aleinikoff and Rumbaut, 1998; Waters, 1999; Portes and Rumbaut, 2006; Rumbaut, 2008). The concentration of poverty in inner cities, the lack of welfare policy and the exposure of youth to a subculture that is frustrated and sceptical about upward mobility and the value of education cause negative or downward mobility. This is made worse by the lack of the buffering effect of a tight family and community:

> This process of forging a reactive ethnicity in the face of perceived threats, persecution, discrimination, and exclusion is not uncommon. It is one mode of ethnic identity formation that highlights the role of a hostile context of reception in accounting for the rise rather than the erosion of ethnicity...
>
> (Rumbaut, 2008: 110)

Second-generation youth who have experienced discrimination or expect to face discrimination in the future are less likely than other groups of second-generation youth to identify themselves as part of the mainstream (Portes and Rumbaut, 2001a, 2001b). The rise of ethnic identification as a result of unreceptive attitudes from the mainstream is not the only response from some minority group subcultures. In the face of discrimination, exclusion and stereotyping, young minority groups develop reactive subcultures as a result (Aleinikoff and Rumbaut, 1998; Portes and Rumbaut, 2006).

If these youth identify with the mainstream, citizenship becomes a crucial aspect of identification. Citizenship is important because it underlines the relationship between individuals and the state. The concept is a very broad term, and is intricately tied to that of civil society – both formal and informal relationships which work outside the control of the state. This informal contract that binds citizens to the state helps build trust, efficacy and a sense of both duty and rights:

> Citizenship is a set of norms, values and practices designed to solve collective action problems which involve the recognition by individuals that they have rights and obligations to each other if they wish to solve such problems.
>
> (Pattie et al., 2004: 22)

In multicultural and heterogeneous states, such as the United Kingdom, where the flow of migration is constant, a society must have a gel to glue its citizens together, to link the varied groups and peoples. It is imperative to build on communal values that unite peoples of a state. A sense of national pride assists in building a politics of identity, recognising the similarities (especially citizenship) which tie them together:

> If citizenship is such a good thing, why are we not all citizens of the world? The answer is because individuals are more likely to cooperate

with people like themselves than with those who are very different, and there are no overarching transnational or multicultural values strong enough to bind together individuals from different nation states to offset these effects.

(Pattie et al., 2004: 21)

Religious group identity

Research exists that considers religion as a part of ethnicity; however, though they are closely linked, ethnicity has a specific frame of reference – that of common descent: 'We shall call "ethnic groups" those human groups that entertain a subjective belief in their common descent because of similarities of physical type or of customs or both, or because of memories of colonization and migration' (Weber, 1978: 389) – while religion may be a global 'imagined' community and one can choose to join or leave. This research considers religious and ethnic identity as separate identity facets, and distinguishing ethnicity and religion is a key factor in the research design.

Since the 1970s, world events have highlighted the strong influence of religion on political and social movements – the rise of Christian fundamentalist movements in the United States, the Zionist movement in Israel and the increasing fervour of extremist Muslims. There have been lengthy conflicts in Northern Ireland, Sri Lanka, Palestine, Bosnia and India. All such examples underline the impact that religious influence has had on the international political landscape.

> Since the terrorist attacks of September 11, 2001, the public debate about religious cultural differences and immigration has focused on the experience of Muslim immigrants. Given the ways in which Muslim immigrants to Europe have felt marginalized and discriminated against, the question in the United States is whether immigrants from Muslim countries will face systematic discrimination, thus hardening the boundaries between Muslims and other groups and preventing assimilation. Few of our respondents are Muslim, but their experiences do seem markedly different with respect to intermarriage and intergroup relations.
>
> (Kasinitz et al., 2008: 270)

However, in order to understand the possible influence of religious identity on individual action, we must query how religious faith functions. When exploring the function of religion in society, the discussion can be split into two camps. Durkheim and his functionalist followers were mainly interested in the social integration phase of religious belief. For Durkheim, religion and society are fused. He believed that humans act out their religious enthusiasm and loyalty through society. On the other hand, Weber, Parsons and others were concerned about the role that religion plays in providing a sense of meaning to its followers. Religion impacts society by shaping individual consciousness and setting basic ethical principles and values. This sense of meaning can be seen clearly in the case of Islam and its expectations of the individual. It offers its members a whole way of life:

> The distinctiveness of Muslim politics may be said to lie rather in the specific, if evolving values, symbols, ideas, and traditions that con-stitute 'Islam'. These include notions of social justice and communal solidarity that have been inspired by the founding texts of Islam such as the *Quran* and the sayings (*hadiths*) of the Prophet.
>
> (Eickelman and Piscatori, 1996: 21)

Religion also provides believers with a sense of belonging. Similar to eth-nic identity, this sense of belonging to a group is a mobilising force of social support at times of crisis. For Muslims, they identify with other Muslims internationally as part of the ummah.[7] Eickelman and Piscatori (1996) argue that the concept of a transnational religious community is influenced by the fact that non-state actors have emerged to promote the 'call' to Islam, which goes beyond class boundaries and beyond national boundaries. Islam is also transnational because of an escalating anxiety over the troubles of Muslim minorities worldwide. 'Muslim'-specific issues have grown in the political sphere. These issues often play a part in Muslim politics. Examples of such issues include Afghanistan, Palestine, the Rushdie affair and Bosnia. 'In each, transnational concern is aroused because of the shared perception that Muslims and Islam are under attack and require defence' (Eickelman and Piscatori, 1996: 146).

Research on British Muslims and identity has found that Islam is con-sidered an integral part of identity. Hutnik's study (1985) found that Muslim identity was listed by 80 per cent of South Asian Muslims as an important identity item. Modood (1997) found that 83 per cent of Pakistanis mentioned religion as important. Modood argues that the positioning of Islam as primary identity by young Muslims expresses a new confidence that is 'sometimes a religious revival, sometimes a political identity, sometimes both' (Modood, 1997: 386). Saeed et al.'s (1999) self-identification surveys in Glasgow amongst second- and third-generation Pakistani Muslims found 'Muslim' chosen nearly three times as often as Pakistani, 'First, because it is the Muslim aspect of their identity that they feel is under attack, and second... that Islam is a more useful vehicle for political mobilisation' (Hussain, 2008: 6); while Ceri Peach (2005) employed data from the 2001 census to reveal that 74 per cent of Muslims gave primacy to Islam in terms of their identity.

In order to understand the diverse views held by Muslims regarding issues of identity, belonging and citizenship in this research, it is essential to understand the points of reference that these young Muslims use. Most points of reference lie in scripture – that of the Quran and the sunnah.[8] However, theological approaches differ depending on which interpretive tradition is followed. In simple terms, there are three distinctive theological approaches taken by Muslims:[9]

1. Islam as non-existent: These are Muslims who (though born Muslim or define themselves as Muslim) do not allow Islam to play any role in their lives whatsoever. Their world views and practices are not prescribed at all by religious obligations, values or religious doctrines. Islam to this group is merely a distant faith that has no impact on their day-to-day life.
2. Islam as peripheral: Influenced by secularisation in Europe, these interpretations argue for the separation of state and religion. These explanations insist that religion plays a superficial and more private role in the lives of Muslims. People following such traditions avoid wearing distinctive religious clothing or behaving in ways that would identify them as Muslims. Some also believe that in today's society the Quran and sunnah are void as reference points, as they are not relevant when it comes to today's norms and behaviour.
3. Islam as fundamental: These Muslims follow the scriptures (Quran, hadith, sunnah) in most aspects of their lives. However, they are represented by diverse forms of Islam because of the variety of interpretations that can be found within religious teachings. While some Muslims follow a literalist interpretation (a conservative form of interpretation, following the ways of life of the first three generations of Muslims), others follow one of four schools of thought[10] that were developed between the eighth and eleventh centuries by jurists. Some Muslims follow modern interpretations that have been developed during this century and are continuing to be developed by jurists – a dynamic contextual form of interpretation that considers modern challenges and the progress of modern societies.

This overview will assist in understanding the differing stances used at times by second-generation young Muslims in explaining their view of religion, ethnicity and nationality.

Many of the issues and aspects relating to the impact of ethnic, national and religious identity will be covered below, based on the material from the fieldwork (including autophotography, see Figure 2.1). The following sections are split into typology groups (see Table 2.1). What must be emphasised is that these categories are not judgements regarding respondents 'Muslimness', nor are they critical notions regarding lifestyles. This typology aims simply to describe the groupings found amongst the sample and attempts to find explanations for how these identities were forged and why.

Table 2.1 Typology group chart

	Group 1 Symbolic ethno-religious identity group	Group 2 Multicultural identity group	Group 3 Dual identity group	Group 4 Mainly Muslim Identity Group
Identity	British	Multicultural	British Muslim	Muslim
Home	Britain	World/Locality	Britain	Nowhere/Foreign
Loyalty	Britain	World	Islam and Britain	Islam and World Muslims
Ethnic culture	Symbolic: choose when to participate or not.	Varied: participate in various cultural practices.	Practised: participate in ethnic culture.	None: do not participate in ethnic culture.
Customs/ Traditions/ Behaviour observed[11]	Occasional ethnic and religious practices such as prayer, fasting Ramadan, celebrate Eid; read Quran; ethnic clothing. More liberal or secular approach to religion. Religiously prohibited is practised: drink alcohol; pre-marital relationships; etc.	Multilingual; wide network varied friends; ethnic intermarriage. Intermittent religious and ethnic practices such as prayer, fasting; mosque attendance; ethnic clothing; free mixing; music.	Modest Western clothing; cultural dress; practise five pillars Islam and more; attend Quran classes; attend mosque regularly; free mixing; music, headscarf; bilingual.	Mainly Muslim networks; segregation; Headscarf/ *Niqab/jilbab*; religious style clothing; Muslim education; *Khilafa*.

Table 2.1 (Continued)

	Group 1 Symbolic ethno-religious identity group	Group 2 Multicultural identity group	Group 3 Dual identity group	Group 4 Mainly Muslim Identity Group
Customs/ Traditions/ Behaviour avoided[12]	Regular behaviour that is identifiably Muslim or ethnic: Headscarf, ethnic clothing, long beards, regular mosque attendance.	Anything Islam prohibits: alcohol; premarital sex; forced marriages; breaking law, non-halal food. Any ethnic cultural behaviour that goes against British lifestyle: forced marriages, clan culture, arranged marriages, etc.	Anything Islam prohibits: alcohol; premarital sex; partners; forced marriages, eating non halal food; breaking law. Any ethnic cultural behaviour that goes against British lifestyle: forced marriages, clan culture, arranged marriages, etc.	Through religious contextualisation they avoid[13]: Free mixing, music, 'immodest' clothing; religious school assemblies; mixed swimming classes for children, sex education for children; democracy; mortgages; plus anything Islam prohibits – alcohol; eating non halal food; premarital relationships etc.
Word sorts/ Auto-photography	City locations, friends, family, food, gender, books, prayer, moderate, hajj, jewellery, hair.	Language, values, music, clothing, makeup, friends, family, gender.	Prayer, ethnicity, Britain, religion, dual nationality, football shirt, *Quran*, values, history, prayer mat.	Foreigner, conservative, moderate, books, *Quran*, prayer, values, skin.

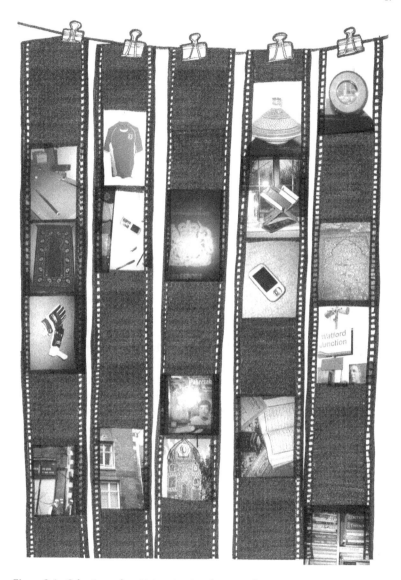

Figure 2.1   Selection of participant auto-photography

3
Identity Typology

As the discussion in Chapter 2 highlighted, identity is a multilayered and fluid phenomenon that is perceived in varied ways. This chapter explores the identification of the participants as self-defined during their interviews. The descriptions were grouped by their similarities into a typology. Though these categories are ideal types, in practice they have fuzzy edges, resulting in blurred boundaries. Though respondents are mainly located in one category, there may be certain aspects of their identity which lie in another category. Time is also an added factor; the respondents are by no means limited to belonging to one category for the remainder of their days, as identity is an evolving and fluctuating phenomenon; and though these respondents have been placed in these categories, time plays an influencing factor in placing them in another. Identity in itself is a complex and multilayered concept, so any attempt at fixing categories is futile unless they are allowed to overlap and fuse.

The categorisation in the typology (see Table 2.1) is by no means exhaustive, but is reflective of the respondents interviewed during this research. Had the interviews included young Muslims who were far more conservative than those in typology group four, then another category would have had to be developed. However, within the realm of the research possibilities, the typology groups accurately represent and reflect the young British Muslims interviewed.

Group one: Symbolic ethno-religious identity

The easiest way to describe this group of respondents is as individuals who downplay their Muslim identification to the level of inner belief, with little outer appearance. This depiction is not unusual among ethnic minorities; it has been described as 'Symbolic' identification (Gans, 1979; Waters, 1990). Waters (1990) explores the symbolic choices of

the descendants of white migrants in America, highlighting the importance that choice plays as an appealing strategy for people who have the
option to choose: 'I have been describing symbolic ethnicity throughout this book as embodying a great deal of choice. Even among those
who have a homogeneous background and do not need to choose an
ancestry to identify with, it is clear that people do choose to keep an
ethnic identity' (Waters, 1990: 151). Waters highlights the attractiveness
of this element of choice 'because having a symbolic ethnicity com-
bines individuality with feelings both of community and of conformity
through an exercise of personal choice' (Waters, 1990: 151). Being part
of the minority group makes people feel special and unusual, as well as
belonging to a group, while belonging to the wider non-minority group
provides conformity and normality. This was mirrored in the responses
of my first typology group of participants.

When asked to describe their identity via either the auto-photography
method (see Figure 2.1) or using word sorts, this group of respondents
referred mainly to non-ethnic/religious-specific words and symbols.
They described their identity via photographs of city locations such
as London and Leeds; of family members and friends. They generally
chose words such as books, jewellery, gender, values and food. When
probed, their responses had little ethnic and religious specifications.
When they did speak of religion or ethnicity, they mentioned occasional prayer, intermittent reading of the Quran and participating in
a few other events, such as Eid and Hajj.

During their interviews, these respondents named numerous activities
that they referred to as behaviour that Islam considers forbidden or sin-
ful but are considered the norm in wider British culture, such as drinking
alcohol or having a partner/boyfriend/girlfriend; or actions that are
questionable, such as celebrating Christmas and Easter or attending
church mass. But these choices were accepted by these respondents
because they are the norm in wider British society; these are activities
which British people participate in daily, and so the respondents feel
like part of the majority. This aspect of their lives provides them with a
sense of conformity and normality.

17. Noora

Yes, as you can see [photograph] my sister's hijabi, yet I'm drinking
[alcohol]; although my family are straight-laced and Islamic, I'm not.

We [friends] do a lot of partying and drinking, I went out with their
mate, and we're still friends.

45. Hana

Okay, well the first one is my boyfriend, **** and me on a ****
trip. I chose it because my relationship with him is very important
to me, and it's sort of a symbol of how I've moved away from the
values of my parents, by going out with a non-Muslim, and also by
the fact that I'm going out with him rather than marriage to him.

Participants who belong in this group are quite 'symbolic' in their usage
of the minority ethnic and religious identity. In *Ethnic Options* (1990),
Waters notes how descendants of migrant Catholic ethnic minority
groups in America were symbolically identifying with their ethnic identity by choosing when to identify with the group based on either
expediency or cultural reasoning. The respondents in this category similarly symbolically participate in minority events and choose whether to
participate or not:

3. Dalal

Yeah, that's the good thing...Christmas and Eid which is great...if
I married someone who is a Muslim I would still like our children to
go to church on Christmas and stuff, even though I'm a Muslim like.
I don't want to forget that little bit. Christmas is great.

These respondents participate in some religious and cultural practices at
times when it is suitable for them. Jacobson's (1998) research into young
Muslim British Pakistanis suggests that one of the strengths of Islam is
that even for Muslims who do not practise their religion thoroughly,
the religion is an ideal towards which these people can strive. They can
make subtle participatory gestures which allay psychological fears of losing all sense of being Muslim, 'such as occasional mosque attendance or
abstinence from alcohol – which indicate their underlying commitment
to the Muslim community' (Jacobson, 1998: 128). This is like Hana who
prays occasionally, or Noora who intermittently reads the Quran. They
hold what would be considered secular or liberal attitudes to Islam; religion is an aspect of their life that is personal, and when practised, it is
practised in private:

17. Noora

I know a lot of people who say they are Islamic but they have never
read the Quran and things like that, I've read the Quran and though
I know that I'm not a practising Muslim right now, I know it will

come to me eventually. I am quite close to God, I see Islam as a personal thing between you and God, it's not for you to say to other people, in that respect, I don't see it as something to rush... I'm Muslim.

45. Hana

I try and pray, I don't usually do five times a day... for me the principles of the religion are more important than the rules as such, and I consider the principles to be the same as most other religious traditions, and so by that measure just sort of being a good person, acting ethically, thinking of other people's interests... I think at that bit of it I'm very good and I consider myself to be a Muslim in that respect... and it is something that I think about a lot, but as I said, practising I don't do very well.

I don't outwardly appear to be Muslim very often, but the sort of inner meaning of it and the personal relationship to Allah, those things are more important to me.

61. Zayd

I don't see myself as religious whatsoever, I try to practise what I can... very religious is based on the stereotype of wearing hijab and having a beard, praying five times a day, praying Quran once a day, knowing the hadiths and sunnahs... I don't do a lot of that.

They decide themselves to what degree they would like to participate in the rituals of religion or in cultural practices, especially those practices that are outwardly obvious such as cultural clothing or the headscarf. Hana, for example, decided to go to hajj,[1] which is no small decision – hajj is very crowded, expensive and takes time to prepare for. However, here she describes why she dislikes and does not wear a headscarf (hijab); Dalal talks about her discomfort in cultural clothing; and Wafa, who was forced to wear a headscarf by her parents, is now questioning the reason for wearing it, especially since she left home:

45. Hana

It did feel strange when I went on this training weekend before the hajj, and it was a group of British Muslims – we were all going together – and most of them converts to Islam, they were all wearing headscarves and I wasn't... I think because I've been brought up Muslim, as I said before, like, the rules and things like that are not as important to me as the way that you act in your life, and so I don't normally wear a headscarf – I just find it complicates things unnecessarily...it feels uncomfortable in certain situations...I find it physically annoying sometimes...I guess the issue about clothing is a lot to do with fitting in with other people.

3. Dalal

Yeah, I...when we go to Pakistani weddings I wear salwar kameez and stuff but I still feel a bit uncomfortable in it, like I do like wearing all the jewellery and stuff...

24. Wafa

I was forced to wear it when I was 13 [headscarf], so I've worn it since then. I could have taken it off when I left home at 19, but at that point I felt I couldn't – probably because just too much had changed and I needed something to be constant...do I really want to wear it and...I mean, do I really care? I find myself not caring enough if I'm showing a bit of skin or a bit of hair and that's why.

However, at times these respondents do want to feel part of the minority community, and to be acknowledged as such. This can be seen where respondents mention that they are exasperated at not being acknowledged as part of a minority group – Hana is also frustrated because she does at times like to mix with and be involved with her Muslim family and their friends, but because of her choices and past decisions, she feels that an element of distrust exists:

45. Hana

Like family friends that have known me all my life, I think some of them are very wary of me because I had that background [Muslim] and then rejected it – to an extent – and then they're worried about the effect on their own children, you know, whether I'm a bad influence or something.

The reasons they give for why they do not identify completely with their minority ethnic or religious group are based on issues of difference and compatibility with wider society. These participants feel that the minority ethnic and religious community they come from is too different, distinctive and exclusive from wider British society. Because of these perceptible differences in values, concepts and, most importantly, practices, they feel that the minority group is different from wider society, and this difference in their minds is what pushes them to make the choices they do. They highlight mainly cultural differences in terms of language, values and class:

3. Dalal

I find that the majority of Muslims, especially Asian Muslims, I have nothing in common with whatsoever... I mean not in a snobby way but I think it's kind of a class thing to be honest... rather than a race thing...

17. Noora

I speak it [Urdu] but I've got nothing to say, their culture is completely different, what they talk about, they are very personal, very objective about who you are, but that's not the society I come from.

61. Zayd

Especially for our generation, there is a clash, our parents have come from... wherever it may be... and they came over just to make a living, whereas for us it's about making a living, being educated, integrating into society. I don't think my kids will have this problem, they'll be Brits.

24. Wafa

My mum doesn't even speak English, so it's almost like we're talking different languages, we're poles apart... I mean obviously it limits her and what she can do and what she reads and therefore how she thinks and it just means that we're poles apart – on different planets really.

Wafa does not identify solely with her minority ethnic culture because of the ethnic and religious conservatism that had impacted her life. Her father was an Imam and is orthodox Hanafi; her two elder siblings are religiously educated; and her mother is very cultural and does not speak English. Her childhood was restricted – limited education, no television, no music and so on. Her only option in order to attend university was to leave home; she had limited contact with her family in the meantime as they disapproved. Her response as an adult is to enjoy much of what was prohibited for her when she was younger – her friends, the places she eats and her image are all aspects of her life that she now has control over, and these are decisions that go against the conservative upbringing she had.

These respondents feel British, with a connection to the wider world, rather than specifically connecting to Islam and Muslims. When asked why he felt British, Adam said that his educational background and British upbringing leads him to feel more connected with English people, rather than with people of his own ethnic group. Some of the behaviour references which these participants mention are activities they participate in which they consider being distinctively 'English' or 'British', such as playing classical musical instruments, travelling to certain destinations and participating in sporting activities such as skiing.

In summary, this group of respondents prefer one dominant identity, that of mainstream British culture. The other aspects of their identity play a minor role in their lives; they use their minority identity when it is suitable for them. This strategy of maintaining a non-Muslim, non-minority ethnic identity places them in tricky relationships with family, childhood friends and the wider minority community.

They refer to themselves as Muslims, but acknowledge that the traditional values of Islam are not necessarily mirrored in their daily lives. Ethnic and religious practices are usually conducted in their private lives and outward expressions of religious or ethnic belonging are symbolic. Most believe that practising Islam is not all that makes one Muslim, but that the important issue is to recognise oneself as a Muslim. Their relationship with Islam is a constant battle; they do at times take part in behaviour that is prohibited by their minority ethnic and religious group. Respondents who fit in this group have a primary allegiance to Britain as well as a preference for British culture, but they participate symbolically in some Muslim religious or cultural practices.

Group two: Multicultural identity

These respondents describe themselves as being cosmopolitan, internationalist, citizens of Europe and citizens of the world. Though they do describe themselves as British, they mention that they associate with many different cultures, languages and people. Their identities are constantly fluctuating because of the many facets of their personalities, the variety of their networks and the diversity in their backgrounds. These respondents were less likely to pick one aspect of their identity as being more popular than others.

When asked about their identity, they respond differently from the other three groups. Though they do identify Britain as a home country and British culture as their own, and as Muslims most certainly, they also referred to themselves in a wider context, as cosmopolitan or internationalist. The reasons behind such attitudes seem to be travelling widely, having a variety of different social networks and being brought up with numerous cultural references. Examples are respondents Ghazal and Sami:

8. Ghazal

I feel, like, more cosmopolitan I suppose because of my mixed race background, like I feel more internationalist, like I feel I can understand large parts of the world better and I'm not like a die-hard patriot and could never be, but at the same time, my British identity is the identity I have if you are asking about a country.

42. Sami

Multiple [identity] ... because I've a Scottish father, [Spanish] mother, but I'm born [in ****] ... but then I'm a Muslim so that means I don't necessarily hold as much in common now with either **** or Britain, so I have a more cosmopolitan identity. I feel very comfortable in various environments – I mean, when I'm with ****, I feel I'm ****; when I'm with Brits, I feel like I'm a Brit ...

This group also included respondents who mentioned that though they were British-born and would live out their lives in Britain, they felt their allegiance was larger than just specifically for Britain – they identified with people of the world.

51. Zaki

I just see myself as a citizen of Europe, citizen of the world – I don't actually have any strong allegiance.

This was expressed in a way by respondents who identified with a large multicultural British city rather than with being British – they identified with fellow Londoners rather than with British people, for example. This was the response by Sami, who had said he felt 'cosmopolitan' (quoted above) and also described himself belonging to 'London' (below). His reasoning is that he married into a different ethnic culture; he grew up in various places both around the globe and in the UK; and he also has a wide variety of friends from diverse cultural backgrounds.

42. Sami

I identify with London... Not necessarily with England, or even Scotland, I feel I'm a Londoner... London it's where... especially in our side of London – **** – it's like most of the people are like us, people who have multiple levels of identity and... and mixed cultural backgrounds. I mean most of our friends are incredibly mixed... Russian married to American, a Yemeni Somali married to Danish... it's like the whole community – that we hang around anyway – are all like this.

Similar responses were found in the research conducted in New York on ethnic minority groups by Kasinitz et al. (2004). They found that while respondents identified with New York as a multicultural and diverse city, respondents were less likely to identify with being 'American' because of the connotations and the geographical variety that encompasses the USA. This is also the case because London, like New York, is very cosmopolitan; they are 'world cities':

Many respondents sidestepped this ambivalent understanding of the meaning of being American by describing themselves as 'New Yorkers'. This term is open to them even as blacks or Hispanics or Asians, and it embraces them as second generation immigrants. A New York identity reflects the dynamic cultural creativity familiar to them, but not necessarily the larger white society. 'New Yorkers' for our respondents, can come from immigrant groups, native minority groups, and they can be Italians, Irish, Jews and the like. The changes necessary to become a 'New Yorker' are not nearly so large as those required to become an 'American'.

(Kasinitz et al., 2004: 17)

These respondents have very pluralistic outlooks. The mixture of cultural influences on their lives causes constant adaptation because of variety in their environments and surroundings. Their identities are constantly fluid; they do not like to identify with specific identity groups, but allow their identity to adapt. These respondents were also unwilling or unable to choose a main identity. Some respondents are not willing to make a choice, some are confused about their identity and some are happy having such a variety of facets to their identity. Tuqa, a young woman of Kashmiri-Pakistani origin, explains several times how varied she feels her identity is, and refers to it as being 'schizophrenic':

18. Tuqa

Pretty much, yeah, I'm schizophrenic (giggling)

I don't think it would be very easy to, kind of, box me...because it is like most of my cultural references are British, they are not like the stereotypical Asian things, I don't watch Bollywood films, I watch French films; I listen to French CDs sometimes...

I wouldn't say I have like...I don't sit there and think 'I'm British' or 'I'm Muslim' or 'I'm this...' but it's sort of like, with my French friends I'm British because I talk in English, I have a British accent; with my English friends I'm British but Asian; at work I'm known as 'the Muslim girl' because that's who I am, I've got different types of behaviour...

Most of these respondents find it difficult to identify with one identity group either because of mixed backgrounds or because they live varied lives. Some respondents, Tuqa for example, play different roles depending on their environment and surroundings. At home, the ethnic cultural expectations of her family lead her to dress and behave in a certain way. Once in her work environment she has a different persona, and in between her social life is just as flexible.

18. Tuqa

they're all different facets of my personality...They're all natural states and I think that's why it's really difficult to say 'I'm this or that'. I don't feel I'm two people, I feel I'm a million different people with whoever I'm hanging out with.

As Tuqa has shown, these respondents do not necessarily come from mixed ethnic backgrounds. Even among the respondents who do have two ethnic backgrounds, it is not necessarily that variety which makes them multicultural. Ghazal grew up with parents from two different ethnic backgrounds, but felt alienated from both ethnic minority groups. She grew up speaking only English without either second language; she did not feel she was welcomed by the communities her parents came from. This has had a lasting effect, leading her to feel she does not identify specifically with either ethnic minority group that she comes from.

Yet the cultural mixture in her upbringing, the variety of social networks she has and the travelling she has done all lead her to consider herself as a 'cosmopolitan' and 'internationalist', and she identifies with a variety of different parts of herself – her gender, her femininity and Islam among others.

The multicultural layering of identity for this group means that they participate in and act on many different aspects of their identity. They are comfortable and happy to connect with their varied identity facets, without wholly belonging to one or dedicating themselves to one or two. They do this by connecting to several aspects of their identity, without wholly committing to them.

This multicultural and varied attitude to identity is mirrored by Warikoo's work on Indo-Caribbean youth in New York City (Warikoo, 2008). Through 'cosmopolitan' ethnicity she describes second-generation teens who are able to pursue multidimensional identities through a variety of music, ethnic clothing, films and social networks.

> ...given that the youth I studied expressed security and no 'identity crisis' with their multifaceted identities, we should question the notion of ethnic identity as one coherent, essential core of the individual. Second, individuals choose different types of identity in different realms of their lives, as I observed in the differences between Indo-Caribbean young men and women, as well as in the differences in individual identities in different situations and realms of life.
>
> (Warikoo, 2008: 385)

It would seem that these respondents are content to use the many identities they have developed or gained and implement them in their daily lives. The extent to which multiple aspects of identity are used is dependent on the extent to which their networks vary, and reliant upon the identity dimensions and facets they wish to hold on to. Unlike the 'symbolic identity' group, these respondents do not mind repeatedly participating in religious endeavours, such as going to the mosque or attending a religious event. However, unlike groups three and four, they do not like to 'limit' their identities to one or two specific choices – they enjoy participating and identifying with many aspects of themselves, whether they are gender-based, cultural, national or religious.

Unlike the other three identity groups, this category preferred to keep as many avenues or channels of identity formation available as possible; they frequently changed and exercised their identity facets in order to keep them accessible. The methods they used could be via their mixed culture parents or partners, a multicultural network of friends and acquaintances, or their globe-trotting exploits and career moves. To this group, identity most certainly only exists in the plural.

Group three: Dual identity

This category in the typology encompasses the largest number of participants – those who identified themselves in the main as 'British Muslims' but also identified with aspects of their ethnic background. No respondents suggested they felt ethnic and religious alone without feeling British. This section looks at each of the three main identity groups they mentioned separately – Islam, Ethnicity and Britishness.

> In a multi ethnic, multicultural country such as contemporary Britain, there are inevitably many potential layers and sources of identity. People can clearly espouse many identities simultaneously. An individual can in principle feel 'British', 'Scottish' and 'Bangladeshi' – or whatever.
>
> (Heath and Roberts, 2008)

Muslim me

Participants in this category, no matter how 'practising', said that religion was their number one identity marker, but usually teamed it together with being British. This dual identity approach highlights the importance that both group identities play in their lives. The British aspect of their identity will be discussed later on.

> 41. Suhail
>
> When I say I am a British Muslim Islam being, well we all have multi identities...I'm British, Pakistani, Muslim...**** as a place to live...you've got your age, skin colour – but I think religion for me is the biggest value, it makes me the person who I am.
>
> 13. Kawthar
>
> A picture [auto-photography] of a Quran – basically representative of – maybe a bit cheesy – of this religion obviously being a major part of life, and necessary really.

For these respondents, religion is an integral aspect of their lives. They attempt to implement as much of the religion as they can.

However, though Islam influences their major day-to-day interactions and behaviours, they leave space for other identity facets, especially those that do not clash with their moral obligations. Jacobson (1998) highlighted how boundary maintenance has assisted in preserving Islam as a source of social identity among young British Muslims. One major reason was because 'Islam survives as a source of meaning in the respondents' lives partly because the content of its messages is accessible and appealing to the young people' (Jacobson, 1998: 126). This is accurate in that these young Muslims can understand the practical aspects of their religion; they associate these practices as a 'way of life'. It influences all aspects of their lives, their family, neighbourhood, local community and even national outlooks.

10. Huma

The number one thing that I believe my identity is based on my religion if anything, the way I think, the way I dress, the way I walk; it makes up who I am.

7. Farah

Islam is my way of life and it gives me a focus in my life and gives me answers to questions that I didn't even know I had sometimes so religion, religion is me a lot of the time.

33. Bashir

I think that being Muslim is something you should be proud of...I don't reckon that young Muslims like myself in a British Western society we should be hiding our identity because at the end of the day we live in a multicultural society, you've got people of different races, creeds, different social classes so in that sense you shouldn't just say...there's one ideal that everyone should adhere to, everyone should celebrate their differences...

These respondents recognise that political circumstances and government initiatives have led to a consistent media spotlight being aimed at Muslims. Unfortunately this has meant that young Muslims are forced not only to consider their identity, but also to try to change the preconceived perceptions they feel society has of their identity.[2] Whereas many other minority religions and cultures in the UK today are able to wear special clothing, speak particular languages, attend religious places of worship and follow religious observances without questions, these young people do not perceive that this is the case for them. The male respondents in this category were concerned about the image of Islam and the stereotypes that young Muslims – especially men – have after 9/11 and the 7/7 London bombings. For example, Yunis, a young Bangladeshi from Tower Hamlets in London, highlights the concern the general public have regarding young bearded men on the Underground, especially those (students, for example) carrying a rucksack.

6. Bilal

Okay, well I think it's important, firstly, to identify that I'm a Muslim because religion nowadays – especially since the events which have taken place since September 11 etc. – takes a big priority because whenever someone asks who you are, if they find out that you're Muslim they'll immediately have certain ideas about you . . .

47. Yunis

Everyone's afraid if you're a Muslim; your religion preaches this and preaches that . . . they'd get scared if someone with a beard jumps on a train, someone jumps on a train with a big rucksack on his back, he might only be going to work or som'in'!

Using the word sorts and auto-photography methods, the respondents were asked to describe what was important in their lives. The majority of this bicultural group described religious symbols or actions. These respondents raised identity symbols such as the Quran, prayer and hijab as being important to their identity:

15. Leyla

Prayer is important to me as a Muslim, because I'm a practising Muslim, I pray five times a day, even at work I will try to pray.

10. Huma

I chose prayer because prayer is a big thing for me, obviously being a Muslim I pray five times a day anyway, but we pray all the time even outside the prayer times, it takes a big chunk of my time.

Many of the female respondents mentioned and discussed the hijab as an important aspect of their religious identity. Hijab to them means differing things; the responses have a sense of sacrificing elements of beautification for religious observance. The majority stated that it was not a cultural or parental decision to wear the headscarf, but their own. For some respondents, such as Arwa, it was a forced decision made by her parents and she has had to adapt to it. From the female respondents in this category, one-third did not wear a headscarf (Kawthar, Bushra, Emel, Mona, Rana), and only one wore a jilbab with a headscarf (Farah). The remaining two-thirds wore a headscarf, usually with modest fashionable clothing such as jeans and tunics or maxi skirts and jackets. I was surprised not only by the degree to which these young women believed in wearing their headscarf, but also by the degree to which they believed in making it stylish and acceptable to their British lifestyles, as Farah and Sana mention below. Some are careful not to wear black as it portrays 'a poor impoverished look, just feel sorry for us' image as Sana says. The headscarf is not only an aspect of their Muslim identity, but indirectly intertwined with their British identity.

20. Sana

In terms of identity now, it's important to me for people to see who I am now, it's PR, not to see someone who is submissive and not to cower with the scarf and to be bold. I remember when I started to wear the hijab, I chose not to wear any black scarves because it seems like you are blending into the background, and that shouldn't be the purpose of it. It is a poor impoverished look, just feel sorry for us.

10. Huma

I chose clothing because people see my clothing all the time, as I wear the hijab, my religious dress, and I dress modestly, it's a part of who I am and part of my identity.

7. Farah

Clothing, clothes are ... for me because I am a big fashion queen but I also wear the jilbab so that means that I sacrifice my ideas of clothing for what my Islam teaches me and so I wear that instead. That doesn't mean that I don't fashionise underneath.

Unlike the first and second identity group, religion to this group of respondents is far from merely symbolic or peripheral, it is fundamental. Religion plays an integral part in their lives, and is a blueprint which they try to follow. Though there are boundaries of difference between the religious followings and teachings and aspects of Western culture, such as drinking alcohol, premarital relationships and so on, these are not seen as difficulties or barriers. They are seen as minor differences because Britain is a diverse society (see the discussion regarding Britishness). The aspects of their religion which they do practise, such as wearing a headscarf, praying five times a day and so on, are fitted into their British lifestyles and made compatible, in an attempt to combine the two identity facets.

Ethnicity

When discussing aspects of their ethnic background, the respondents were fairly nonchalant about their identification. It is not a purely symbolic gesture, nor is ethnic identification something they feel very strongly about. Those who spoke a second language could only speak it, rather than read or write it. Travelling to the country of their parents' origin was spoken of as a holiday, rather than as a regular trip. Traditional ethnic clothing was only worn for special days or in order to impress the elders. However, they also practise aspects of their ethnic culture because they see it has an asset or capital to have and hold on to.

> 2. Banan
>
> I don't feel Indian...I think the point is that I identify with Indian culture and it is a part of me, I appreciate my heritage, and I would be a more boring person if I didn't have that, but it's not my be all and end all.

Most of the respondents in this group mentioned travelling yearly. Most go to their parents' home country to visit extended family networks, some merely because it is a cheap holiday destination where they are familiar with the language and culture.

> 32. Ali
>
> When I go Pakistan, you know people it's like they see different because you know like the accent, the way we speak the language it's different. You know like in England we speak English, English is my first language. You know when I go to Pakistan I speak the language but my accent is different. So...they differentiate me.

Speaking a second language for most of the respondents was seen as an asset that they have grown up with. Some have not had that opportunity, but have attempted, with difficulty, to learn it as adults. For some respondents such as Bashir, speaking a second language is the difference between communicating with parents and extended family or not, as some of the first generation or elders do not speak English. Huma also sees having a second language as an asset; only realising as a young adult that she could lose out on the potential of a second language, she set about relearning and improving her language ability, which later came in useful in her work environment.

33. Bashir

Language, I agree that language is important because my parents they don't speak English but they understand English but it's like as kids we used to do all the translation.

10. Huma

Predominantly I speak English but I also speak Arabic, when I was younger English was more a part of me than my Arabic was, it was only when I was growing older that I realised the Arabic was disappearing and I thought to myself stop, I need to work on my Arabic. I dream in English, I read books in English, I speak in English, I speak to my parents in English... and I thought to myself, although I'm British, I still am bilingual, so I started to speak Arabic only at home, with my parents and so it improved my Arabic. I also deal with people in Arabic in my workplace; it relies a lot on my language. That's why language [word sorts].

Ethnic clothing seems to be an arena that only the female respondents had issues with. Cultural clothing was deemed by most as a hobby, a part-time set of clothing they wore mainly to please the parents, grandparents, or community 'aunties'. Cultural clothes are seen as aspects of identity that respondents may have grown up participating in, but have chosen to withdraw from out of choice. They wear cultural clothing on symbolic grounds, for celebratory events as well as to keep the peace.

7. Farah

Because it's [salwar kameez] not a massive part of what I wear, I mean I do wear Asian clothing, but it's not like a main part of me. Maybe because I don't see it massively significant, clothing I suppose because under a jilbab it's more comfortable to wear trousers and a top than it is to wear a big salwar kameez with massive trousers under it.

I'll give you an example, my grandma is adamant that we wear Asian clothing and you know, if we ever wear a skirt she'll be like 'why are you wearing that? Where's your Asian clothing?' Coz obviously in her generation it wasn't the done thing, it's a cultural thing, she sees it as us losing our culture when we wear Western clothes. And I think for her it's more important obviously coz that's what she's brought up with, for us it's not such an issue because we don't feel that clothing is the only thing that makes us Kashmiri or Pakistani or whatever. Clothing can be one part of it but definitely I mean out of respect when she comes over I do wear the clothing to keep her happy.

4. Emel

Clothing…it's like when I'm at home, my mum is like 'when you're at home you should wear salwar kameez'…a lot of them wear headscarves and salwar kameez, and I don't have an issue with wearing salwar kameez outside…but people wear the headscarf out of culture, not because they have reached a spiritual enlightenment, because they have grown up with it…my mum's like that…you know Aunty G's going to talk, and I'm like it's okay, I'll talk to her myself about it…People judge you initially on what you are wearing, and I've kept that in mind, but not give into that pressure. It's a way to express who you are…

16. Mona

When I was really young my mother used to insist that I wear the traditional [salwar kameez] like a baggy sort of overshirt, you know, which I didn't mind until I realised she had awful taste! (giggling)…and sequins so it was the old aunties that used to come over with clothes and they were gifts so you would have to accept them! And it would be bad if you didn't wear them! So you know, it's a catch 22 – I mean, it is! – so, I mean, traditional attire I'm perfectly happy with, I actually like the salwar I think it's a very practical piece of clothing, but just as long as I'm left to choose what I have to wear it with.

There were aspects of ethnic identity culture which these respondents disagreed with and stood up against. This was most popularly ethnic minority cultural practices that the respondents either disagreed with on principle or felt were incompatible with their British values or religious beliefs, mostly regarding forced marriages and clan culture.

54. Maha

Forced marriages, that is predominantly still within the Pakistani culture, as they don't have the understandings of the religious teachings, they assume that what their forefathers did was correct, and they assume that it's part of religion, but because they have not had the knowledge and they have not read the Quran and hadith they don't know any better, they assume what they are doing is right...

And clans... in our Pakistani culture there is a lot of clans, people who are associated with a certain caste and status, if you're not part of that status then you have nothing to do with me, again, not religious, cultural and traditions, that's all it is, but it does affect, completely affects the way of life of many young Muslims in these families.

61. Bushra

Marriage is a big tension... in Islam there is no caste system, but with Pakistanis especially, also with Bangladeshis and Indians, but Pakistanis especially since they are the majority Muslims in England, they feel very strongly about castes and I don't understand it, and if you look at where the caste system has come from, it doesn't make sense why they are so proud! We're of **** origins and my mum's 'oh you have to marry a****'... she knows there should be a 'Muslim' option, but she's scared of the society around her, of the Pakistani community attacking her, of my uncles, my grandma and everybody else, she's scared of that element. She'd say if your cousins do it, you can do it, so there is that tension...

None of the respondents in the dual identity group were completely detached from their ethnic background. They all have a working knowledge and understanding of their culture and traditions. They can communicate, respect and identify with their extended family and wider ethnic community. However, religion has arisen as a stronger identity reference in recent years, eclipsing that of ethnicity, notably since the events of 9/11 (Samad, 1992; Ahmed and Donnon, 1994; Werbner, 2000; Bagguley and Hussain, 2005; Lewis, 2007).

Similar to the attitude taken by the symbolic identity group, ethnic identity is used in a voluntary sense in that some traditions are practised and some discarded. The voluntary nature explored by 'symbolic' identity allows these respondents to disregard aspects of their culture which go against the stronger aspects of their other identity facets – Islam and Britishness:

There are parts of these past ethnic traditions that are sexist, racist, clannish and narrow minded. With a symbolic ethnic identity an individual can choose to celebrate an ethnic holiday and refuse to perpetuate a sexist tradition that values boys over girls. The selective aspects of symbolic ethnicity are in part what makes it so enjoyable to so many individuals.

(Waters, 1990: 168)

It allows the second and consequent generations to disentangle themselves from certain cultural shackles (forced marriages, clan culture, lack of education, etc.) and argue their cases for living their lives in a British culture with Islamic references. This allows women to become educated, youngsters to wear Western clothing while retaining modesty and young men to choose their marital partners.

> The younger generation, especially the women, demonstrate sophisticated understandings of how religious and ethnic traditions intersect and use these arguments to challenge parental perspectives or expectations... Second and subsequent generations of Muslims are reclaiming their religious identity and rediscovering Islam. Their ability to read English fluently allows them to research in the dominant tongue, the language of the web and text books. This diasporic awareness reconfirming yet also redefining their roots, and some made subtle distinctions between the religious and cultural strands, bringing to the surface their own reflexivity in this process.
>
> (Bagguley and Hussain, 2005: 217)

The difference between the first typology group and this one is that these respondents strengthen their British Islamic identity, while retaining a respectful understanding of their culture and its assets; while the symbolic identity group chooses to symbolically identify with both religious and ethnic aspects of their identity, maintaining a mainly British reference point. For this group, ethnic identity is mostly seen as an asset. Though they disagree with aspects of their cultural background, they are not willing to forsake it altogether. Though these respondents are born into these cultures, they grow to manipulate the situation by picking and choosing when and where to exercise these cultural practices. While many of these are seen as harmless, such as clothing and travelling, there are others such as forced marriages and caste systems which are repeatedly being challenged by these youngsters, based on both religious and British values. In this way they are forging the ground of a new understanding of their chosen identities.

Being British and belonging

What does it mean to be 'British'? Is 'Britishness' a given or can it can be gained, developed and grown? The responses were interesting, and covered a wide variety of areas, mostly cultural aspects including music, scenery, holidays, history, values, language and education. The young people in this group have a sense of inclusiveness and belonging because of the values, education and upbringing they have had. Almost all of them had positive statements about being British, and the negative comments mainly referred to discrimination and stereotyping. These respondents are part of what Jacobson (1998) terms as 'upholding inclusive cultural boundary of Britishness' (Jacobson, 1998: 69). The exclusions, they felt, were in relation to some cultural aspects of British culture which they could not or would not participate in, such as drinking alcohol and having premarital relationships.

> Any decline in British identity might have important consequences for British society. While most residents of the United Kingdom and Northern Ireland officially hold British citizenship and a British passport, British identity is more than an official category. It may also provide a sense of attachment to the state and this may have a role in promoting social cohesion within the nation.
>
> (Heath and Roberts, 2008)

Being British for this group of respondents was sharing British values of fairness, justice and equality; identifying with cultural landmarks, historical events and culture; living in a diverse mixed society and feeling comfortable to be themselves. Understanding cultural jokes, associating with TV shows and understanding cultural pastimes such as musicals and theatre are all aspects of identifying themselves as British rather than any other nationality. These are the aspects that they felt made them British. They did not suggest that flying a flag or celebrating St George's Day made them feel British. It seems that the subtlety of feeling British lies in socialisation, upbringing and feelings of belonging and connectedness.

11. Iman

I'm not a patriotic person, but I'm very proud of being British. For me the idea of being British is different from being patriotic. I don't agree with the wars, with the policies that are coming out in the country ... I'm not about hail Britain or hail England ... I'm proud of the fact that I'm British, it makes me a unique individual, because I'm British and Muslim and ancestral roots in Bangladeshi. That's why I chose the passport [auto-photography].

41. Suhail

I stand firmly for British values with regard to fairness, justice, liberty which Britain has acquired over many many years of wars and difficult periods... for example our Parliament, our sovereignty, taking part in politics, that's being British, to understand how things work, to understand the significant history behind our country to know about it...

30. Zayneb

I feel British because I am British, it's just a fact, and I feel... that I can relate to... this culture is my culture in many ways, i.e. you know, I switch on the TV, I can understand the jokes that they're making and someone who's not from this country probably won't. I feel, you know, a lot of the landmarks here have historical relevance to me, they're part of my heritage, you know, I've travelled around Britain, I'm familiar with places here, you know I can locate the accents... they're part of me.

The values of fairness, justice and equality that these respondents mention are closely linked to the other aspect they like about being British – diversity. The respondents mention that feeling a part of this country lies in acknowledging that Britain is made up of many different people, of varying ethnic, religious, sexual, cultural and gendered backgrounds. The freedom to practise is a strong issue for Muslims here, especially when compared to the situation faced by other Muslims in other European countries – including, notably, the ban of religious insignia in France.

62. Salim

Being British means to me... having freedom... taking an active part in society, viewing people as human beings, regardless of race, age, gender, disability, faith, belief, sexual orientation... regardless they are all human beings...

It is also an interesting note that the respondents repeatedly chose to identify with a British identity rather than an English/Welsh/Scottish identity, mainly because these identities are perceived as racial groupings. These attitudes are matched with large-scale survey results, most notably the latest 2011 Census results, which also emphasised that in a subjective view of national identity, almost all respondents (99.7 per cent) of the 'White: British' ethnic group census category selected 'English Only' as a national identity, while 71 per cent of 'Asian/Asian British: Bangladeshi', 63 per cent of 'Asian/Asian British: Pakistani' and 58 per cent of 'Asian/Asian British: Indian' associated with the 'British only' national identity. Sikhs (62 per cent), Muslims (57 per cent) and Hindus (54 per cent) are all more likely to report British only national identity than all other religious groups. Among religious groups, Christians (15 per cent) are least likely to describe themselves only as British and are much more likely to identify with only an English national identity (Christians 65 per cent and Jews 54 per cent).

The perception of 'British' identity as an all-encompassing national identity rather than a racial identity could be partly related to the far-right discourse, which has seen a targeted ownership of an 'English' identity belonging only to 'whites', but could also stem from a historical trajectory that sees 'British' as a safer option for some visual ethnic minorities to identify with:

20. Sana

I say I'm British. When you say English you get a picture of what an English person looks like, but when you say British, Britain is full of people of different ethnicities and different backgrounds of people, I think that British explains Britain more than English explains Britain.

Not only do this group of respondents feel British, but they also consider Britain as 'home'. This sense of 'home' is repeated and very important for this group, unlike the fourth group in the typology. Feeling British is more than an instrumental or accommodative respect for British practices; for this group, Britain is the one country they consider 'home', where they feel comfortable and welcome – they understand and feel part of the culture. The sense of Britain as home is also starkly obvious when respondents travel abroad and feel foreign (see Asif and Sana). When abroad, their accent may define them as being British; their dress code may hint that they are British; their attitudes to various cultural practices may indicate that they are British.

5. Asif

Britain, again, I mean I feel like Britain is my home, it's like...now when I travel outside the UK I always feel like coming home, you know, home is the UK – you know, there is no other place in the world where I'd rather be than in the UK...this is the one place that I think is home and it's only in the last...since the whole issue over Muslims and integration has kind of blown up, that you begin to feel like your place in this country is under scrutiny...

20. Sana

I'm British, I feel like a lot of white British people, you feel more British when you are abroad than when you are in this country. With language you can speak English, and the fact that you have a British passport it defines your identity by placing you as a person and communicate with them.

These responses are mirrored by quantitative research that found that though Muslims identify themselves as Muslim, they also identify themselves as British:

> The article claims that...Muslims and South Asians are almost as likely as whites to identify themselves as British. In addition, factors such as socio-economic difficulties and ethnically and religiously segregated networks that supposedly contribute to Muslim and South Asian alienation have been shown to be insignificant...and despite retaining ethnic and religious social and political networks, Muslims and South Asians have also actively built integrated networks and consider themselves part of the larger British community.
>
> (Maxwell, 2006: 749)

Is 'belonging' in or to Britain influenced by the way a person is made to feel by wider society? Or is 'belonging' dictated by the way a person chooses to engage/disengage in wider society? Is it wider society or the individual who makes the decision whether they 'belong' or not? When talking about belonging, many respondents referred to feeling a sense of belonging themselves, but also feeling at times ostracised and excluded from wider British society. Aspects of prejudice and discrimination were discussed – that no matter how British they feel, or how many times they state it, their allegiances are questioned. Stereotypes of Islam and Muslims in the media reinforce this paranoia.[3]

As mentioned in Chapter 1, the cases of stereotyping, discrimination (Ameli et al., 2004; Abbas, 2005; Masood, 2006) and Islamophobia (Runnymede Trust, 1997; Allen and Nielsen, 2002; Allen, 2010a; Allen, 2010b; Goodwin, 2013)[4] have increased in recent times, and government policies regarding the prevention of extremism have also meant that Muslims are wary of surveillance and increasingly sensitive about external perceptions and assumptions regarding Islam and Muslims. This can cause defensiveness, similar to the case that taxi driver Musa describes:

36. Musa

I'm a cab driver, a taxi driver, I picked up someone yesterday – three English youths – they don't seem all that good to be honest, drunk and all over the place. He was saying he's in the army, in Iraq, gonna go back on Monday to Iraq. As soon as he got in the car he said 'are you Muslim?' I thought to myself, why d'ya have to ask that particular question as soon as you see me? I'm a taxi driver, do you want a taxi or you don't? He said 'don't take it offensive' but I'm taking it offensive already, the way he commented...asking if I'm Muslim, that means you got something against Muslims the way I see it, you trying' attack me? That's the way I see it straight away...

Some of the unfortunate violent, extremist, terrorist incidents perpetrated by those who refer to themselves as 'Muslim' leads to a focus on Muslims in the West. There is a weight of responsibility placed on the shoulders of British Muslims to somehow either explain the behaviour of this inexcusable minority or to denounce their behaviour as 'un-Islamic'. This pressure on everyday British Muslims can be difficult to shoulder, especially when it is seen as double standards that other ethnic and religious groups are not asked to take responsibility or denounce the behaviour of these who do wrong in the name of their groups:

41. Suhail

I think at times certain incidents take place in Britain where I think not just myself but certain groups of people are looked on and called upon to act or make comments and to speak about certain issues, I don't think that's fair really because for example...bombing on the 7/7, I feel as though I'm not being looked upon as British when they ask me for advice, I mean I can only give the same advice as any non-Muslim white person on the street, so in instances like that I think oh I think I'm not welcome because I'm being picked out, I've been chosen to give my verdict on an extremist attack which I don't have anything to do with anyway and I don't regard them as part of my moderate values and my religion of Islam. That's the time when I feel that I'm seen as non-British or made to feel like that.

These respondents were also very keen to point out that though they are regularly quizzed about whether they are Muslim OR British, they feel they can be Muslim AND British, and that these two identity facets are not in contradiction or conflict.[5] They argue that belonging to their state is part of religion, because Islam urges Muslims to belong and contribute to the community and society they are from. So far, none of the respondents could find any situation they had faced where they had felt a conflict between their religion and their nationality. The difference between the religious views on nationality among this group of respondents and typology group four lies in different interpretations of religious scripture. The views represented by this group can be described as 'to protect the Muslim identity and religious practice, to recognize the Western constitutional structure, to become involved as a citizen at the societal level, and to live with true loyalty to the country to which one belongs' (Ramadan, 2004: 27).

11. Iman

I do feel quite strongly about being a British Muslim, there is a lot that I can offer to this country as well.

56. Zain

Being British...that is part of my religious identity, because Islam teaches me to be part of the community where I reside, of course if there is a conflict between a British value, although there is a debate about how to define Britishness, they are universal values, if there was a uniform consensus on definition of being British and if there was an aspect contradicting Islam, I don't see any, then the Islamic teachings would outweigh the British, if there was any.

65. Nabil

British means being involved – values, being involved, helping out, not being segregated and closed off, but contributing and being involved in the society that you live in and where you come from, and respect the law of the land.

These respondents follow contextual interpretations and understanding of how citizenship and nationality fit into their modern lives as Muslims living in the West. An example of such interpretations is the response of the deputy head of the European Council for Fatwa and Research, Sheikh Faysal Mawlawi. When asked about citizenship on Islam Online, he said:

> A Muslim can affiliate to a non-Muslim country and he or she can also give his or her loyalty to such a country. This is rooted in the *Sunnah* of the Prophet (peace and blessings be upon him)...The religious duties required from a Muslim living in a non-Muslim country... are to live with other people by Islamic morals, to cooperate with them in whatever is necessary or permissible, to deal with them justly, even if it is against himself, to comply with the obligations he undertakes in a way that does not contradict his religious freedom and duties. A Muslim also must not betray the society where he lives or the country to which he belongs. Betrayal is never permissible.[6]

When asked if they had faced any irreconcilable differences between being British and being Muslim, all the respondents in this group said no, and none of them could think of examples. When asked to imagine any possible situations where two identity issues could clash without any hope of resolve, only one young imam (Zain) described what he imagined to be a potential case where halal and kosher meat would be prohibited under British law. Taxi driver Tahir highlights that the only major clash that could be detrimental to both identity groups would be if life in Britain becomes unbearable to the degree where freedom is severely restricted; under that extreme circumstance he would consider leaving his British home and migrating.

In conclusion, these respondents feel Islam is the most influential aspect on their lives. They also have a geographical and emotional attachment to being British – Britain is 'home', they feel British, they act 'British'. They respect the British way of life, and even though they may not be able to participate in every aspect of the British lifestyle, they do not see any conflict between being Muslim and being British. Being Muslim encourages their sense of citizenship and communal belonging. The interpretations they follow support their involvement in their civic community, and promote their civic ethics and their sense of national belonging.

Ethnicity is in the main a symbolic aspect in their lives, but they voluntarily participate in aspects of their cultural background because some of it is an asset; at other times they abide by the requests and pressures of the community out of deference for their elders and out of respect for their parents. Ethnic identification is held on to in order to recognise history and heritage; they use some aspects of their ethnic culture to their advantage, such as the bilingual element and opportunities to travel.

Group four: Primarily Muslim identity

The respondents in this group comprise a small number of the overall group of respondents, but their antipathy and oppositional attitudes are starkly obvious. They have little emotional attachment to their nation state. Unlike the dual identity group, where being Muslim and British is compatible, where they identify geographically with Britain, this group of respondents is very clear that being Muslim comes first. For most, being British comes second; to others, being British means little more than speaking the language and holding a passport. Being 'British' is an instrumental identity; they use it for practical purposes.

Nationality plays a diminutive role in the life of these respondents. There is little sense of any geographical attachment; any civic engagement is rooted in religious engagement rather than a sense of citizenship. Being Muslim comes first, ethnic and civic identity is secondary. These respondents have an accommodative stance to living in Britain – their allegiance is to Islam foremost, and they feel that being a 'good' citizen comes from the values and ethics of their religion.

26. Rashid

The only sense of belonging I have is to the Muslims firstly, and within the Muslims, it's to those who are working to achieve the same goals, there is certainly no sense of geographical belonging.

12. Jamila

Britain... In the way I speak, walk, dress, yes I'm British. But in the values of Britain, no, allegiance to Britain... shock horror... my allegiance goes to Muslims first. My allegiance will always be to Islam and the Muslims first, but that doesn't mean that I'm going to be a bad citizen. My Islam makes me a good citizen.

57. Yahya

My answer will always be as a Muslim, I explain to them that I see myself as a citizen of this world for a very short time, but I see myself as a citizen of the hereafter for a long time, so first and foremost I need to get my priorities right, and my priorities go beyond borders.

Though they pay their taxes, obey the laws and are loyal, they have little emotional attachment to Britain. These respondents use their national belonging in a rational manner in order to survive, while using a more emotive approach in mobilising their religious group sentiment. The use of citizenship and Britishness is merely an instrument in order to fulfil certain goals, such as making a living, having a home and bringing up children, rather than wanting or feeling as if they belong. Uthman, for example, highlights that living in the UK is better than living in any other European country because of the freedom to practise faith here. Such positive aspects of living life in Britain are why they consider themselves 'good' citizens, but this does not cause them to hold any emotional attachment to being British. The material also underlines a certain amount of isolation from and antipathy towards British people and society.

29. Tufayl

For me, if I look at it, I've never really associated with them [British people], for me I've never really, ever, looked at myself as British – I understand that there's a place to be British, there's a place and value to have a passport on a clinical level such as travelling abroad, such as being in this state, living in this state, paying your taxes...

27. Sa'il

I've been here all my life. In terms of being British, I don't see myself as being British, I'm British in that I live in this country and I'm labelled with the nationality of British. I have no qualms about living in this country, in terms of what it offers me it's fine.

Tufayl argues that being British to him is not about national symbols such as flags or football; but having grown up in Britain, it becomes part of you whether you want it to or not. He highlights that although he can say he does not associate himself with being British, being British is part of who he is – it is all that he knows, he is used to it, he is familiar with it. Because these respondents were born and brought up here, they feel it would be difficult to give up the lifestyle and system they are used to.

29. Tufayl

Growing up in this country, whether we like it or not, we are so used to a standard of living, we are so used to the culture, and that's the

ironic thing of this whole thing – I say I'm not British but I'm probably more British than I can ever imagine – and it's only perhaps when
I leave this country I will really realise how British I am, and when
I mean British, I'm not saying that I'm going to, sort of, stick a flag on
my car and support England in football, I'm talking about on another
level, where there are certain values that exist in this society, there are
certain norms that exist in society, certain nuances within humour,
within language, within a way of thinking, within watching a television, that you are so...you are so absorbed in, without realising it,
that it's only when you leave it that you will realise that these things
existed.

These respondents believe that the values that they live by are Islamic
values, and that these are what make them good citizens. There are
'British' or 'Western' values that they disagree with and do not accept.
These conservative or literalist interpretations of Islamic sources (see
the theory in this chapter) lead individuals and even groups[7] to reject
what they consider to be Western concepts such as democracy, human
rights, freedom of expression and so on. Jamila raises concerns over (her
interpretation of) differences between British and Islamic concepts of
freedom, democracy and respect:

12. Jamila

Values...my values come from the Islamic beliefs. Some values which
all people seek, like respect on meeting people, courtesy, feed the
hungry, basic things...kindness, not being rude. But some confusion
in that, although all humans seek these values, I think as Muslims
we do have unique values, and the media mixes it up that we have
all the same values, we don't! I don't believe in the values of freedom
because it goes against my belief, the word *Abid* in Islam means slave,
the whole meaning of Islam is submission, so I don't believe in this
freedom and democracy. I don't believe that human beings can make
up the laws, which is what democracy is.

I believe Allah is the only lawmaker, I take his law. My values are different to that of other people. My truth is different, they seek things
for some benefits, some people who give to charity are selfish, they
really do it for self-fulfilment...But in Islam, that action has to be
purely for the sake of that, you don't want anything back. You are
nice to somebody not because they were nice to you, but because
Allah required this from you. That's why our values as Muslims are

unique, we don't have the same values in freedom and democracy and this point should be clear amongst Muslims, that's why Muslims are not clear about their identity.

If I took to this 'freedom' it means my child can speak to me as he wants, but in Islam he has to respect me and I respect him, I'm not free to neglect him, yet that is the core Western value. Or other things like we don't believe in freedom of speech, that you can go and insult somebody, yet the Western values, yes you can – even the prophets (PBUH). My core values I seek from Islam, not from Western values.

Feeling 'foreign' for some of these respondents is usual. They do not all consider Britain as 'home'; however, they do not consider anywhere else as home either. They suggest that only in mainly 'Muslim' countries do they feel a degree of comfort or homeliness. These attitudes are in stark contrast to the Dual Identity group who believe that Britain is their 'home' and being abroad enforces the feelings of foreignness. This group sees Britain and most Western states in pessimistic, binary terms. They envisage that life here is challenging to their faith, to their values and to the upbringing of their children. However, having been brought up here and having no other state to call 'home', they continue their lawful and practical lives here, while feeling emotionally distant.

25. Salman

But looking at this word in front of me, foreigner [word sort], which is what I feel like now, I feel like I'm a foreign body in this country, it's come so far, I almost feel like a prisoner in this country, trying to break out, not necessarily from the people, but from the certain way of life, the structure, that's how far it's come to. My sense of belonging now is very confused, because although I'm a foreigner in this country, there isn't really anywhere I can go where I won't feel the same way. I can ameliorate it a little by going to a Muslim country, or going to Pakistan where I have an ethnic identity or an Arab country where I have a Muslim identity, but I'm still going to be a foreigner, and that's quite intimidating.

12. Jamila

If I felt like a foreigner, it's probably in all the non-Muslim countries...it's a very difficult question. I feel like a foreigner in non-Islamic lands actually, that's why Britain is part of my life because I live here, but because the Islamic aspect is not here, it's difficult to say ... on holiday we looked for a beach, we ended up on a military beach, training, those planes might be going to Iraq to kill my Muslim brothers, so that causes a problem for my identity, the foreign policy of this country.

29. Tufayl

I don't want to admit it now because in my heart, I do feel to a certain extent a foreigner here, and to an extent, you know, and I do feel, like, in this country that, you know, Muslims are looked down upon, times are hard for them, the government's not necessarily very ... Muslim-friendly, work environment is not very Muslim-friendly, the attitude – denigration of Muslims has increased, I can only go in public with my wife and see people looking at her because she wears a hijab or me wearing an abaya – all of these factors certainly make me feel more, less of a citizen, despite being born here, than anything else. But then I think about where I want to go, I don't feel that I'm linked to anything.

These respondents also have very little affection for national borders or ascriptions; they consider themselves global religious citizens (members of ummah).[8] There are three issues that have led to these respondents feeling disenchanted and disengaged with a specifically British identity, and more prone to overlook national borders. One is that there are specific political events in this cohort of young Muslims which have shaped their lives and caused them to feel this sense of alienation and detachment from a civic sense of belonging. From the Salman Rushdie affair onwards,[9] there are numerous – mainly political – grievances which these respondents have taken personally and which hold the key to their attitudes. This has recently become exacerbated with government community-based policies regarding the prevention of extremism, anti-terrorist measures, increased policing powers, media stereotyping of Muslims and perceived double standards in government foreign policy:

25. Salman

... it takes something to trigger that [identity] off. That was the Rushdie thing, it was a seminal moment for British Muslims. That really changed my thinking where my loyalties lie. From that point onwards it was a balance between how Asian I was and how Muslim, it was the percentage difference ... It does take an external impetus sometimes to make you realise what your identity is, it was certainly the case, it was the politicisation of Islam, the foreign policy of various countries, things that are going on in the world, it makes you question your identity, it makes you question where your identity lies.

26. Rashid

When the Salman Rushdie thing happened... that didn't change much, but it... we could have gone one of two ways, either you go this is wrong and integrate completely in society from that point of view or entrench ourselves or myself a bit more as an outsider, as someone who doesn't quite fit in here. That's the direction we took, that yes this reaffirmed my identity as a Muslim, we've got these views and these guys the British are different, their society is different.

29. Tufayl

Yes, whether it be Bosnia, whether it be, you know, whether it's Chechnya now, whether it be Palestine, whether it be Iraq, whether it be Kashmir, whatever it was, you kind of felt – yes, it's Muslims that are getting victimised, Muslims that are getting trampled on, so you, kind of, almost suddenly develop this idea of an ummah. If there were no problems in the world, if Muslims were not trampled all over, do I think people would have this strong sense of an ummah? – probably not.

22a. Kamal

Yes... it's good to be talking about Islam, yeah, but not in the other ways... as gory [white] people make out... white people... it's like everything's about terrorists and Islam, it's not.

22b. Munir

Skin colour is the most important thing in England anyway, coz white people they are bad, they make Islam bad, Muslim people bad. They always on about black people, black people this and black people that, and then we have bad names from it, and then we have to fight back, and we get a bad name then... you know what I mean.

Secondly, some of these respondents have consequently joined organisations which look at Islam as a political ideology (Ramadan, 2004; Akhtar, 2005; Hamid, 2007; Macey, 2007a, 2007b).[10] They strongly feel that a movement is needed to encourage the development of an Islamic government – a pan Islamic state or *khilafah*. Tariq Ramadan says:

> The discourse is trenchant, politicized, radical and opposed to any idea of involvement or collaboration with Western societies, which is seen as akin to open treason. The *Hizb ut Tahrir* and *Al Muhajirun* movements are the best known in Europe, and they call for jihad and opposition to the West.
>
> (Ramadan, 2004: 27)

Castells' (1997) description of the 'resistant identity' encompasses this group of respondents, in that they communicate within their own network but not with the state. They only communicate with the state when in pursuit of their interests and goals – the revival of Muslim identity though solidarity with the global ummah and the attempt to create an Islamic state[11] (Lewis, 2007). Similar to the 'reactive' ethnicity,[12] these respondents also reject mainstream values and norms, creating their own rules and ideals which they believe will lead to a better life, community and indeed nation.

26. Rashid

Islam is inherently political, the way I see it going this sense of identity will be transferred to a sense of state level or an international political level, where a sense of identity [...] some sort of Islamic political structure[...]A *khilafah* or *khalifa* for lack of a better word. While the *khilafah* exists then the identity of the Muslims of the citizens of the *khilafah* will be as opposed to the other countries of the world. The purpose of the *khalifa* is to implement Islam internally and to spread the rule of Islam to the rest of the world. Hypothetically speaking, up until that we can achieve that your relationship with the rest of the world will be defined by that and the citizens will probably be inculcated with that viewpoint and that sense of identity of the citizens will be along this line. Come the point when the state takes over the world, the identity would still be Muslim because that is what it would be ...

29. Tufayl

I do identify with ummah – for me, the ummah does exist, on a spiritual level, on a ... on an emotional level, on a practical level, I do think that it can only really, really manifest itself when there is a state, I do believe that, coz I think that is what gives the greatest form of definition.

Thirdly, their interpretations of Islamic rulings regarding citizenship are different from those followed by others (see group three). As Chapter 2 highlighted, the traditions of textual references can be crucial in understanding the differences between Muslim attitudes.[13] Some of the respondents in group four follow certain interpretations of religious scripture – for example, that God has presented them with membership of a global Islamic community – the ummah. This belonging and allegiance to the ummah is above and beyond national borders, and thus above British citizenship. They are 'good' citizens because their religion expects them to respect and abide by the rules of society, but this in itself does not help in developing any national sentiment. Here, Jamila and Sa'il (both members of Hizb ut Tahrir) highlight how they believe that nation state boundaries are illegitimate constructs, intending to split people up along nationalist lines and divide groups. They believe that Muslims do not belong to nation states, that the global ummah is far more important, and that this is what Islam requires of its believers.

27. Sa'il

When you say the ummah, I take it on board as the global ummah, as in every single Muslim who exists in the world, that's more important than a country to label you as being part of that country. I feel like I have a close affinity with the Muslim ummah simply because Allah (SWT) has told us that we have to. In this country, this government pushes you to a certain nationality, but that's not who we take our ruling from, our rulings come from Allah ... Allah says you're not meant to be British, you are meant to be part of a global ummah.

12. Jamila

Ummah is part of our belief; we believe that Muslims are one ummah, one nation. It's a very powerful concept, and it's one which Tony Blair wants to pull out of Muslims, there was a leaked document two years ago, he said he wanted to destroy this concept of ummah amongst the Muslims, because it creates problems, because of this ummah concept, my allegiance to Britain is not there. It comes to the ummah first. But I don't think that Tony Blair will be successful in this ... Islam transcends all nationalism and boundaries, the flag should be the Islamic flag, that flag is what is missing today, because for countries nationalism comes first, I don't associate with any national flag, because I don't associate with nationality, that's how my Islam has changed my identity. People talk about the radicalisation of Muslims, this is radical, but Islam says nationalism is *haram* [unlawful within Islam]. This is clear.

These respondents have a complex and differing understanding of religion from those in the Dual Identity group. These respondents are British by name, citizenship and birth, yet they hold little belief in a need for allegiance and loyalty to national borders. They feel foreign on British soil, though they have no other place to call home. They identify with Islam in the main and with no other identity. They highlight that political issues, foreign policy, discrimination, stereotyping and their contextualisation of Islamic references are the reasons they feel the way they do. The civic engagement they participate in is rooted in religious values and ideals. Their boundary maintenance of 'otherness' is clear throughout the discussion. They justify their attitudes on religious rather than ethnic grounds, but reject most of British culture and even some values as being secondary and substandard. They are, in the main, Muslims – but Muslims with different attitudes from the other three groups.

Conclusion

The aim of this chapter was to tackle the concept of identity, because it is the root that the research project is based upon: how does identity feature in the lives of these young second-generation British Muslims? In understanding identity from their viewpoint, the chapter found that religion and national identity as well as ethnic belonging held meaning in the lives of these respondents.

Identity is a flexible, fluid, and multifaceted aspect of life. It is not concrete and it is not always consistent. It may change through time, and it may be reassessed and re-evaluated in the minds of the respondents. Through the use of varying research methods (word sorts and auto-photography) via the interviews, the research was able to elicit the attitudes, views and beliefs the respondents held regarding their group identity.

Religion played a key role in the lives of many of the respondents. The way in which Islam acts as a significant source of meaning in their lives and the reasons behind this attachment formed a considerable part of this chapter. For the first group, religion was found to be peripheral –

it was symbolic in nature. Religion for the other three groups was more important. It mediated aspects of their personal and social lives. This is clearly seen across groups two, three and four. The difference between group two and the others lay in the flexible attitude given to the practice of tenets such as prayer and fasting. Though respondents in group two do consider themselves Muslim, and Islam has a role in their lives, the role of religious practice is flexible. Religion is as important as other aspects of their identity, including gender, age, femininity, nationality and so on.

Religion was a main source of guidance for respondents in the third and fourth group. Among these two groups the participants were clearly independent with regard to their feeling for their religious and ethnic identity. Islam influences their lives. For these two groups religion is not just a personal choice, but also has a strong impact on their daily decisions and outlooks, as can be seen in their day-to-day lifestyle. The difference between these two groups of respondents lay in their religious interpretation. This meant that the third group held more inclusive views of citizenship, Britishness and belonging; the fourth group, in comparison, was more exclusively Muslim and felt little connection to an ethnic identity or nationality.

During this chapter, distinguishing between religion and ethnicity as sources of identity was important. As mentioned earlier, the differentiation between ethnicity and religion is because ethnicity is a part of the respondents' lives that they are born into, and specifically relates to similar people and a specific geographical place, whereas religion is an aspect of their lives that they can choose to belong to (or not), and it can have universal significance for people of diverse backgrounds. Evidence of ethnic identity attachment was low among these respondents. They spoke of holding fluid and hybrid ethnic identities, which has no space for complete ethnic group belonging. The role of ethnicity was most influential in groups two and three. Respondents in both of these groups considered their ethnic identity as another facet of their identity, and strove to keep aspects which they saw as assets alive, such as speaking another language. Both groups of respondents chose to forsake aspects of ethnicity that they felt no longer played a role in British society and could not fit in with their faith – issues such as clan culture and forced marriages, for example. For both groups, their elders, extended family and their parents have an impact on the role that ethnic group culture plays. As the second generation they still feel unable to be disrespectful about the culture of their parents and sideline their heritage, so they maintain a certain amount, while using both religious and British points of view to persuade their elders that certain aspects of the culture cannot be maintained. As the generations develop, we may find that ethnic identity attachment may indeed diminish and that participating in aspects of ethnic culture may indeed become symbolic.

Being British was meaningful to respondents in groups one, two and three. For these respondents citizenship plays a role in their lives – values, socialisation and expectations are important – more so for groups one and three. The second group of respondents, though identifying themselves as British, have greater connection beyond borders, with people of many diverse backgrounds and cultures. Members of the fourth group also have a connection beyond borders (the ummah), but lack an emotional attachment to their nationality. They consider their citizenship as enabling them to live a certain independent lifestyle where they can maintain their mainly religious identity. This relationship is instrumental in nature, and there is little emotional attachment to a British identity. For group three, Britishness is meaningful and undoubtedly tied to their religious identity.

The relevance of this four-group typology lies in setting a framework from which the political motivations of the respondents can be noted. Chapter 4 will use the typology-based identity framework in order to analyse the varying aspects that may or may not motivate political participation. It will explore how the respondents make certain decisions regarding political action, and will uncover whether their identity facets play a role in decision-making. The chapter will follow the extent to which the respondents participate politically. It will also underline what the respondents consider to be political in nature, and why and whether these actions are deemed to be effective or ineffective.

4
Impetus for Engagement

Catalysts to action come in many varied forms – a misguided foreign policy decision, a new tax or the sale of green belt land, for example. The stimulus to engage in a political activity is rooted in the human psyche: at times, it is an incident that alters an individual's attitude towards action, on other occasions it is a value system that individuals have been taught and believe in. Many experiences can generate political interest – being socialised in a highly political environment, whether it is a home, school, church or war zone, can affect the political outlook of individuals; however, we can also search for concrete patterns of motivation through discussions with individuals regarding the source(s) of their political motivation.[1] This chapter explores these sources and the commonalities and differences between the participants, finally recognising the common themes that motivate political engagement. Understanding the roots of political motivation is useful in contextualising the forms of action taken, the popularity of certain political activities and the role that motivation plays in the choice of those political issues that are popular among the respondents.

The process is all about choice: siblings may be socialised in the same highly politicised family, yet not be motivated to engage in politics to the same level or in the same way unless they identify with the values to a similar degree. This underlines the importance of individual choice in reacting to the stimulus. This chapter explores the foundation of participants' commitment to political issues which results in engagement. What spurs these young Muslims to politically engage? And does the drive to participate in politics derive from the identity facets discussed in Chapter 2? In Chapter 3, the links between the various typology groups highlighted that the fluidity of identity is a continuous process and that the identity groups do not function in and of themselves, but link together and overlap. This chapter will continue the story – how identity impacts on behaviour; specifically on political action via motivation. It explores what motivates or helps to initiate political action. It attempts to understand how identity influences interests and concerns in the political sphere.[2]

There are several theories of political motivation that are based on participant choices.[3] First, there is the rational actor and economic approach. This includes selective incentives that benefit an individual or group. Rosenstone and Hansen (1993) distinguish three types of selective incentives: Material (e.g. Employment opportunities from engagement); Solitary (e.g. Recognised as a leader among the group); and Purposive (e.g. Sense of having done duty). Whiteley and Seyd (2002) also create a synthesis of rational choice theory and social psychological theory in order to develop a model that explains high intensity types of participation:

> The general incentive theory of political participation postulates that a number of distinct factors are at work in explaining why people join a political party or become active once they have joined. These are selective incentives, group motivations, and affective or expressive motives. Some of these are grounded in rational choice theory, but the theory goes beyond a narrow rational choice conception of participation to examine broader motives for involvement, derived from the social psychological theoretical tradition.
>
> (Whiteley and Seyd, 2002: 56)

> People participate in politics because they get something out of it. The rewards take many forms. Participants sometimes enjoy material benefits, tangible rewards that are easily converted into money, like a government job or a tax break. Those active in politics can also receive solitary benefits, intangible rewards that stem from social interaction, like status, deference and friendship. And participation can also yield purposive benefits, intrinsic rewards that derive from the act of participation itself, such as a sense of satisfaction from having contributed to a worthy cause.
>
> (Rosenstone and Hansen, 1993: 16)

'Material benefit' (Rosenstone and Hansen, 1993) and 'Outcome incentives' (Pattie et al., 2004) are political activities that are motivated by the prospect of material gains for the participant. These could include employment opportunities, rising through the ranks and being elected into office. This form of incentive underlines that individuals at times are motivated to be politically involved for personal benefit. Material selective benefits such as employment opportunities, tax cuts and university grants constitute very material gains and losses by groups of people. Social class-based political behaviour could constitute this form of incentive – people make choices based on their class background and socio-economic status.[4] The self-interested motivations also include those who are driven to take action out of psychological benefits, such as demonstrating because it is therapeutic or thrilling (Tullock, 1971; Opp, 1990).

Then we have the altruistic models, which argue that value/moral/quality-based motives are distinct from the self-interested rational actor ones. One example is engagement because of civic motivations (Heath, 1985; Whiteley and Seyd, 2002; Pattie et al., 2004). People who participate in voting, political campaigning or lobbying out of a sense of British pride, engaging in the democratic rights of their country out of loyalty rather than the benefits they may receive from doing so, are motivated by altruistic reasoning.

> An ideal citizen is the person who has a sense of belonging to a community and feels a sense of obligation and commitment to other members of that community. The community is most likely to be contained within a territorial unit.
>
> (Pattie et al., 2004: 34)

> Some people hold beliefs and preferences that motivate their participation internally. The most common is a sense of citizen duty. Because of their socialization by family, teachers, or friends, some people believe it is their responsibility to participate in politics – and in particular to vote – regardless of whether their participation has any effect on the outcome.
>
> (Rosenstone and Hansen, 1993: 19)

Finally we have the group that is construed of both moral and self-interested motivations. A fusion of choice-making and social psychological attitudes, these theories suggest that people are encouraged to participate through both moral incentives and self-interested motivations.[5]

Under the identity-construction approach, moral motivation in politics and political behaviour is regarded neither solely as rooted in a self-interested calculation of costs and benefits, as in rational actor accounts, nor as based solely on altruistic or self-sacrificing impulses, as in the 'beyond self-interest' approach. Rather, the identity-construction approach points to types of concerns that are morally relevant and self-regarding at the same time...

(Teske, 1997: 74)

This is the case for global concerns linked to 'new' value politics and Postmaterialist issues, such as the environment, anti-poverty (Mueller-Rommel, 1989; Roots, 1991) and human rights campaigns, which are difficult to frame as either self-interested or moral incentives. These global concerns are materialist in that they benefit everyone; they are essentially altruistic in nature.

Inglehart's (1990, 1997)[6] work on Postmaterialism argues that an increase in affluence has led to changes in the political issues by which people are motivated. People have become more concerned with Postmaterialist values such as 'belonging, self- expression and the quality of life' (Inglehart, 1981: 880). This is most obvious among the young, especially with improvements in standards of living, better education and increased awareness of global political issues. In *Modernization and Postmodernization* Inglehart (1997) highlights that new concerns such as the environment, rights (minority, human, gay, abortion, etc.) and freedom of speech have taken precedence over traditional salient group behaviours (such as social class). In *Citizen Politics* Dalton (1996) also supports the argument that there has been a move away from politics based on economic success to 'quality'-based concerns such as environmental issues, mainly owing to social mobility (weakening the identification between new generations and the social class of their parents), cognitive mobilisation (voters are better equipped to evaluate political policies) and the individualisation of society (shifting away from group solidarity towards Maslow's (1943, 1954) self-actualisation thesis).[7]

Similarly, people who participate for the benefit of the group, at a potential cost to themselves as an individual, are motivated to do so for the greater good of the group or the greater benefit of the group at large, also benefit as individuals who are part of that group. Thus this motivation is both altruistic in nature as well as self-serving (Whiteley and Seyd, 2002; Pattie et al., 2004).

A second approach focuses upon the group itself rather than its group related class position and emphasizes attitudes related to group membership per se that mediate the effects of socio economic position on participation. A particular group subculture might be viewed as either encouraging or discouraging to political participation; or those who have a sense of group identity or consciousness might be more active.

(Verba et al., 1993: 458)

Much research has been conducted highlighting the importance of group identity as a factor impacting individual political behaviour (Shingles, 1981; Bobo and Gilliam, 1990; Tate, 1991; de la Garza, 1992). According to the Social Identity theory discussed in the earlier chapter, people tend to categorise each other according to labels, identify with certain groups ('our in-group') and compare and contrast 'our group' with other groups (out-groups), with favouritism towards their own group. By categorising people into groups, people are drawn to their particular group because of the differentiation between groups and the perception of the differences, and how they identify with their particular group.

> ... collective identity confirms that one belongs to a particular place in the social world. At the same time, it also affords distinctiveness from those other social places (or people) to which one does not belong. It further signals that one is like other people, though not necessarily like other people ... collective identity signals that one is not alone but can count on the social support and solidarity of other in-group members, so that, as a group, one is a much more efficacious social agent.

(Simon and Klandermans, 2001: 321)

Dawson (1995) also studies the role that such group incentives play in motivating people to choose group identity over alternative groupings. He questions why African Americans remain politically homogeneous to their race even though within the group they are economically polarised.

One theory based on the theory of relative deprivation[8] is called the equity-fairness theory (Pattie et al., 2004). Based on relative deprivation (Runcimon, 1966; Gurr, 1970; Muller, 1979; Dalton, 2002), the equity-fairness theory is an explanatory approach which attempts to explain political motivation by exploring the relationship between groups or individuals who compare themselves to other groups/individuals; this comparison usually results in frustration and/or aggression in political participation because of perceived inequalities and disadvantages.

It is far more likely to explain unorthodox political behaviour such as riots than conventional political engagement such as voting. The model argues that such behaviour is more likely among minority groups, because in comparison to other groups they will have strong group consciousness as well as an ability to mobilise based on the comparative inequality and disadvantage they feel. The groups are then able to orchestrate political action and motivate their members to engage in order to improve the situation (Olsen, 1970; Verba and Nie, 1972; Miller et al., 1981).

> The equity-fairness or relative deprivation model is based on the idea that individuals who perceive a gap between what they expect out of life and what they actually experience are likely to suffer from psychological deprivation... this perception of relative deprivation may in turn mobilize them to participate, particularly in protest activities.
>
> (Pattie et al., 2004: 166)

The evidence from this research highlights that the moral language, value-based judgements and explanations the respondents give to their political activity indicate that value-based motivation is highly relevant for understanding their political behaviour. As will be seen, there are variations in the 'values' that are preferred among the respondents, but also there is a variation in motivations, impacting on the actions taken. So one respondent will be motivated by different values, resulting in different political actions and multiple interests/issues.

Civic motivation

Citizenship and civic behaviour is discussed readily by respondents because it is in essence exploring the relationship between an individual and the state. Earlier in the book, we found groups one, two and three in the typology were identifying themselves as British.[9] Such information contextualises the feelings towards citizenship of many young Muslims.

Civic motivation for political participation is mainly focused on the format of electoral voting. Voting is a brief activity that occurs with an intense amount of social and political activity that builds up to Election Day. The amount of information that is provided for voters and the pressure to engage – being persuaded, manipulated and cajoled into the voting booth in order to add a cross in a box – is high. The irony is that voting occurs at such a mass level that one vote does not necessarily influence the outcome. However, people do vote in their masses. Understanding the context and attitudes behind such political behaviour is steeped heavily in civic attitudes – gained during childhood socialisation. Also, voting is more popular among people with high levels of efficacy and belief in the democratic system.

> Education functions in a more complicated way as a political resource: formal education itself fosters organizational and communication skills that are germane to political activity and imparts attitudes such as a sense of civic duty or political efficacy that are associated with political involvement.
>
> (Verba et al., 1993: 457)

Civic political participation is usually focused on voting, though potentially it can incorporate other political activities such as volunteering as a local councillor, campaigning for a local political issue or fundraising for a local political campaign. Voting is the most popular civic political action because is the one activity that is strongly linked to rights and duty; while it is less affected by resources (it is free and very quick), it is affected by political outlook and perception. The more respondents felt British, felt they belonged and felt a sense of duty to the state, the more likely they were to vote and feel positive about the democratic system. This is typical for most British voters as well (Parry et al., 1992: 188). Pattie et al. (2004), however, found that political engagement beyond voting is not seen as a sense of duty by their respondents:

> Overall then we can summarize that people's sense of civic obligation encompasses obedience to the state, a willingness to undertake voluntary actions, such as participating in a Neighbourhood Watch or a local renovation project, and a willingness to engage in civic service, such as going on a jury or giving blood. But for most people their sense of duty does not extend to more obvious political undertakings, such as becoming a school governor or standing for the local council; on such matters, their commitment is much more limited.
>
> (Pattie et al., 2004: 53)

With regard to the typology from earlier in the book, groups one, two and three all display significant attention towards civic duty as a form of political motivation – especially for electoral voting. They recognise that voting is part of a healthy democracy and believe it shows their political allegiance towards the state. This civic motivation does not explain how they vote, but it does explain why they vote. It is only some members of typology group four who refuse to recognise civic motivation as important, which is not surprising considering the outcome of Chapter 3.

The respondents are motivated by their civic identity because they see the democratic system as their prerogative and privilege. It highlights their positive feelings towards a democratic government and towards engaged politics. Some respondents reflect on historical moments when the vote was fought for by women for women; others reflect on current political climates where democracy is a façade or not reliable. A feeling of appreciation towards a democratic system which in essence attempts to consider the political outlooks of the masses is popular.

11. Iman

The way I see it is that we live in a democracy where every opinion matters, or is supposed to matter. By me being a resident in this country it is absolutely my right to have my opinion heard. I'm fortunate enough to have this right, so why waste it.

3. Dalal

I think voting is very important...I always want to use my vote, because I think there are places where people aren't given the chance to vote, I think we're very lucky to be able to vote.

2. Banan

Well the last general election was the first time I was eligible to vote, I'd turned 18, so it was quite a romantic action, I'd always wanted to vote...reading about the suffragettes, and how they died getting us the vote that made me want to go out and exercise my democratic right.

31. Adam

I'm a big fan of voting, it's an absolute, absolute, absolute must that we should vote and participate in a democratic environment or engage in democracy.

The deep-rooted feelings of civic duty are highlighted alongside the feelings of voting as a right and privilege. Engaging in the democratic processes is perceived as a responsibility that includes engaging in elections in order to advocate views and choices, and to avoid candidates from parties such as the BNP being elected.

> Voting is represented as being not merely a right but a duty. Secondly, even if few voters read the full party manifestos, virtually all receive an electoral address from the candidates along with other literature. If they ignore these, they can scarcely avoid entirely the media coverage and the posters.
>
> (Parry et al., 1992: 292)

44. Leyan

I basically feel completely unrepresented by the party political system in the UK... and for that reason I feel a duty to vote.

58. Uthman

I feel strongly that people should vote, because people not voting means people like Nick Griffin become MEP, people should vote based on what is closer to their faith rather than just voting on loyalties they might feel they have with someone.

It is quite clear from the respondents that though they are motivated by differing concerns in the political arena, when it comes to electoral voting, the majority keenly feel a psychological sense of civic duty and a communal right to vote. They understand the potential impact they could have, even though voting occurs in masses. The expressive nature of these incentives is important to its psychological success in building a sense of belonging to a state and feelings of active citizenship.

Global catalysts

Global concerns are a political catalyst for individuals who value ethical, humanitarian and environmental causes and are motivated to engage in the political sphere owing to the expressive nature and potential of political activity. This set of political motives is representative of wider British society.

These global concerns as political stimulus were most popular among the first two groups in the typology. The responses from the respondents can be described as Postmaterialist values and concerns. Concerns they hold regarding war, humanitarian causes, inequality, political injustices, human rights, the environment and so on are all examples of Postmaterialist tendencies. The theory of Postmaterialism (as discussed earlier in this chapter) was developed in the 1970s by Ronald Inglehart,[10] who argues (1990) that there has been an increase in the salience of lifestyle issues and a decline in social group bases such as class and religion; and that these have led to newer patterns of political behaviour. He argues that a shift has occurred via gradual cultural changes in societies, with the result that issues relating to quality of life and self-expression (Inglehart, 1990: 66) are far more popular, and traditional religious, moral and political values have declined.

> The term 'Post-materialist' denotes a set of goals that are emphasized after people have attained material security, and because they have attained material security. Thus, the collapse of security would lead to a gradual shift back toward Materialist priorities. The emergence of Postmaterialism does not reflect a reversal of polarities, but a change of priorities: Postmaterialists do not place a negative value on economic and physical security – they value it positively, like everyone else; but unlike Materialists, they give even higher priority to self-expression and the quality of life.
>
> (Inglehart, 1997: 35)

When these interviews were conducted, the economic recession of 2009 was not in sight; neither was the banking crisis that went alongside it. Whether the responses from the respondents regarding their political motivations would have differed had they been interviewed under such circumstances is another matter. However, Inglehart (1990) argues that even short-term economic adversity does not diminish these long-term and long-standing values: 'Postmaterialism did not dwindle away in the face of diminished economic and physical security. In most countries, its numbers grew, and in many ways its political influence seems greater now than it was a decade or two ago; but its character and tactics have changed significantly' (Inglehart, 1990: 67).

Both respondents from typology groups one and two discuss being motivated by injustices (Hana, Dalal, Adam, Noora), conflict (Dalal, Noora, Wafa), inequality (Hana, Zayd) and green issues (Hassan, Wafa). These are issues that are equally popular among Postmaterialists in wider British society, and in general the attitudes from this group of respondents fit in well with views, interests and causes supported by Postmaterialists. These concerns are clearly issues that affect everyone (and so people are engaging at a cost to themselves because while a few engage everyone benefits). It is also clear that these issues are not directly affecting the respondents; they participate because of psychological values – a sense of injustice, sadness at loss of life, frustration with inequality, lifestyle values:

45. Hana

I'd be more influenced to go if...obviously it's an issue that I care about a lot...Global issues, more than local, yeah, definitely, sort of political injustices...Again, the international aspect is, yes, and also my feeling that we need to do everything to help people and to...equalise the way that things are so it...I don't want to be making us richer at the expense of poor people.

3. Dalal

...I was quite passionate about that, and quite emotionally passionate I think. I don't think that it's even the fact that it was a Muslim country that was invaded; it was just the fact that there were people who were going to get killed for no reason.

31. Adam

For instance the Guantanamo Bay, my local MP was very slow to take up that issue with the government...to me that was an issue of justice nothing to do with Muslim or not but I felt it was a social [issue].

9. Hassan

...I don't often see it as a Green political thing, I see it as a Green value thing and, you know, part of a frame of how you live, that's the bigger [issue]...me joining the Green Party...it was also about how you see your spiritual side, and I think, innately, it's about the environment, about people.

It is also interesting that at no point did the respondents in this research mention instrumental incentives. This may be linked to the fact that people do not like to admit to materialist or self-centred incentives – the social desirability bias 'in which cognitive dissonance can lead to a rather consistent distortion of memory in order to reinforce continued perception of oneself as a good citizen' (Cahalan, 1968: 621); or it may be linked to the time frame of the interviews, but as it stands the material highlights a keen interest in Postmaterial causes. These young British Muslims are driven to express themselves far more than they are motivated by personal gain or interest. As discussed during the introduction to this chapter,[11] there are self-expression-based motives that people use as a form of political motivation. Though they as individuals may not achieve any material gain from taking part, they benefit from other expressive and emotional achievements. Some find certain political action remedial, expressing their emotions and venting their anger; others enjoy being at the heart of an event and experiencing political action first hand; Dalal mentions enjoying the 'atmosphere' of demonstrating. These psychological gains, the sense of fulfilment from engaging in political activity, are in themselves a motivation for engagement – suggesting a revolving door effect for political motivation: the more a person attends and engages, the more they gain and the more often they become involved. In this scenario, instrumental calculations regarding the likely effectiveness of a given political action seem obsolete, while the psychological gain becomes more relevant than the effectiveness or ineffectiveness of the action.

17. Noora

It's my emotions, how passionate I am about the subject, how angry I am about an issue...Demonstrations, in the society we live in, it's the only way to voice our political frustration, only channel we've got, but it doesn't do much, it's just a vent, and I got frustrated with that because I want to do something.

3. Dalal

I actually quite enjoy demonstrations...I think that the atmosphere is really good. That's quite a shallow, one-dimensional thing about thing about them...

Although the respondents are motivated mainly by Postmaterialist concerns and expressive behaviour, there is also an element of enduring childhood perspectives. The respondents mention how they are influenced by their socialisation as children – from seeing international conflicts to boycotting goods that their parents boycotted. Inglehart's thesis argues that childhood experiences are never lost, and that adults are influenced by childhood outlooks and experiences that continue into adulthood. This is relevant for these groups, who mention that religious upbringing still influences their outlook, even if they don't identify with the group completely. For example, Hana, Dalal and Adam report that they are influenced by their childhood upbringing in terms of parental influence as well as where they grew up:

45. Hana

Yeah, I think a lot of the feeling of being interested in international politics comes from my upbringing. My mum's also from Zimbabwe as well as being... as well as that connection with the Middle East (my parents have both lived in the Middle East) as I said; I've done a lot of travelling, so those are really issues that interest me.

31. Adam

[Dad] influenced in shaping my perspective on life, he was one of the people who brought the best out of you and he always emphasised on communication and on getting and engaging with us from a very young age in order to make us better tune to what's happening in the reality of situations [international conflicts].

3. Dalal

Actually... since we were little we don't buy any Nestlé or L'Oréal stuff, my mum's made a point of not doing that, because of the... to do with the dried milk scenario and Nestlé giving out dried milk in countries in Africa, and then the kind of breast milk of these mothers in Africa dried up, so and L'Oréal basically is Nestlé I think, like Nestlé owns L'Oréal or L'Oréal owns Nestlé, whichever one... we still don't buy Nestlé, but it's more of a habit more than anything...

This continuing influence of socialisation is also interesting to note with regard to religious attachment. Interestingly, Inglehart's (1990) thesis highlights that people with Postmaterialist preferences seem to have weak relationships with traditional or institutional religion (unlike Materialists). However, like Materialists, people who fall into the Postmaterialist camp have strong tendencies towards religion in more relaxed, spiritual forms:

... the linkage between the rise of Postmaterialism and the decline of religious orientations more generally is conditional, not inherent. As we have noted, despite their detachment from traditional religion, Postmaterialists are significantly more likely than Materialists to spend time thinking about the meaning and purpose of life. In this respect, Postmaterialists may have more potential interest in religion than Materialists do. A religious message based on economic and physical insecurity finds little resonance among Postmaterialists – but one that conveyed a sense of meaning and purpose in contemporary society might fill a need that is becoming increasingly widespread.

(Inglehart, 1990: 211)

This is mirrored in the responses of respondents in this category. Identity categories one and two were, in comparison to the remaining groups, less religiously orientated, less attached to obligations and more likely to be symbolically Muslim. However, as shown in Chapter 3, they still held aspects of religious feelings and some followed limited religious observances. Overall, this fits well with the analysis that Inglehart (1990) discusses regarding members of wider society who hold Postmaterialist perspectives.

Noora says that socialisation and upbringing is an important part of who she is as an adult; that even if she is no longer practising (see Chapter 3 on identity group one) she is still influenced by her Muslim upbringing and the values that were instilled in her, and to a certain degree she feels that upbringing politicised her. Both Adam and Dalal also discuss the parental influence, being Muslim and political interest. Being Muslim was part and parcel of their upbringing and it affected their political socialisation:

17. Noora

I was brought up as a Muslim, with certain beliefs, America's bad, Israel's bad, blah blah blah, you know, my mum said if I became a policewoman she'd disown me, etc. ... brought up ... hate is a strong word ... but not to trust the government's actions ...

31. Adam

when I was young, in fact my father from the age of, God knows, the earliest I can remember is the invasion of Lebanon by Israel in '82 and I remember discussing with my father who was a big proponent of engagement on all topics, be it politics, the majority of the time it was politics but it could be issues which are traditionally taboo in Muslim households but it was discussed out in the open with the female members present as well.

3. Dalal

I got a lot of my political views from my dad, but the fact that I'm a Muslim, I think that automatically makes me quite left-wing in some ways in this country ...

Whether respondents were brought up in secular or religious environments, religion has played a varying role in their political motivations as adults. Though they are more motivated by global concerns and Postmaterialist value-based choices, religious identity still holds sway over the causes they support and the actions they take. Similar to the quotations from respondents above, here Ghazal is saying that though she has shifted to more value-based decisions, the political choices she has made in the past have been strongly influenced by being Muslim.

8. Ghazal

They [causes] were more international issues, mostly Muslim-based. I'd like to think that I'd be the type of person who would have enough motivation and, like, a social conscience to get involved in international issues that weren't related to religion, but I think that inevitably religion has played a really important part in deciding what...you can't protest about everything that's going on...in deciding what was worthy of my time...

The respondents who fit into this category are clearly motivated by Postmaterialist values and concerns. This group is motivated by altruistic incentives, where many if not all people benefit, even though only a few people engage, participate and act. This is a noticeably altruistic form of political motivation, which fosters a sense of group participation for mass benefit. They have a psychological preference for expressive forms of political engagement, which also motivate them to engage. In addition, these respondents are motivated by emotional responses to mass or collective concerns. They feel that expressing anger and frustration over injustices and inequality, for example, is what motivated them to become involved or take part in political activities. These psychological motivations are altruistic in nature, yet fulfil needs for self-expression.

However, childhood socialisation influences the concerns they are keen on, and socialisation has impacted on their political landscape through political group consciousness. Though in the identity group typology these respondents were either symbolically identifying as Muslim or Islam played a peripheral role in their lives, owing to their upbringing and socialisation, being Muslim does have an effect on the Postmaterialist causes they choose to engage in. These respondents have been brought up with a different world view and approach.

So what does this tell us about the bigger picture? Identity is reflected in the political motivations the people in these typology groups express; indirectly, identity has an impact on their political views and perspectives and their psychological attachments. Some young British Muslims have similar motivations to wider society – large-scale global concerns – though group identity is also an influence on their political motivations as adults.

Religious incentives

Political sociology literature documents that religion provides an important source of social capital and democratic skills that facilitate democratic participation (Putnam, 1993; Verba et al., 1995; Wood, 1995). Faith provides believers with a sense of belonging in a society and a sense of moral meaning to the life they lead. These psychological, social and spiritual attachments are the possible explanations for understanding the political action of religious communities. Political culture for these respondents most clearly encompasses what is mainly a religious reference point. Religion and politics have intricate relationships the world over, and for this group of respondents, as for many other cultures across the world, religion plays a pivotal role in influencing their political outlook.

> it would be a mistake to conclude that religious faith is unimportant for politics in contemporary Britain. Political discourse rooted in faith continues to matter a great deal. Many people's thinking about right and wrong, and about the kind of society they want to live in, is deeply influenced by religious faith and values instilled by faith.
>
> (Rt Hon. Stephen Timms, MP. Foreword
> in Birdwell and Littler, 2012: 11)

There is also evidence to suggest that minority group matters can often trump economic concerns. Similar to those arguments, this category highlights that politicised religious collective identity has resulted in religiously motivated political action. With regard to this group of young British Muslims, group identity heightens the likelihood of political mobilisation.

The first consistent aspect that these young Muslims discuss in relation to political motivation is the 'purposive' and 'expressive' motivations of religious duty. This was mentioned during Chapter 3 when exploring issues relating to British citizenship and Islam for group three, who felt that Islam inherently supports citizenship because it urges Muslims to belong and to contribute to the community and society they are from. This is very similar to the responses below, which argue that being Muslim means that being involved in politics is imperative – and a duty. This attitude includes respondents from the fourth identity group, who do not identify with being British. They believe, like respondents from group three, that religion is the motivation and influence in political involvement.

These attitudes very much fit in with the theory mentioned earlier of group motivations – people who participate in political activities because of a group consciousness, for the advantage of their group and at a possible cost to themselves (both material and other). It also encompasses (in a similar way to civic duty) a 'purposive' motivation – a group mission to act.

12. Jamila

I would voice my opinion, from the Islamic perspective, to stop the wrong that is happening, the *munkar* [something that is forbidden] that is happening, I regard it as my obligation as a Muslim in this country who is fit and able to voice my opinion for my fellow ummah and help out, for those who can't do it in the Muslim world. I go for the purpose of raising awareness about oppression happening in the Muslim world, exposing something that has happened like injustice of a war...

56. Zain

Whatever I do that is defined as political would be religious otherwise I wouldn't do it.

65. Nabil

I think it's important that Muslims get involved not just when it's Muslims but people joining together wherever they see injustices happening around the world, on behalf of Muslims we shouldn't only go out and demonstrate when it's just Muslims, but if they find any injustices happening around the world, we should have the same desires, same motivations to bring about change and justice.

In Chapter 3, we found that group three identified as much with their British identity as their Muslim identity. Why is it that when considering political motivation, they are more motivated by their religious identity than their national identity? As was discussed earlier with regard to civic motivation, most group three respondents vote through civic motivations, but civic motivations do not seem to encourage their participation in any other political regard. The answer to this question, I believe, may lie in Social Identity theory as discussed in Chapter 2. Social Identity theory highlights that not all collective identities are salient at the same time. Some identities stay inactive depending on the social context. In a context where a religious group identity is threatened, it becomes more apparent, significant and poignant. Strong emotional attachment to a group identity is dependent upon the identity group that is most meaningful at a given time.

> Young people may be claiming an Islamic identity for themselves because this places them within a global community that means they no longer feel so marginalised. This connection with a global Islamic identity, one which has a rich and powerful history, may serve to undo local stereotypes of Islam, which may be particularly negative.
>
> (Spalek, 2007: 201)

A second aspect which has relevance to the political motivation of young British Muslims is the persistence and prolonging of historical myths, symbols and stories specifically related to the concept of the ummah. The ummah in Islam refers to the community of believers or diaspora of Muslims worldwide. It is questionable whether the term is a theoretical concept, or a real community of people. In *Imagined Communities* Benedict Anderson (1991) talks of the idea that communities can create imagined consciousness; an abstract connection that has no actual territorial location. Anderson (1998) also criticises the development of the 'long distance nationalism' that is created by this transnational political consciousness. For these respondents, the ummah exists, even if theoretically. They believe that political actions on behalf of the ummah are part and parcel of their belief. Through these feelings for the ummah they feel it is their duty to participate and act; otherwise they will be held accountable.

50. Numan

Yeah, I think the ummah is...is not this utopian, kind of, mass of people that all hold hands and make human shield against evil – it's broken people and it's people who need help and everyone...everyone needs help in their own respect – I need nurturing and development in the same way that a single mother might need some support, in the same way that, you know, someone like a drug dealer might need support and help.

23. Umama

It's ... it's [ummah] peaceful because ... it's almost like the heavenly idea ... of perfection, of us being a brotherhood all together. Ummah's like back in the Prophet's time, you know, of us ... of brotherhood, of looking after one another.

28. Yara

My ideas come from the Quran and sunnah, many hadiths that Muslims are one brotherhood, 'Muslims are one body, if one dies, the rest of the body hurts'. That's something I have taken on board strongly, I feel like I have a close affinity with the Muslim ummah simply because Allah (SWT) has told us that we have to.

The use of stories, traditions, symbols and reinvented myths in political motivation are not unusual among minority groups; religious culture and meanings can directly mobilise members into political action (Harris, 1994). Harris notes several cases where religious expectations and values are used in a political context in order to influence the political engagement of religious individuals in the African American community: 'In one example ... introduced Danny Davis, the black mayoral candidate for the 1991 Democratic primary, he drew on African American religious language, culture and symbols ... ' (Harris, 1994: 49).

Similarly, the concept of the ummah revolves around the tradition of brotherhood; built upon stories and symbols referring to the ties that link Muslims beyond national borders and transcend ethnic and linguistic variations. The references that are found about the ummah in both the Quran and hadith refer to Muslims being one group, one brotherhood, whereby each is responsible for others and has a duty to care for and to support other members:

And verily this Ummah of yours is a single ummah and I am your Lord and Cherisher: Therefore Fear Me (and no other). Quran, sura 23: verse 53

An Arab is no better than a non-Arab. In return, a non-Arab is no better than an Arab. A red raced man was not better than a black one except in piety [hadith Prophet Muhammad]

The ummah is a fundamental concept in religious observance for the respondents, and this has tangible implications for their political motivations. The connection with other Muslims around the world is also affected by the perceived ostracism of Muslims and a disaffection that Muslims feel about the international political context: this leads to a strengthening of these ties and a stronger connection to their religious group and perceived commitments.

> In the Muslim world, there has been an important and highly visible resurgence of Islam. This affirmation of faith and identity is a powerful force in all aspects of human life and is reflected in clothing, changing social lifestyles and the arts, as well as in the more visible arena of politics and political power. Concurrent with this resurgence is a growing demand for greater popular participation in the political system.
>
> (Esposito and Voll, 1996: 16)

The discussion of relative deprivation and the equity fairness theory is pertinent here. The argument is that a feeling of alienation (as seen in Chapter 3, even among group three who identified themselves as British), together with feelings of discrimination and a feeling that their grievances are not being addressed, builds group antipathies.

In relation to these young British Muslims, the responses of religious zeal in the political sphere and insistence on political changes are collective responses to feelings of inequality among their group worldwide. In the equity-fairness theory people react to material inequalities; they are motivated to improve their group situation in an attempt to become equal with compared groups. This could explain motivation to politically engage in activities that endeavour to assuage injustices among the ummah worldwide.

2. Banan

... but the question you are asking is whether I identify more with Muslim issues ... to a certain extent I do ... I feel sorry for anyone, but most of the time the underdog seems to be Muslim. I'm not going to not feel sorry for someone just because they are Christian or have no faith, but it just seems that Muslims have always been persecuted in recent history which is why I tend to sympathise with them more.

10. Huma

My beliefs as a Muslim that my brothers and sisters are being killed or being affected in a bad way is enough for me to go ahead and do something.

14. Mosab

Issues that I'm very interested in are like influence of British Muslims in politics, is the war in Iraq, war on terror, the stigmatisation of Muslim community, and the most important of which is the Israel-Palestine situation, which I think is the core of everything. It needs to be resolved.

Again, relating to relative deprivation or the equity-fairness theory; the use of the concept of the ummah is crucial in the discussion of political incentives for young Muslims. As we discovered above, the ummah is perceived as a worldwide community of people, transcending ethnicity and geographical location. This sentiment of attachment to the ummah causes young Muslims to be motivated to act in the political sphere because of the duty they feel not just towards other members of the ummah, but especially towards those who they feel are marginalised, victimised and are facing injustice.

56. Zain

Of course the ummah exists, it has always existed and will always exist until *yawm al kiyamah* [Day of Judgement] *inshallah*, and it's very important for the wider community and the government to appreciate that the Muslim community, despite all their attempts, we have not disengaged from the global Muslim community. So if there is an issue in Palestine, in China or elsewhere, and though the government wants the Muslim community to blindly follow its policy, that's not going to happen. And it's not just the Muslim community, if the Muslims in the UK see an injustice – the non-Muslims in Saudi Arabia, then the Muslims must stand up and fight for that cause. So those are the values that Islam teaches us, compassion and mercy, fighting for justice – that applies across the board.

The impact of the concept of the ummah on political activities and engagement in certain political causes has a two-fold explanation according to the responses. One explanation is linked to the relative deprivation or equity-fairness debate – that the respondents become involved in political activities in order to ensure a more equivalent and balanced relationship between two groups or communities. The second impact of the ummah on political activity is the feelings and sentiments drawn out by duty and obligation. The ummah as a concept implies that Muslims who believe in it are to engage on behalf of others who are less able to do so, to support their cause out of duty and obligation to the group consciousness.

This implies that if such inequality and injustice were not occurring at such large-scale level, then sentiments regarding the ummah in political activity would be less obvious and less important to the political activity of young Muslims. It is also interesting to consider the context of the increased usage of media and communication formats as a form of political activity (see Chapter 5 and Chapter 7), because the use of media and communication formats aids the increased awareness of issues and causes around the world, and this in turn fuels the feelings of duty and obligation and the sense of injustice and inequality felt by young Muslims.

The effect that religious duty and values have on the political motivation of young British Muslims is also influenced by social networks and cultural norms. Some literature argues that Islam has helped in politically motivating Muslims through social networks, social capital and political participation (Modood, 1990, 2005; Samad, 1992; Werbner, 1994; Adolino, 1998). Linked to theories of social norms and network mobilisation, the material from the respondents does highlight that childhood socialisation encourages an awareness of political concerns that are assumed to be important to the group – this sense of intergenerational transmission is part and parcel of parenting:

12. Jamila

I think that children are groomed from a young age; most of my friends in school were Conservative voters, because their parents are. The children see the news, they see the bombs, they see the dead people, they see it happening, I'm starting to explain what is happening and to build a sense of ummah in him, he's Muslim. Children are undervalued, not seen for their worth, I value that my grandfather talked to me as a seven year old of what was happening politically.

Social networks also encourage the respondents to be politically active through belonging to organisational and political networks, as highlighted in previous research and literature (Anwar, 1979; Shaw, 1988;

1998; Hussain, 2003). The respondents belonged to organisations[12] such as MCB (Muslim Council of Britain), ISB (Islamic Society of Britain), FOSIS (Federation of Student Islamic Societies), HT (Hizb ut Tahrir) and UKIM (UK Islamic Mission), among others. There are other organisations which the respondents do not belong to but are familiar with and associate with. Belonging to such organisations increases the likelihood of being involved in political activities, as they usually foster group consciousness as well as mobilise their members to be involved in the political sphere.

56. Zain

... We have specific purpose organisations for example like political organisations that lobby for civic participation and media engagement like MPac [Muslim Public Affairs Committee] and Engage[13] [campaign group for Muslim political participation] and also MCB [Muslim Council of Britain], even Friends of Al Aqsa, lobbying groups like ... PRC[14] [Palestinian Return Centre], like Halal Monitoring Committee (HMC) ... and we have specialist Islamic centres which are sometimes joined with mosques, for example OCIS [Oxford Centre for Islamic Studies] which is linked to the [Oxford] University, we also have specific counselling organisations like MYH Muslim Youth Helpline, we have student bodies like FOSIS [Federation of Student Islamic Societies].

26. Rashid

I don't think that any group, including Hizb ut Tahrir who we're a part of is going to provide that leadership, what we can do all the groups is to instil an Islamic understanding in people, so that their reference point is Islam and so they solve their problems by referring back to Islam and by living their lives as 'good Muslims'.

The respondents in this category are motivated by a combination of issues or areas that together explain why religious political consciousness is so evident and strong not just among the group but also reflects wider British Muslim sentiment and feelings. The key issue is that aspects of political motivation for this group of respondents are intrinsically linked to their identity. The link is reflected in their religious group belonging; sentiments of attachment towards the ummah; duty towards the group; reflection on religious sources in a political setting and so on. The psychological and emotional connections to their religious group lead to motivation in the political sphere that is a result of feelings of duty, belonging and emotional attachments. The interviews found a mixture of these issues from each of the respondents, and although to differing levels, the respondents from identity groups three and four raised these four key issues as crucial to their political motivation.

Concluding remarks

The types of motivations that the respondents are encouraged by are very similar – they are based around group participation (collective action oriented). These motivations are not self- interested; rather, the respondents are motivated for the benefit of a larger group at the cost of self. Very few indicate being motivated by material benefits or for instrumental reasons.

A second similarity among respondents in this chapter is that they are motivated by psychological needs for expression of their frustration, anger and discontent (even though the political expressions or causes may be different). All respondents are motivated by some form of group concerns and a need for self-expression. The main difference between the respondents lies in their varied group belonging (linking back to Chapter 3), which explains how it is that identity is in fact a key justification for differences in political motivation – it is seen in the causes they choose to support, in the intentions they express towards their group and in the accounts of their political behaviour:

> Thus, the benefits of political participation appeal to different people in different ways, depending on their interests, preferences, identifications and beliefs. People who perceive more at stake in politics – because policies affect them more, identities beckon them more, options appeal to them more, or duty calls them more – participate in politics.
>
> (Rosenstone and Hansen, 1993: 20)

This result is interesting in that it reflects on similar survey research conducted on American Muslims. Ayers and Hofstetter (2008) used large survey data of 1,846 American Muslims (funded by Pew Charitable Trust and conducted by Zogby International on behalf of Muslim Americans in the Public Square – MAPS). They found that in the aftermath of 9/11 the environment has become highly sensitive towards Islam and Muslims, and that American Muslims became politically interested and engaged because of higher levels of anxiety regarding how they are perceived, and also because of their alienation.

It is likely in the current climate of 'guilty until proven innocent' that anxiety may motivate American Muslims 'political action'.
(Ayers and Hofstetter, 2008: 8)

They argue that against a backdrop of alienation after 9/11 and the negative political climate that followed, instead of becoming insular and disenfranchised, American Muslims have increased engagement in order to engage with the democratic system (Ayers and Hofstetter, 2008: 22). This is reflected in this research: that against a negative backdrop described in Chapter 1, British Muslims are political motivated and active, concerned with the portrayal of the religious as well as feeling that as citizens engagement is the only plausible method to create change.

American Muslims, like British Muslims, have a strong interest and are motivated by foreign policy issues and concerns, especially when compared to the views of the wider public (Read, 2008: 41). The key findings in this research is that for identity groups one and two, though they consider global concerns to be of utmost political importance, the influence of their roots is apparent. The impact that socialisation in a religious context and in upbringing has on the formation of their views, on the causes they choose and on their outlook in general is less obvious than that found among groups three and four, but it is evident. For identity groups three and four, the importance of belonging to a religious group and the political context have resulted in strong feelings of duty to the group – especially in the sense of a wider ummah. Together with feelings of lack of representation in the political sphere, marginalisation of certain key issues as well as political mobilisation via social networks has increased the politicisation of religious issues and resulted in a perceived increase in religious identity politics.

Overall the evidence in this chapter suggests that political culture is relevant to the discussion of political motivation. Political culture is found in differing forms, and is meaningful to different people in varying ways depending on their socialisation, cultural upbringing and value-based expectations. However, it is influential for all the respondents in the same way – the political (sub)culture influences their political motivation, though they are motivated to engage in slightly different ways.

The political culture approach today constitutes the leading alternative to rational choice theory as a general explanatory framework for political behaviour. The political culture approach is distinctive in arguing that (1) people's responses to their situations are shaped by subjective orientations, which vary cross-culturally and within subcultures; and (2) these variations in subjective orientations reflect differences in one's socialization experience, with early learning conditioning later learning, making the former more difficult to undo. Consequently, action cannot be interpreted as simply the result of external situations: enduring differences in cultural learning also play an essential part in shaping what people think and do.

(Inglehart, 1990: 19)

It is also clear, though, that most of the respondents (except some from identity group four) share a mainstream political culture – that of civic and democratic norms. The endurance of civic norms in political involvement signals that socialisation in a British civic context does influence the expectations and norms of political behaviour among the majority of young British Muslims.

How much the respondents psychologically identify themselves with their normative group corresponds with their political concerns, and what motivates them to engage. Chapter 5 will explore more specifically the political actions, how political activities are decided upon, and which are popular and why, together with further exploration of identity and political activity.

5
Political Participation

Political participation in a modern democracy is a seal of approval on individual citizenship and state belonging; it is important for the integration of citizens and the well-being of the state. Identification with the state through political engagement means accepting national institutions, rules and state symbols by understanding their roles and expectations and acknowledging their legitimacy (Maxwell, 2006). Through political participation, the communication of individual and group needs can be represented and understood. Political participation is a foundation of citizenship and of fundamental importance to belonging as a citizen. Political engagement also helps guide political education and further civic and political involvement; it helps to promote certain skills such as communication, organisation and management, as well as psychological characteristics such as trust, confidence and efficacy (Sapiro, 1983).

Engagement in political activities is important for minority groups because it helps the articulation of needs between the group and political institutions, and caters for the smooth running of the state for its citizens. If certain groups of citizens refuse to take part in the democratic system, long-term consistency and trust in the democratic system could be at stake. This is especially important for British Muslims because the media regularly portrays Islam as fundamentally in opposition to democracy, freedom and tolerance. If this were the case, citizenship, political participation and belonging to Britain would be troubling for young Muslims in this research. Their lack of political participation would be hazardous to integration, and this is of greater significance when age is taken into consideration, as over 50 per cent of the British Muslim group demographic are youth.[1]

The aim of the next two chapters is to explore what is considered by the young Muslim respondents to be a political action and which (if any) political activities are popular or unpopular. A wide framework regarding the conceptualisation of 'political actions' has been used – this is especially important when exploring the perspectives of minorities, and these respondents are members of minorities on several levels – ethnicity, religion and age. Their views regarding what constitutes a political action may not be the same as the traditionally held views, and thus exploring political action from their perspectives is imperative. It may be that the participation of young people in political activities is undetected because they may be using unconventional forms of engagement in the political sphere (O'Toole, 2003; Marsh et al., 2007; O'Toole and Gale, 2009). It may also be the case that traditional forms of political engagement do not consider generational changes and innovations. The development in global communication, internet usage and new media formats could affect the forms of political involvement that these young respondents engage in.

> Generation effects arise from the fact that successive generations face new challenges of which previous generations have no experience. Thus, the political issues and arenas familiar to other, older generations and foci and sites of political activity may well have little relevance to young people.
>
> (O'Toole, 2003: 6)

In early literature on political engagement, electoral politics was the main concern of political scientists (Lane, 1959; Milbrath, 1965). Since then, developments have led to many more political activities being accepted as methods of political engagement (Verba et al., 1972, 1978; Barnes et al., 1979; Pattie et al., 2004), including protesting and petitions. A number of potential additions to the political engagement landscape such as consumer politics and internet politics are possible contenders in the future.

> Political participation is typically equated with voter turnout, although citizens participate in a variety of political activities, with varying levels of involvement over time. We will improve the theoretical rigor of our models of participation by studying this variety of political acts and how it changes over time; focusing on voter turnout alone – as discrete acts structured by the electoral calendar – offers no such advantage. We must therefore shift the focus of our study to alternative forms of participation.
>
> (Leighley, 1995: 181)

Newer forms of political activities have become more popular, while some traditional forms of political engagement have waned (Dalton, 2002; Norris, 2002). Traditional methods of engagement have changed and modified; activities that people participate in or find effective and popular have altered. There are even arguments suggesting that the institutions that exist in order to represent and address the issues about which citizens feel strongly are no longer effective, leading to shifts and developments in the styles and forms of participation (Inglehart, 1997; Norris, 2002).

> To understand the trends in participation we must recognize the full impact of social modernization and other social and technological developments on contemporary politics. Greater political sophistication does not necessarily imply a growth in all forms of political activism; instead, rising sophistication levels may change the nature of participation...A sophisticated and cognitively mobilized public places less dependence on voting and campaign activity as the primary means of influencing the government.
>
> (Dalton, 2008: 54)

Many varied definitions of political participation exist in the literature,[2] including wide variation in what constitutes political activities.[3] The acknowledged conceptual definition of political activities includes actions that are taken by citizens, not politicians; actual political actions – not simply taking an interest or having views on the subject; and actions that generally refer to government and politics (Verba et al., 1995; Brady, 1999). However, the pictorial vignettes[4] that were chosen in this research for questions about political activity were not all related to government or politics. Some of the scenarios depicted were of the socialisation of children, the education of children and other 'social' or 'civic' endeavours. Most of these were not considered to be political actions by the respondents,[5] so the socialisation of children and other such concepts will not be discussed further.

During the discussion with respondents about political activities, the effectiveness of political actions was an aspect that was repeatedly referred to. Effectiveness comes in many guises – it could be in venting frustration, gaining media interest, getting public attention, policy change, getting representation in decision-making and so on. It was interesting to note whether their perceptions on the varied forms of 'effectiveness' had a role to play in the choices they made when participating in the political sphere.

Acknowledged in the literature at the same time is the fact that different activities anticipate different costs, demands and skills (Milbrath, 1965). While a participant may sign an online petition which is simple, easy and relatively costless, its effect is also less obvious. Whereas attempting a sit-in could be costly, with a risk of being arrested, gaining a criminal record and possible public infamy via media sources, the rewards could be seen as potentially higher. Some actions are more expressive, such as protesting, while others are instrumental, such as campaigning on behalf of a political party.

Expressive and instrumental reasons for the justification for political participation (Parry et al., 1992) are repeatedly referred to in the context of political actions, because this highlights the costs and benefits or effectiveness of the various political activities according to the respondents. In instrumental actions, the participants can achieve the goals they want through minimum cost and maximum effect. These goals may not necessarily be selfish (they could be altruistic, such as lobbying political representatives on behalf of a charity), but the individuals consider it ineffective to use certain expressive political activities, such as flag burning, while they may consider it more instrumentally effective to participate in other political activities, such as lobbying.

Barnes and Kaase (1979: 526) broke away from the instrumental argument and argued that expressive forms of political participation have taken priority over instrumentality as a motivation for citizens to engage. Expressive motivations for political participation include the manipulation and use of symbols (such as flags), engaging in political activities because it is fulfilling (such as attending a protest) (Milbrath, 1965), actions that are focused on expressing feelings or views, and engaging in political activities in order to support either other participants, or the cause – a solidarity form of action (Hardin, 1982).

Aside from expressive forms of political engagement is political activity as a signalling mechanism. Signs, symbols and signals are among the many concepts explored by Erving Goffman in *The presentation of self in everyday life* (1959). He discusses 'appearance signs' which intend to communicate personal stances and views; the 'manner' in which individuals communicate prepares the observer for an expected response or reaction – shock, awe, impassivity, for example. A political setting such as a demonstration is a sign; add to it symbols such as placards, political chants and clothing with messages, and the audience (i.e. policy-makers, media, potential supporters) consider the whole social setting as a signal. The words and actions of the participant influence how others see and think of them, and encourage a response. Unlike political expression, signalling is a two-way communicative mechanism; it encourages a dialogue or negotiation – whether to encourage fellow supporters, gain further media publicity or negotiate with policy-makers.

As mentioned above, expressive, signalling and instrumental motivations are blurred at times, because the original aim in attending a demonstration or vote may be expressive but it could have an instrumental or signalling impact. Some political actions can be construed as self-interested and others as selfless – such as going to a demonstration in order to 'be there' (Hardin, 1982). At times, events occur which in a given cohort are known to be special and not likely to recur in that period, such as a revolution, a riot or a large-scale demonstration. Motivations to participate in these activities, based on building memories of having attended that event, are expressive in nature, though they may look like instrumental motivations (attending to increase aggregate numbers in order to affect change) to those observing.

Political participation in this study encompassed many varying forms of action. The traditional forms of political activities are included as a given, including voting, campaign activity and protest activity. Activities that were once considered unorthodox or unconventional such as boycotts and lawful demonstrations (Marsh, 1977) are now part of normal political activities. There is a very wide variety of actions that could potentially have been construed by respondents as engaging in political acts, and it was inevitable that not every one of them is included; however, a great effort was made in attempting to include as many forms of participation as possible. The two main political actions that were not included because they were not thought of during the interviewing phase, but were repeatedly referred to during the interviews, were the use of media and communication formats as a political action and lobbying.

Voting is a large-scale yet individual action that requires little initiative. Participation in the electoral process, specifically voting, is considered a gauge for the integration of ethnic minorities. In communities where voting is relatively low, various reasons and theories have been debated to explain this, and explanations have included alienation, political exclusion (it makes no difference who wins) and apathy (lack of interest in the democratic system).

Over time, the political activities that communities have participated in have changed and been modified. Whereas electoral participation was once the focus of most political engagement research, what was once considered unconventional has now become the norm. Before the 1960s, most protest political activities were considered to be linked to the most deprived, marginalised and alienated members of society voicing their demands. However, since then the political climate has changed and protest is no longer considered a marginal political activity, nor is it participated in by only the most disadvantaged in society (Parry et al., 1992; Dalton, 2002; Pattie et al., 2004).

Protests have become more popular (Barnes et al., 1979; Dalton, 2002, 2004; Norris, 2002). They are more popular among younger people and more popular among males than females (Marsh and Kaase, 1979; Topf, 1995; Dalton, 2002; Rucht, 2007). Protest activities usually go through phases of popularity depending on the issue of the day. However, demonstrations, marches and protests are part and parcel of political life in Britain. They cannot be ignored as a form of engagement (Parry et al., 1992). These protest methods have become more popular since the upsurge in internet communication. The speed at which information can travel through cyberspace, across time zones and borders has influenced the speed at which protest activities have spread. This was the case in January 2003 when anti-Iraq war protests were coordinated to occur simultaneously, and continued over long periods. Demonstrations spread across the world, and within days over 50,000 people were marching in Washington, San Francisco and other US cities; while there were also demonstrations in many other countries, such as Japan, Turkey, Pakistan, Syria, The Netherlands, Egypt, Russia, France, Britain, Argentina and Mexico.[6] During the fieldwork period, large demonstrations and protests in the UK ranged from anti-war marches against the invasions of Iraq and Afghanistan to protest marches against the Danish cartoons mocking the Prophet Muhammad in 2006 (made political by the refusal of the Danish government to ban their repeated publication), protest against the invasion of Gaza by Israel in 2008, and the violent protests during the G20 summit in 2009 – and numerous others in between.

However, protest movements have the potential to, and do, become violent actions. This in itself is a question that has not yet been resolved – should violent activities be considered political action? The early researchers held that such actions were not political (Milbrath, 1965: 18; Verba and Nie, 1972; Verba et al., 1978). However, more recently, violent forms of actions conducted with political intentions have been seen the world over, and cannot be ignored as potential political action (from French rioters to British northern riots, flag burning in Trafalgar Square to G8 summit clashes with police and destruction of property). It is interesting to note that not all violent actions were considered political actions by the respondents.

Historically, protest and contentious actions arose from feelings of frustration and deprivation. Concentrated among the socially disadvantaged, repressed minorities or groups alienated from the established political order, protest was an outlet for those who lacked access through conventional channels... the nature of protest is, however, changing in advanced industrial democracies. Protest has broadened from the disadvantaged to include a wider spectrum of society... In the past, protests often challenged the basic legitimacy of political institutions... Modern protest is typically a planned and organized activity in which political groups consciously orchestrate their activities to occur when the timing will most benefit their cause. For many individuals and groups, protest has become simply another political resource for mobilizing public opinion and influencing policymakers. Protest was once considered distinct from conventional forms of democratic political participation, but it now appears to be an extension of conventional participation by other means.

(Dalton, 2008: 48)

The more conventional political activities are easier to acknowledge as such, but many theorists and commentators are less enthusiastic about newer forms or potential political activities. While some see political discussion or debates as borderline political engagement (Parry et al., 1992), others have considered them political activity (Almond and Verba, 1963; Milbrath, 1965; Barnes et al., 1979). It is difficult to place the influence of political debates and discussions – a conversation may not persuade a person to vote a certain way, but it may in the long term affect his or her views regarding certain foreign policy initiatives, which may have an impact later on political actions taken. As far as this research is concerned, if a meaningful discussion regarding political issues is construed as political action by respondents, then it will be taken as such, and will be discussed further later in the book.

If the frequency of political discussion is, indeed, a measure of the health of a democratic political system... then the evidence so far is that the West European patient has been in a remarkably stable state, at least over the last twenty years.

(Topf, 1995: 66)

The use of media and communication formats for political engagement is also a recent phenomenon.[7] The internet has had a strong part to play in the development and spread of the use of media as a format for political participation (Grossman, 1995; Bimber, 1998; Ayres, 1999; Norris, 2002; Bimber and Davis, 2003; Micheletti, 2006; Oates et al., 2006). Cyberspace promotes ideas, assists in spreading tactics and collecting resources across borders and time zones. It is easily accessible and has a very fast impact. This communication technology revolution is having an impact on forms of political action; both individuals and organisations can orchestrate internet campaigns which affect policy-making decisions through pressure; people are able to correspond with representatives and policy-makers, and access (at times concealed and guarded) political information at the press of a button. There are websites that provide users with hourly news updates; discussion boards for like-minded people; email reminders for events; the ability to sign mass petitions and send letters online; and political analysis via bloggers. The speed at which these tactics can be used is a means of political empowerment.

> E-mails are now the most common and rapidly growing form of communications from constituents to members of U.S. Congress. Web sites were unheard of in the 1992 campaign, but today they are a standard and expanding feature of electoral politics. A wide range of political groups, parties, and interest groups use the internet to disseminate information...The blogosphere is a still newer source of political information and commentary that potentially empowers individuals as rivals to the established media. The internet can also be a source of political activism that occurs electronically.
>
> (Dalton, 2008: 53)

The development of websites such as YouTube enables users to upload messages and videos, which are available worldwide within minutes. Some of these videos have an audience of millions and spread like wildfire. They can be used as propaganda and campaigning, as protest and critique. President Obama's most popular YouTube message on race has been watched over three million times. Facebook and Twitter, as well as numerous other networking sites, enable political enthusiasts to launch campaigns, spread invitations and advertise events with the minimum of fuss and almost no financial expenditure, gaining a mass audience with minimal effort.

> Communicative participation involves citizens hands-on in politics. This is good for democracy. Googling, blogging, clicking, forwarding, downloading, and constructing websites are important

forms of participation, just like voting and membership in political organizations. The only difference is that they are more individualized, DIY forms. Online involvement and cyberactivism offer growing numbers of citizens abundant and flexible occasions to participate by creating, reconstructing, interpreting, and critiquing information to re-craft politics worldwide today. They unite people by aiding them to develop a political understanding locally, nationally, and globally. Perhaps it is not at all startling, then, to consider blogging a new people's movement.

(Micheletti, 2006)

Other types of media, such as films, documentaries, music, and written media, are also popular formats among younger generations. This has been recognised as a potential method for recruitment. The low number of young people voting before the 1997 general election led to the launch of Rock the Vote UK, a political advocacy attempt to engage young people via youth culture and to encourage them to sign the electoral register. The campaign was launched in 1996 at the Ministry of Sound club in London, and featured a mix of political, music and entertainment personalities. The campaign was taken to cinemas and concerts, and promoted via videos. This is just one way in which political campaigns have used facets of the media in order to mobilise and encourage political participation.

'Political consumerism' (Micheletti, 2003) is yet another political activity which has become a popular phenomenon in the last decade (Bové and Dufour, 2001; Levi and Linton, 2003; Micheletti, 2003; Pattie et al., 2004; Micheletti and Stolle, 2006; Dalton, 2008).[8] Some people use boycotting and purchasing products as a form of criticism or support of brands, businesses or governments (notably Nestlé and McDonalds), based on ethical political stances. Country-based boycotts were also popular during the period of apartheid in South Africa (Seidman, 2003) and the Israeli boycott during the 2000s was fought by university campuses, academics and faculties across the world (Micheletti, 2003). For young Muslims, the most noteworthy country-based boycotting occurred during the 2005 Danish cartoons incident, when Muslims across the world were asked (mainly via internet campaigns) to boycott Danish goods in protest over the government stance on the incident.

The choice that individuals and even groups make to boycott certain products is based on their personal attitudes, views and values. This is usually advocating values such as justice, equality and fairness. Within a political framework, the decisions relate to an assessment of government practices. The phenomenon of political consumerism has been all but ignored in many contemporary analyses of political engagement (Verba et al., 1995; Skocpol and Fiorina, 1999; Putnam, 2000).

> People who view consumer choice in this fashion see no border between the political and economic sphere. For them, the market is an arena for politics. They also believe that their private choices have political consequences.
>
> (Micheletti, 2003: 2)

One of the issues with political consumerism is that it is a very private activity. Consumption choices are usually made on an everyday basis. The traditional forms of political action have been fairly public forms of engagement, or at least publicly convened, whereas political consumers defy this usual format, and challenge the norms of political activity as a public form of activity.

There are problems that have been highlighted with new forms of political activity. One issue relates to the blurring between activities that are undertaken with a political motivation and the same actions with another motivation in mind. Consumer purchasing or boycotting can be ethical or political. Blogging about a political issue could be entertainment or it could be politically motivated. Such complicated motivations can only be clarified through listening to respondent justifications for their activities, which is the intention of this chapter.

> Can such engagements be interpreted as political participation? Take the example of e-mail petitions. How can we distinguish between someone who regularly visits political websites, participates in chat room discussion and signs e-mail petitions of a political nature from someone who sends the petition along as it comes from a friend that he trusts, even though he is not very aware of the actual political problem for which he gave the signature? Or how do we establish the difference between someone who doesn't visit McDonald's because she doesn't like hamburgers and someone who boycotts the golden arches because they are seen as a symbol of economic globalization? ... the distinctions are important because, if these activities are not sufficiently political, the link between citizen and the political system might not be successfully guaranteed through these forms of participation.
>
> (Stolle and Hooghe, 2004: 278)

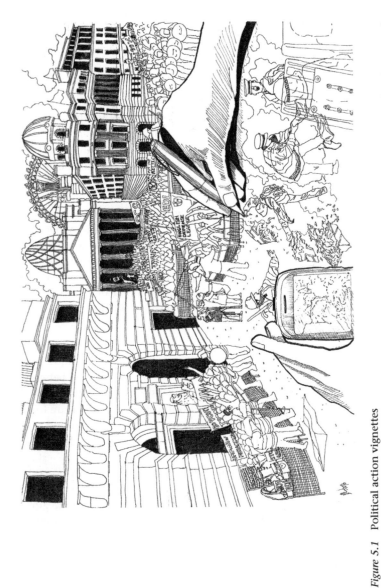

Figure 5.1 Political action vignettes

Note: **Political Activities**: This is an illustrated image designed for this book from a selection of the various political activities discussed during the research.

This research began with a long list of varied activities, some conventional, some not, some traditional political actions, others newer forms, some actions that could be construed as civic or social rather than political. The intention was to listen to the views and experiences of these young British Muslims and understand what they consider to be political activities and whether they have participated in any of them. The research attempted to explore why they choose specific political actions to participate in and not others – linking to Chapter 4, which discussed what motivates people to participate in political activity in the first place. Chapters 6–8 discuss the political activities which the respondents participate in, and actions which are popular among all the respondents, regardless of their identity groupings (defined in Chapter 3); contextual activities; and the political activities which are unpopular among the respondents, with an exploration of why these actions are out of favour.

6
Politically Engaged and Ready for Action

From Suhail the Labour councillor in a Northern ward, Hassan the rucksack-toting Green party activist and Sana the hijab-wearing Respect party campaigner, to Salman the HT member advocating a ban on democratic voting, Noora the non-practising Muslim female who admitted to torching a Union Jack flag and the angry youth from Halifax who believes that military violence is a justifiable political action, the next few chapters explore the variance in activity, opinions and disengagement of young British Muslims.

This research intended to understand what motivated young British Muslims to politically participate, and also to recognise the forms of political activity which they prefer and engage in. This chapter explores the choices which the respondents make regarding favoured forms of political engagement; investigating the reasons why they prefer these activities over others. A comparative element can be found in the following chapters, which focus on political activities that are unpopular on varying levels, and explores why they are considered as such. The conclusion is that popular political activities are the same as those found in wider British society, voting, demonstrations, boycotts and petitions; and the reasons these activities are preferred among the young respondents are their convenience, expressive nature and group or public dynamics.

This chapter explores the political activities that are more popular among the group (voting, demonstrations, petitions and boycotting). Chapter 7 explores four activities that are more nuanced and distinctively new in the political arena, including the use of particular media formats, discussions and graffiti as potential political activity. Chapter 8 discusses unpopular political activities, including young Muslims' views about why they are not methods used to engage in the political arena.

Voting

Voting is a foundation stone of democracy. It is a simple action which does not require much motivation and little cooperation with others. It varies in frequency from state to state, and whereas it is compulsory in some countries, it is a voluntary political action in Britain. Voting rates vary among ethnic minority communities, and statistics are often out of sync with current trends; however, on average Muslims are in line with statistics for the white non-Muslim population. This is also the case among American Muslims, who vote similarly to wider American society (Ayers and Hofstetter, 2008). While the South Asian community as a whole is said to have lower voter registration rates in comparison to the white population, voting rates are high among Indians who are more likely to vote than other Asian groups such as Bangladeshis and Pakistanis (Saggar, 1998; Anwar, 2001; Electoral Commission, 2002). However, for those registered to vote, Muslims are as likely to vote as the wider British population; Muslims are more likely to be registered in areas where Muslim populations are in larger numbers; and are more likely to vote in areas where they are concentrated (Fieldhouse and Cutts, 2006). Again, compared to American Muslims, who are also slightly less likely to be registered to vote (owing to the immigrant nature of their cohort), the voting rates of those who can vote are comparable to wider American society (Read, 2008: 41). The recent Ethnic Minority British Election Study (Heath et al., 2013) found that British Muslims did not show a lack of commitment to democracy, nor an enthusiasm for extremist politics. The findings highlight that the wars in Iraq and Afghanistan together with immigration were salient issues during the 2005 general election, especially among Muslim voters. Again, this is similar to American Muslims, who also are:

> ... not entirely in step with the general public in foreign policy, especially having to do with the Middle East. In 2007, for example, the general public was nearly four times as likely to say the war in Iraq was the 'right decision' and twice as likely to provide the same response to the war in Afghanistan (61 per cent compared to 35 per cent of Muslim Americans).
>
> (Read, 2008: 41)

Most respondents in this research argue that voting is a privilege, that to vote is a right that should be appreciated and that everyone should vote.

There were a handful of respondents who avoided voting – because they cannot be bothered, because they consider their vote will not matter, or because they consider voting in a non-Muslim state to be impermissible in their religion.

Like many other studies (Parry et al., 1992: 42; Verba et al., 1972: 36; Barnes et al., 1979), this research found that voting is the one activity in which the majority of respondents have participated. Over two-thirds of the respondents acknowledge that they vote. About 5 per cent say they would vote but they are under age, or were under age at the last general election. The majority feel extremely passionate about elections and the right to vote. They say it is a privilege, that it is a right that should be appreciated and that everyone should do it. The category with the most non-voters is typology group four, which includes six non-voters; though identity group three also holds a few non-voters.

1. Arwa

Yes... I don't bother reading the mandates; I follow the news and the media. I'd vote in all elections, if you're in a democracy, I think you should use it.

51. Zaki

I think voting is a privilege. I say it's a privilege not a right because, in many countries, of course, you don't have free and open elections, so where you do have them, you know, you should make the most of them.

The electoral system of voting as an instrument for change is considered as a crucial reason for voting among the group – once in a while, if enough people agree, then change can occur. There is a certain sense that as a system for change it is effective and trusted. However, trust in specific local representatives is much lower. The respondents blame lack of policy changes on their local MPs rather than on the democratic system itself. They believe that through voting they may change the parties in power – thus mass power exists. However, trusting local representatives to fulfil the promises they make during the campaigning stages of the electoral process is much less likely. The respondents are sceptical of the representation they receive – with an underlying sense that their views are not represented and an underlying slight distrust of the political system. These young respondents are not uninterested in electoral politics, nor are they uninformed about what goes on in Whitehall, but they distrust the procedures and outcomes of elections. This is similar to a small longitudinal study in Nottinghamshire (Henn et al., 1999), which also found that young people felt that elected representatives were only interested in their views at election time. The respondents in that study felt that they had very little influence on the system, and this resulted in low levels of trust in the electoral system.

59. Usayd

It's important to vote, sometimes it's stressful, you vote for a party that comes to power and x amount of things are promised, deliverance is minute, it doesn't exist sometimes, it's important to get your vote heard...

17. Noora

It's fair enough, but there is never going to be one party that represents my ideas or beliefs, so in that way, there is no point coz I'm not being represented, people are never actually gonna have a choice... Yes I vote but it's not gonna change anything, we don't have much of a choice...

The fact that the participants feel they have a 'right' to vote or that it is a civic duty highlights their identification with their status as citizens. However, while trust in institutions and the process of democracy seems moderate, the respondents distrust many political individuals and political parties. This is not dissimilar from patterns among the wider population (Pattie et al., 2004), and it is considered to be a healthy set of attitudes to hold:

One way of explaining this apparent paradox is that a healthy democracy requires people to be basically loyal to the system and to some extent to be proud of it. At the same time they should have a healthy scepticism towards their elected representatives if government is to be held accountable.

(Pattie et al., 2004: 263)

Similar to voting patterns among non-Muslims, there were a handful of respondents who avoided voting. There were three main reasons why this seemed popular – because they cannot be bothered, because they consider their vote will not matter, or because they consider voting in a non-Muslim state to be impermissible in their religion. These views are in fact similar to the views of those respondents who *were* voting, though expressing elements of political exclusion – the idea that it does not matter who wins, because all political parties are the same, no real choices exist and current political parties are not representative of their vote. The respondents below all express the same views, but state that they do not vote. The group of three young teenage males from Halifax (Kamal, Munir and Noori) and the Tower Hamlets young men (Umayr, Yunis and Zubair) hold relatively despondent views – that representatives and parties make and break promises and thus cannot be trusted. Other reasons for disenfranchisement are the similarity of political parties to each other (Naji) and the lack of policy changes (Ali).

22. Kamal/Munir/Noori

Would you vote?

No

Why?

Because they never do the right stuff for us.

They say they will do this and do that, but they get into power, they scrap the plans that they made.

You know like Tony Blair and them, they got into high power coz of us lot, when we voting them, they go to high positions, so why should we vote people who are going against our religion and going against stuff that we don't like to do, doing them things, and so I won't vote.

They don't do the right stuff... they chat shit innit, just leave it to them.

47. Yunis

I think it's just a way that the higher powers, the government and stuff to give normal citizens normal people have their say, but I don't fink it really counts, coz they just wanna keep us happy. Like we've got a bit of say in this country and how things are run in this country, givin' us hope – but I think it's just fake really. Fake dreams, fake hopes.

There are always people out there who are running everything and we're voting just to show like, yeh we got power in our hands, wow [sarcastic] they know everything...

37. Naji

No. No I don't, no I don't vote, but then there's a reason for that, because I think what you're buying in with political parties is they're actually offering very similar things, and the things that they're offering don't really attract me.

32. Ali

Voting, to be honest with you all these governments in England basically the same so there's no point in voting so anyone who wins is not really gonna change the policy so I think...

Other reasons for not voting were varied, but few reasons were as consistent as the views above. Apathy – lack of interest in politics; convenience – time consuming; impact – viewing individual votes as not counting: none of these were mentioned much among the group. Then there are the few who believe that voting in elections is prohibited for them religiously. Those that held this view were in the main members of the Political-Islamic group Hizb ut Tahrir, or ex-members. As we discussed in Chapter 3, one foundation of citizenship is an identification with the state, and though non-voters are found in all typology groups the highest number of non-voters were respondents from typology group four.

27. Sail

I don't vote. I think it's *haram* to vote in this society... In terms of voting for a political party in this country I think it's *haram* and I wouldn't do.

29. Tufayl

Because now, whereas before I thought it was pointless, now it's a creedal issue for me... the change is that on a creedal level I believe that this act is tantamount to telling somebody in this country 'you, as a man, can legislate and make the law', when I believe that the only one that can do that is Allah.

12. Jamila

I don't vote in this country because I would only vote for a Muslim government, or a Muslim election like in a *masjid* [mosque] or something, I wouldn't vote for a non-Muslim, I think there is an *ayah* [sign] in *surah* Al Nisa 'Allah will never give authority to the disbelievers over the Muslims' that makes it quite clear that you are not to allow or to accept to have a non-Muslim authority over yourself.

In Chapter 3 (typology group four), these respondents stated that they never break the law, but at the same time do not identify with being British. When asked via an email how they would react if Britain made voting compulsory for all citizens, the response received was:

It is unlikely in the extreme that obligatory voting would occur in this way and still I would guess that registering an 'abstain' vote would still be an option.

The respondents mainly choose to vote because they feel a civic or moral reason to do so. After acknowledging this expressive desire to take part in an action they consider important, the respondents then seem to use instrumental reasons in their decisions.

Voting is a popular political action among these young British Muslims. The smaller number of respondents, who chose not to vote, did so because they distrusted parties and their representatives. They feel that their views are excluded and never considered seriously.

Overall, the views held about voting are similar to those found among non-Muslims; the majority of respondents signalled a commitment to democracy, considering it a right and duty to vote. The marginalised views of political representation via the electoral system are paralleled by similar views among white lower-class non-Muslims, such as those who choose to support the BNP as a protest vote. The popularity of voting as a political action lies in its ability to be convenient, expressive and influenced by a sense of civic identity.

Boycotting

Just as voting is signalling to a government how voters feel regarding policies and parties, boycotts are also signals – not only to a government, but to corporations, foreign states and individuals. Studies have found that boycotting is popular across the industrial world:[1]

In today's world many campaigning organisations recommend people to use their purchasing powers to influence global corporations, and clearly a large number of people, whether as a consequence of such prompts or on their own initiative, are taking such action.

In other words, in their day to day consumption behaviour they are acting politically.

(Pattie et al., 2004: 77)

This research found that boycotting goods in order to signal dissatisfaction to companies and countries is a popular method of political engagement. Boycotting was a very popular political action among the group, with over 50 per cent stating that they boycott certain brands. Levels of education did not seem to play a role in the likelihood of boycotting, but among non-boycotters, males were predominant. The respondents are savvy boycotters. They don't always boycott; they make political choices based on monetary value, effectiveness of a given action, its potential usefulness and so on. They are aware that boycotting is not always effective, nor is buying fair trade a solution. However, they believe that state-sponsored boycotting together with individual boycotting is more effective than individual boycotting alone. Boycotting Marks & Spencer, Starbucks and Nestlé are the most popular individual boycotts, while the boycotting of Danish goods was the most popular recent state and individual boycott.

The respondents used financial means as a political action in an expressive rather than instrumental way. The boycotting of goods was symbolic of their stance in relation to the politics of the company, its CEO or the state in which it was produced. However, the respondents used economic forms of participation as a means only if they benefited from it – thus the expressive intentions and instrumental outcome lead to a blurring of the motivating boundary. By boycotting one product, they are expressing a stance. However, they must be able to choose an alternative. Through boycotting, respondents are getting a product and easing their conscience at the same time. In cases where, for example, the alternative product is expensive, respondents are more likely to back down from their boycott and purchase the cheaper option – thus making their choice quite instrumental.

17. Noora

In boycotting, I could boycott Marks & Spencer quite easily, but I couldn't boycott Coke coz I like the taste...I could boycott Coke I guess, I haven't drunk it in two months, but boycotting something big like M&S is different, can't explain it...

Consumer boycotting can be considered as 'an attempt by one or more parties to achieve certain objectives by urging individual consumers to refrain from making selected purchases in the marketplace' (Friedman, 1985: 97). While voting was the way that respondents chose to make their views known regarding their own government, money talks, and can be a way in which people express their frustration about international governments or corporations with regard to foreign incidents that have little to do with their own government.

> Consumption can in certain instances be a venue for political action. It offers people an inroad – venue – into policymaking that otherwise may be rather closed to grassroots citizen participation. It can create a venue because consumer behaviour is difficult to regulate ... this means that people excluded from such policymaking communities as corporate board rooms, diplomatic circles and legislative arenas can use their market choices as a means for political expression and as political action.
>
> (Micheletti, 2003: 2)

Country-based boycotts are usually followed because frustrated people want to express their anger and frustration about the policies of another country. People use their financial choices to attempt to sway opinions or to make an impact on the country directly, or to sway companies who supposedly help to fund those countries. This was seen in South Africa during the Apartheid era, for example. For these young Muslims, one recent case was the boycotting of Danish products after the printing of cartoons in Danish newspapers that were deemed offensive by Muslims.

> The trigger for the latest clash of cultures was the publication by the Danish newspaper Jyllends-Posten on September 30 of 12 cartoons of Muhammad. A biographer of the prophet had complained that no one would dare to illustrate his book, and the newspaper challenged cartoonists to draw pictures of the prophet in a self-declared battle for freedom of speech. One submission showed Muhammad wearing a bomb-shaped turban; in another he tells dead suicide bombers that he has run out of virgins with which to reward them. Any portrayal of Muhammad is blasphemous in Islam, lest it encourages idolatry. But the issue began to boil this month after the cartoons appeared in Magazinet, a Christian newspaper in Norway, and on the website of the Norwegian newspaper Dagbladet. Supermarkets in Algeria, Bahrain, Jordan, Kuwait, Morocco, Qatar, Tunisia, the United Arab Emirates and Yemen all removed Danish produce from their shelves. Arla Foods, a Danish company with annual sales of about

$430 million in the Middle East, said that the boycott was almost total and suspended production in Saudi Arabia.

(Browne, 2006: *The Times*)

Although most of the impact was thanks to several country-based boycotts by countries with Muslim majorities, such as Saudi Arabia, Iran, Jordan and Malaysia, individuals (such as the respondents in this research) who were based in non-Muslim countries were also able to make the personal choice to boycott certain Danish products and services, such as Ecco shoes, Lego toys and Lurpak dairy products. This case is just one example of group identity interplaying with political preferences. The fact that a religious matter became politicised led many Muslims, including the respondents in this research, to use their financial empowerment and ability to make a choice when purchasing items in order to make a statement or take a stance. Thus, identity has a strong impact on the expressive stances taken by these respondents. 'Historically, consumers often preferred products for reasons other than classic economic calculations. This connected consumption with their religious, ethnic, racial, national, class and other identities' (Micheletti et al., 2003: x).

16. Mona

For example recently there was, like, a huge controversy across the Western world when pictures of the prophet Muhammad were printed – offensive pictures of Muhammad were printed and reprinted – in two European countries... [boycotting] that's really, really effective because Danish government actually sat up and listened to that, because they had to send... Danish politicians, you know, they immediately saw the impact on Danish business, the Danish economy is suffering because of this, we have to do something... that boycott had an impact and a very visible impact – it made them sit up and think, so I thought it was very, very effective, and that's just one kind of example [of effective boycotting].

Other popular products which the respondents boycotted were Marks & Spencer, Proctor and Gamble and Starbucks coffee. These were also choices that were influenced by the respondents' identity. Any products or companies that are rumoured or deemed to be pro-Israeli are boycotted in an attempt to support the Palestinian cause. The boundary between what is religious and what is political is blurred (in a similar manner to the discussion in Chapter 3 regarding identity). Starbucks and Marks & Spencer boycotts relate to reports or rumours suggesting that money or percentages of store profits are invested in the state of Israel, or that CEOs of companies take pro-Israeli stances which indirectly lead to funds being invested in Israel. For example, Starbucks coffee is guilty through its association with its CEO, who has made certain comments; these have caused the boycott of the company by young Muslims across the world (Knudsen et al., 2008).[2]

Many of the respondents could not give any further information about the evidence leading to their boycotts – most of the companies are chosen through hearsay, rumours and the effective tools of mass communication (especially blogs and mass emails). Boycotts are at times backed up by religious decrees (fatwas), such as Sheikh Yusuf Qaradawi's prohibiting of Israeli and American goods[3] and Egyptian Sheikh Mohammed Tantawi's encouragement of the boycott of Israeli products,[4] but none of the respondents mentioned them specifically.

15. Leyla

I do boycott products, I do think it is effective, I have boycotted products. I boycott Nestlé because I heard they give money to Israel and they kill innocent children. Same reason I boycott Starbucks because I can get a cappuccino anywhere and I can live without eating a KitKat.

16. Mona

For example, I don't go to Starbucks coffee because the owner of Starbucks used to make it, like, a certain percentage that – and because Starbucks earns a lot of money that percentage is a substantial amount of money – he's committed that to, sort of, the state of Israel. Now, if it was, sort of, money used for like developmental work, you know, within, sort of, the 1967 borders of Israel, that would be fine, but then because his commitment to this huge...yeah, it's so ambiguous that the money could be used for anything and I have a problem with that because if the money's being used to arm, sort of, military personnel who, you know, go and commit heinous crimes, then obviously I'm not going to be happy about it.

I think I've been quite good at not going to Marks & Spencer recently.

At times, boycotts can have an impact on the importing country. The boycott of Israeli goods, not only on religious grounds but ethically by

wider British society, has led recently to the British government suggesting that supermarkets relabel their goods in order to differentiate
between food produced on illegal Israeli settlements and food made in
the West Bank by Palestinians. This new labelling may attract boycotters
back to purchasing products made in certain areas of Israel;[5] and Tesco,
Sainsbury and Waitrose have announced they will be using more specific labelling. This could be considered a successful impact of long-term
consumer boycotting.

Boycotts also seem to be influenced by lifestyle; if respondents grew
up boycotting certain products, because of the political circumstances
their parents grew up in, then these boycotts were carried on by the
respondents as adults – even if circumstances had changed.

3. Dalal

Actually...since we were little we don't buy any Nestlé or L'Oréal
stuff, my mum's made a point of not doing that, because of the...to
do with the dried milk scenario and Nestlé giving out dried milk in
countries in Africa, and then the kind of breast milk of these mothers
in Africa dried up, so and L'Oréal basically is Nestlé I think, like Nestlé
owns L'Oréal or L'Oréal owns Nestlé, whichever one. I mean it's so
hard now because I was looking at Garnier and it's also tied in with
L'Oréal and it's so hard to boycott one product, because you might as
well boycott them all, but we still don't buy Nestlé, but it's more of a
habit more than anything...

5. Asif

Again, it makes you feel good. It makes you feel like you're doing
something and maybe even if you're not, but it's...for me, it's something that I've always just done even without thinking, like for
example, Barclays – I would never go to a Barclays cash point –
because they were a bank that continued to still be a part of the
Apartheid regime in South Africa, and even though Apartheid ended
15/16 years ago, it's something that I feel very strongly about – that
I would never have anything to do with Barclays.

Ultimately, the reason respondents boycott goods is a form of expression. It is a symbolic stance intending to highlight their disapproval of
the goods, companies and executives. When the respondents boycott,
they know that their choice will not bankrupt such large enterprises,
they are realistic in their expectations – but they are also keen that their

own money is not invested in them, thus they are making a politically conscious decision. As Zayneb says, it is 'therapeutic':

30. Zayneb

Boycotting?... it's a bit like marching, I think it's more therapeutic and I think... I mean, there are certain things, like for instance Marks & Spencer – I never have bought anything from them and I never will and that's just... it's not so much that I think I'm going to put them out of business, but it's just that I don't want my money going there.

20. Sana

Boycotting, I've been doing like boycotting Israeli goods, since around 2001... With M&S it was just raising and distributing information, it's not boycotting their goods, but they give proceeds to Israel, it's on record, so what do you do with that information? You put it in the public domain, people can either choose to act or not on that information. Maybe it will influence someone, like Starbucks, their chairman made a statement against the Palestinians and linking it to the consumer on the street, who might not vote, politics is not just about voting, it's about other stuff as well.

Boycotting was popular among the group, especially among businesses that for generations have been boycotted by either the minority group or in wider society. Ultimately, respondents at times used their social group identity when boycotting; the boundary between religious and political motivation was blurred, especially in the context of boycotts related to international conflicts. This is very different from voting, where social identity did not seem to influence their choices.

However, boycotting was popular because there is a high amount of choice, and thus choosing an alternative has little cost to it – especially when cheap alternatives are available. So instrumental choices underline the expressive intentions of this political action. If products are important or expensive, decisions are made to stop boycotting if the option becomes expensive or no alternative product is available.

Boycotting is an action which is popular above all because, like demonstrations and protests, it signals international dissatisfaction with governments or with policies on which British citizens do not have much impact – especially if the British government refuses to alter its policies. People still boycott partly because of the act's expressive quality, but also because of the signalling mechanism – they encourage a response from the other side; they signal to other potential boycotters the benefit of taking action; and signal possible negotiations, for example based on specific issues with the product. Individuals use political activities such as boycotting as a signalling mechanism as well as an expressive form of activity.

Boycotting is popular because it is expressive, convenient (as long as a number of alternatives are available) and linked at times to group identity through collective action. Group identity influences how the respondents are politically motivated. Identity also influences which political causes they feel passionately about, and thus boycotting is popular not just because it is convenient and expressive, but also because it is based on supporting particular causes – whether on ethical, moral or religious grounds. The difference between the popularity of voting and boycotting as a political tool lies simply in the differing motivation – they are both convenient and expressive, but whereas voting is motivated by civic identity, boycotting seems at times to be influenced by the respondent's group-based identity.

Demonstrations

Non-violent forms of protest are not only popular and seen as politics in action, but many types exist from picketing to marching and sit-ins, as well as covering hundreds of topics from Green issues to anti-immigration. The change in the popularity of protest politics[6] has come with the development of communication technology. Satellite TV globally highlights a plight; the internet helps organise protest across the globe; and cheap travel ensures that a country is mobilised within hours. We do not have survey data confirming the numbers of British Muslims who have demonstrated, attended rallies and so forth, but American Muslim data showed that 35.2 per cent of American Muslims had protested and 44.6 per cent had attended a rally (Ayers and Hofstetter, 2008). It was found that American Muslims in general participated in more political activities than the non-Muslim Americans surveyed.

Overall these young British Muslims participate in demonstrations and protests, mainly on international war issues. They do not think that this is an effective method of changing government policies; however, they feel that demonstrations are both an expressive notion (venting frustration and building feelings of camaraderie) as well as a signalling action (raising media awareness, encouraging further public support and policy changes). Interestingly, the issues which the young Muslims in this research have demonstrated about have mainly been international foreign policy issues – and there were no indications that these varied according to the differing identity groups discussed in the Chapter 3. Those from the symbolic identity group, such as Hana and Noora, attended the same protests as those from the fourth group with the mainly Islamic identity, such as Salman and Rashid. The idea that demonstrations have become a hub of people from varied backgrounds with differing agendas and interests seems accurate:

> Many of the young Muslim activists saw their coalition partners in simplistic, instrumentalist terms, as non-Muslim compatriots, without consideration as to their differing organizational agendas: the Trotskyite left like the Socialist Workers' Party; the trade union movement; the Campaign for Nuclear Disarmament (CND); the anti-globalization movement; dissident journalists like John Pilger, Robert Fisk and Yvonne Ridley; and the maverick left-wing MPs on the sidelines of New Labour like Tony Benn, George Galloway and Jeremy Corbyn. The marches also included the broadest possible range of Muslim opinion, covered by the fig leaf of anti-American imperialism: Muslim liberals, like the novelist Kamila Shamsie, demonstrated side by side with fanatics who had, on one Palestine demonstration, marched with fake plastic explosives around their waists (*The Guardian*, 1 August 2002).
>
> (Birt, 2005: 102)

It was fairly obvious from the start that the demonstrations which the respondents (across the board) were interested in attending were mainly based on international foreign policy issues – wars in Iraq and Afghanistan and the Gaza conflict were those most frequently mentioned. These may perhaps have been easier to remember, because they were the largest demonstrations in recent history.

45. Hana

I've been on lots of demonstrations, particularly of the Iraq wars, when I first, sort of, started getting really into . . . actually no, I went on that 'drop the debt' one as well . . .

10. Huma

I have, mainly political issues, about Palestine, about the war in Iraq . . . I'd been to couple of demonstrations about Libyan politics...human rights. About university fees, about asylum seekers, about Bosnia...too many to remember.

7. Farah

I went to the ones before the war and the ones after that...the bring the troops home; I went to both of those...I think mainly the ones that I went to were the war ones to be honest.

Demonstrations are considered ineffective in terms of policy change, but they are useful for other signalling means. The respondents note that though they consider demonstrations may be ineffective in changing policies, they increase public awareness of issues. Media attention on one demonstration usually has an impact on the numbers of people attending further demonstrations, as seen during the Iraq war and the Gaza escalation.

7. Farah

...Having said that if I knew that they were still going to war, I would still have gone to the demonstration because I think they increase awareness and they can act as a sort of counter-argument for things that might be coming out of the media and things like that.

6. Bara

You take a million people [demonstrating] and still the government didn't do anything about it, but it's important because at least every-one in the world can see (everyone in England especially) can see that, well, there were a million people who came in, just in London, to come and show their views.

38. Yaman

Yeah, I think they're good for one thing, and one thing only, is that the media sees it...

Protests are also a way for people to express their views and opinions and vent any frustration they may hold regarding a situation. At times, this expression becomes violent, as will be discussed later in the book.

17. Noora

Demonstrations, in the society we live in, it's the only way to voice our political frustration, only channel we've got, but it doesn't do much, it's just a vent...

53. Kusay

People want to express their opinion, and if you don't voice that opinion you don't get your message across. But there's only so many times you can voice your opinions, with the Iraq demonstrations they went on and on and on, biggest march in the world, did it make a difference, not really.

21. Jamal

I love them! I'm fond of going on a demonstration … there are people there you can learn from, inspiration … make a lot of noise which is also good if you are angry … the more the better … you go to demos to meet your friends!

Demonstrations are also an active way of putting extra pressure on governments to change their policies and at the same time to show support for a cause. In a way this is linked to media reports, because as more people attend the demonstrations, the more likely it is that the reports will be highlighted across the world, emphasising to any afflicted parties the support they are receiving via demonstrations across the globe.

7. Farah

They are effective at increasing awareness and they're effective at perhaps putting pressure on the government but whether they're effective at achieving their actual motive … and it can put more pressure on the government which is always a good thing.

17. Noora

I went to the march on Saturday against Israel with Lebanon, but I know it's not gonna do anything, but at least we support Beirut. It shows people …

Finally, demonstrations seem to be popular as a form of belonging to a group; feelings of actively participating in a political action such as a demonstration may impart psychological feelings of satisfaction, the easing of conscience and the sense of fulfilling a purpose. Hana highlights this when she talks about demonstrating in Durham on the eve of the Iraq war:

45. Hana

The first thing that comes into my mind is the anti-war demonstrations … actually, I was in Durham … it was on the night...that the war finally broke out in Iraq and I had this sort of group of people in Durham that had been trying to mobilize action – very much against the odds because nobody cared in Durham that we spoke to – and it was like a very small group of us and on the night that the war finally broke out, we staged this sort of demonstration in the market square in Durham and we camped out there overnight because it happened in the evening, and we just sort of slept there in the market square, and there's all these, you know, random Geordies walking past going 'What are you doing?'. It felt very much like it was us against everybody, which is a weird thing to be a favourite political action because it was very much a hopeless situation – like the war had actually happened and we were just showing that we were unhappy with it – and in the situation which we were in, not...nobody was really paying attention to us anyway, so...but it was just...it felt good to be doing something.

Non-attendance at demonstrations seems to be influenced by three differing issues – violence, parents/upbringing and geography. Some of the respondents mention that most protests and demonstrations go hand in hand with violence and vociferous aggressiveness, which puts them off. Again, this suggests that different political activities suit differing personalities and personal circumstances. In a similar way to graffiti and cartoons, which need artistic skills, those who feel that boisterous and loud protests are not suited to their personalities try to find other actions that may suit better.

60. Zayd

I'm very against demonstrations that might lead to potential conflict...but I would personally prefer to challenge them through the means of having relationships...through my MP, through the Youth Parliament...

54. Maha

No. Because of what I see on the TV, it's portrayed, people are shouting and becoming aggressive when their message is not getting across, it turns me off completely.

Some respondents also mention that attending demonstrations is constrained by the attitudes of parents and community, and cultural expectations. Some youngsters only attend when their parents are there as well; others highlight the fact that negative parental views about protests limit their ability to attend, as do cultural attitudes – especially concerning female attendance at demonstrations.

13. Kawthar

The one on Saturday, which was about Beirut, and the war on Iraq one as well and my mum and dad have been on a few other ones with me.

62. Salim

Demonstrations, I've never attended, I've led quite a sheltered lifestyle, it's the sort of thing my parents wouldn't prefer me attending...

11. Iman

My parents were never keen on the idea; they always said it would end up in violence, chaos – that was one reason.

18. Tuqa

I don't know. I mean, I guess from a cultural point of view, you know, women going out in the street and shouting isn't encouraged, so it's never been something I've (from a young age) wanted to do, because I was told it's not acceptable.

Geographical location also seems to be an important consideration when choosing whether to attend a demonstration or not. Most major large-scale demonstrations are organised in the most populated British cities, and those who live in smaller towns must weigh up whether attendance is worthwhile.

11. Iman

The second was that living in ***** ** *****, when Stop the War organised demonstrations I wasn't aware of it, I was removed far from it, it was never in my face so that I would say yes, I'll go.

I had friends who had suggested it, but they were from the same area as me, so distance was also another... people were not talking about it around us, whereas if I lived in London, people would be like... are you going to the march... that unity.

64. Fatima

Demonstrations I attended on tuition fees, fair trade, globalisation, exploitation, issues that I feel matter to me... Palestine, most are in

London, far from where I live, but when I can if I'm passionate about it, then I will.

Demonstrations, like other popular political activities in this section, are popular because of their expressive and signalling nature, their convenience and their public or group effect. The respondents highlight that though demonstrations and protests are considered ineffective in changing government policy, they are useful for expressing support, gaining media attention and venting frustration. They also argue that demonstrations are a good way of meeting friends and fellow enthusiasts in a public setting and gaining encouragement for further activity. Similar to all the political activities discussed above, demonstrations are popular because of their expressive ability and convenience; they also fit in with political discussions and media usage as political activity. Demonstrations are also visual and a public or group activity, where the respondents gain support from others who feel the same way or who have similar political attitudes.

Petitions

Signing petitions, according to survey data, is usually high[7] – but what does it mean to the respondents? Is it considered a significant activity? Positive aspects of signing petitions are that they engage people at the grass-roots level, and they are quick and convenient; but those who sign are sceptical of their effectiveness. People don't know what they are signing, they use fake names and they never know where the petition has been submitted. This form of political engagement is therefore not taken seriously either as a form of effective action or as an action affecting change – even though it is very popular. Even those who sign petitions think they are ineffective – they sign them out of pity or just because of the convenience of having the petition placed in front of them. The increasing use of the internet as a way of spreading petitions has in a way decreased the reliability or trust placed in them, though it has increased the numbers of people that the petitions reach. Petitions are seen as a harmless action that doesn't take much effort – they are a symbolic form of action, expressing support for an issue.

16. Mona

It depends where they go. I've done some work for a Member of Parliament and I've seen that sometimes they go to number 10 and then there's a big hoo-ha about boxes and boxes of signed papers arriving, it's like, you know, 25,000 signatures... I hope that most people, kind of like, think about why they're signing it and then there's some sort of level of engagement, like 'oh I agree with that, so I'm going to sign a petition' as opposed to 'oh yeah, you know, my friend just signed this so I'm going to sign it too'.

13. Kawthar

Petitions are good. I always sign petitions, I always feel good when I've signed them. I don't know, I think a lot of people are wary of them these days and signing them because they don't know where they end up and who knows what you've signed and stuff, but... yeah, I don't whatever happens to them, the end result, you just sign them and they move on and you don't know if they ever get there, if they ever have had an effect.

26. Rashid

I think they have their usefulness, they are less effective because they are easily manipulated, they don't have as much credibility, people put multiple names down and silly names down, don't take them as seriously.

8. Ghazal

... I have signed innumerable petitions... even if I think it's ineffective. Mostly out of pity for the people who are circulating them.

Petitions are only popular because of their immediate convenience (that a petition is emailed and signed at the push of a button) and because they are cost-free, rather than through their usefulness or effectiveness. However, they are also expressive actions, which respondents use at times in order to symbolically support an issue or take a stance. However popular petitions are, the weight they carry among respondents is not the same as other political activities; the gravitas held by voting, demonstrating and boycotting is far and above the popular yet unproductive perspectives of petitioning.

Conclusion

This chapter has highlighted that though these political activities are popular among the young British Muslim respondents in this sample, the popularity of these activities lies in particular elements shared by the activities. Some are expressive and/or signalling political activities, which allow participants to convey messages, to vent frustrations, to display dissatisfaction and so forth. The political activities are also convenient, they don't require specialist skills, they are not expensive, they are not too time consuming and all are legal. These activities are also based on informal groups. Demonstrations, petitions, and boycotting clearly involve group-based support in order for them to function.

As has been seen in Chapter 3, religious identity played a varied role in the identification of these respondents; religious group identity is also significant to varying degrees across all the groups in Chapter 4 regarding political motivations. Religious group identity arises as a commonality among causes and issue support for most of the respondents in the sample, irrelevant of their identity group category (see further analysis later in the book). Religious identity affects the causes the respondents support (as seen in Chapter 5), and plays a role in the type of political activities in which the respondents participate and which are popular among the group. They choose to attend demonstrations, to boycott goods and to hold political discussions, usually relating to (but not exclusively concerning) issues and causes with a Muslim element, as discussed above.

7
Borderline/Contextual Political Activities

The complexity of human behaviour and decision-making is further problematised by the society and social organisations around us. What is considered morally acceptable, legal or etiquette in one country, culture or community may be morally unacceptable, illegal or impolite in another context. This chapter discusses four activities that under certain circumstances are non-political but can become politicised through their symbols, language, imagery and interactions. These activities are not traditionally measured in political surveys; the complexities in their boundaries drive them to be seen as borderline politics, but they are increasingly popular amongst the youth.

Media

New media and communications have vastly changed our world. They have increased the speed at which information is passed on, and the way in which political news has become globalised. Over the last few decades, political actions which were once popular have become less so, and those which were deemed as unconventional have eclipsed the more popular forms. There are activities which are still viewed sceptically by academics and policy-makers alike, but which, owing to the popularity of particular media and communications methods, have the potential to become the conventional political actions of the future.

Respondents suggested that activities they participate in using media and communication formats are considered to be political action. Respondents felt that those who produce and make political messages via certain media and communication avenues are taking a political action – these include writing a blog, loading a video on to YouTube, producing a TV documentary and making a music CD. However, the respondents who listened to, tuned into or bought these items were not necessarily considered to be conducting a political action.

Media as a format for political action was not something the initial research had considered. For example, there were no photographic vignettes depicting music- or video-based political activities. Again, there is little survey data that refers to the political activities of Muslims via the internet or other communication formats. US survey data from the Pew Charitable Trust found that 41.6 per cent of American Muslims had used the internet for political activity (Ayers and Hofstetter, 2008). The suggestion that media formats were a form of political action came from the respondents themselves; they suggested the ideas that producing music, blogs and documentaries are forms of political engagement. The young Muslims themselves mentioned that they considered aspects of media output as political action. For example, writing blogs on political issues is considered a political action, as is organising political discussions on radio shows or orchestrating political chat room discussions on the internet.

> The Internet is becoming an important method of political communication and mobilization. The networking potential of the Internet is illustrated on the Facebook.com web site, where young adults communicate and can link themselves to affinity groups that reflect their values as a way to meet other like-minded individuals. In fall 2006 the top ten advocacy groups on Facebook included nearly half a million members.
>
> (Dalton, 2008: 53)

Among these activities the respondents mention internet blogs, chat room discussions and video uploads as forms of political action. Again, they are expressing an interest, informing the 'masses' (see Jamila below), and making people aware of political issues, views, and cases. These formats are a popular method used in the globalised communicative world of today, and an expressive format of political engagement.

23. Umama

> Stuff on the internet as well, that could be quite political...I just saw a bit about blogs – you know, how like, like for instance David Cameron's got his own blog now and stuff like that – I've actually read it, it's so funny – a lot of some really famous Iraqi blogs, some

really good Saudi blogs. I think blogs kind of become the new . . . form of political action.

26. Rashid

I think you need to examine anything and everything that you can utilise and move forward, put videos on YouTube, etc. can be just as effective as getting arrested.

Respondents also highlight that music, films, documentaries and TV shows make people politically 'aware'; they are informative formats which spread and influence viewpoints and make an impact:

12. Jamila

The most effective form of political change is talking to the masses, planning talks all over the place, they affect people's views. I work on the Islam Channel, talking can influence people, their views, why they have those views, press releases, conferences, radio as a means of gaining political understanding.

23. Umama

. . . even music, like that guy who's like on the front cover of QE – I've forgot his name – but he's . . . just bought out an album called 'Jihad blah, blah, blah' and I guess his music is really political. There's loads of political music, even like rappers these days – what they're rapping about – that's really political.

47. Yunis

Like nasheed artists. Like some radical ones they use music to show what's going on in the world right now. Like 'Soldiers of Allah' they use radical ways to show what happened in our history, how Muslims were divided for hundreds of years, and the whole ummah was split-ted up, yeah. How our culture and ideas were destroyed. It gives you a bit of history; it's just a radical way of doing it, shouting and aggression.

21. Jamal

Have you heard of Aki Nawaz from Fundamental? He's in a lot of trouble now . . . he's done a new album, called 'Everything is War: the Benefits of Jihad' . . . cultural jihad through music . . . do you know Gil Scott-Heron 'The Revolution will not be Televised?' Primal

Scream...Manic Street Preachers...one album I listen to now is called Bangla...they are bringing these thoughts about religion and values into the forefront...

When asking respondents about their usage of mass media forms, respondents from groups three and four repeatedly mentioned that they watch international satellite channels, TV channels dedicated to Islam and read internet fatwas by famous Muslim clerics – and when they need religious advice, at times they referred to the internet for answers. This relates to political engagement because some religious scholars have become TV and internet personalities, such as Egyptian Amr Khalid, American Hamza Yusuf and Swiss Tariq Ramadan. They upload lectures, publish books and televise numerous programmes. Then there are the sheikhs who are able to lawfully deliberate and announce fatwas, as mentioned earlier (regarding fatwas concerned with the boycotting of Israeli products). All this information has been translated into numerous languages across the globe and become accessible to millions because of the internet and satellite television. Whether these political stances are influential is difficult to gauge from this research, but it would be interesting for future research to discover whether political stances by these scholars are followed, and to what degree.

5. Asif

I've been listening to...you know, the Radical Middle Way. I've listened to...I mean the kind of people that a lot of Muslims consider, kind of, mainstream appeasers, right...a lot of my own friends consider them to be, like, appeasers of the West...

23. Umama

I recently went to...Amr Khalid who came to London (he's doing like a tour) so like, and people really revere him, and stuff, so I think they do get a lot of leadership from international ones as well.

14. Mosab

I've been influenced heavily by Tariq Ramadan, Dr Fareed Ishaq, these kind of people.

There seems to be a need for clarification in this new arena of communication and political engagement. It is clear that those who write blogs and produce music with a political context are using modes of political participation. However, those who place a political petition, link to their Facebook site or purchase a CD with political lyrics are less clearly politically engaged, according to a traditional understanding of political activity. Producing shows on the Islam Channel to influence the masses is considered a political action by a respondent, but what of those people who are watching it? Are they politically participating as well? Some respondents mention the posting of YouTube videos or the production of politically motivated music as political actions, but are individuals who make a video and upload it to YouTube more active than those who track it down and watch it? Or is it the case that different people have differing abilities and preferences? Some people have the financial ability to purchase a political CD; others have the skills to upload videos or to write politically inspired messages. This all underlines the fact that media and communication formats should be considered as useful and popular methods of political engagement.

It has been enlightening to listen to the views of these British youngsters and to hear that they engage in activities which are not usually monitored or surveyed in traditional large- scale studies. Rather, in individual and personal ways they are participating in the political sphere, using their own creative and innovative ways. Using particular media and communication formats is convenient; many can be designed and adapted in personal spaces and without financial expenditure. These methods of political activity are creative and expressive; they allow young people to explore and articulate their views and opinions, to advise and persuade, and to encourage other like-minded people to engage and participate. The visual and public nature of these formats is also an element that is repeated; similar to political discussions, young people seem to be attracted to political activities which engage with others, because as informal groups they can encourage, inform and support each other.

Graffiti

Graffiti is not a popular form of political activity among the group, and not many of the respondents have attempted political graffiti. This activity is also made more complex because of laws regarding the destruction of property and the fact that as an art form graffiti needs skill. More importantly, there is a blurring between what is considered art and what is considered political graffiti. On this subject there is a strong split between those who consider graffiti as a political action by the graffiti artist, if the messages or slogans have political intentions and outcomes, and those who consider it simply to be a criminal action and ineffective.

Only three of the respondents, all male, acknowledged creating some form of graffiti as a political activity in their past. All three had either graffitied or fly posted on behalf of organisations or political events they were publicising. Respondents who have participated in graffiti were advertising or publicising an event or campaigning for or against political candidates. All three mention some aspect of guilt connected with their actions, even if they had political intentions. They each stated that somehow it would be cleaned (Mosab), and that it was state property so it was justified (Rashid).

14. Mosab

It's all about tactics, the means and ends...do they justify them. I myself have engaged in stuff like that...As part of a political campaign I was running, I spent all night fly-posting, all day I'd canvass. It was fun...what kept me going was the belief that this was jihad. I was trying to unseat a pro – well, the foreign secretary of this country [Jack Straw]. We weren't spray painting, but we were plastering, and it was an important part of our strategy, and it was the hardest thing I've ever done but I felt like it was justified for me to do what I was doing. I didn't feel like I was being a nuisance because the council had a dedicated vehicle taking everything down the next day.

25. Salman

A lot of property is state property, and state property, I don't think there is any hokum [law] against doing that, so if it's effective, I don't have anything against it. And we do use it...I was thinking about fly posting, I don't think the image thing is that important, it's how you go about it, if it's political graffiti, then you're not 'blah was here' on a wall. The few negatives would be outweighed by the massive positive.

Those who considered political graffiti artists to be political activists were clear that some graffiti is simply artistic and other forms are intended to make a political statement. The respondents think that sometimes it is a political activity and sometimes it is not; it depends on the context. The respondents also mention that graffiti is useful as an expressive political action or as a motivational action. It can gain media attention, as well as public attention, and gather sympathy for certain political situations.

Graffiti has limitations as a form of political action because not many people are skilled or creative enough to encompass their ideas in such an artistic format (Iman). It is also illegal in Britain.[1] This means that as a format for political activity it may be admired by some, but it is not plausible as a continued format for political expression.

3. Dalal

I love all the graffiti on the wall in the West Bank. I think that it's amazing, some of the graffiti there, and the murals in Belfast as well... I think that some kind of graffiti that makes you think is really interesting, like... I think... I think it's quite interesting when it's put on the Berlin Wall and stuff.

20. Sana

It depends on what sort of graffiti it is, some can be good, I like in Italy, graffiti is politicised, it reflects people's politics on the street, you can't avoid it. It's rebellious, it breaks laws, I don't like... everyone spraying on whatever they want... it just depends on what it is.

11. Iman

I think graffiti is one of those things that can either be considered an art form or a nuisance. I've had people graffiti on my wall... it depends on the context. If it was political, then it would be political action. I never had the guts, and I don't think I'm artistic either.

17. Noora

I like graffiti... it's funny, it is political action, I've seen a lot of stuff on walls. There is one in Swindon about nuclear power stations, a big bill board where someone sprayed 'climate criminal' with an arrow pointing to it and when trains go past it makes people think and look.

65. Nabil

Graffiti is political, people who don't have a say in the media or the public, having their ways of highlighting their opinions. They feel their voices are not heard and they resort to graffiti.

47. Yunis

Like if someone does it on a big picture and it goes all over the world, it has an effect, it has publicity, he [Banksy] goes on papers and all over the news and look what this guy has done, this is what is going on in the world, some innocent guy with someone shootin' him while he's laying down. I'm not sure who done this one, but it was of some steps of higher power, at the top you see a guy sat with a cigar in his mouth and then it goes lower and lower and at the bottom you see a little black guy lookin' as small as possible, and everyone just trod on 'im. The picture just makes a whole person. It's a clever graffiti, a clever one, it shows what's going on, the status you have affects what positions you are in this society and where your culture stands, if you're in a lower status you don't have nothin' you don't get much.

3. Dalal

Then also Banksy the graffiti artist, he's done stuff on the wall. I think that some of his stencilling is amazing.

Graffiti is usually considered as vandalism, and almost half of the respondents were unsure whether graffiti is a justified political action because of its criminal status. Many of those respondents considered political graffiti as criminal:

2. Banan

Graffiti? No I don't think so, I think it's a crime.

22. Kamal/Munir/Noori

How about graffiti?

That's vandalism.

51. Zaki

It's a criminal offence (laugh).

These attitudes towards graffiti as a political action have not changed over time. Marsh's work (1977) highlighted that decades ago views on graffiti as a political method were very similar to today. It seems this is strongly related to the illegal element, and the fact that creating graffiti is consequently seen as a criminal action.

One very surprising result was the universal condemnation of 'painting slogans on walls'. Superficially, this activity seems harmless enough, sometimes even amusing, and was placed in figure 2.1 among those items now confirmed as acceptable to the majority because 'flyposting' and sloganising is a common feature of political campaigns in both the orthodox and unorthodox spheres. The only reasonable conclusion is that most people regard the activity as a defacement of visual surroundings and thereby a public nuisance, and that many others may associate political daubings with graffiti other than the strictly political. Activists, on the other hand, will regard slogan painting as immature, irresponsible, and ineffective.

(Marsh, 1977: 46)

The unpopularity of graffiti as a political activity lies in several facts: that it requires a level of artistic skill that the majority of people do not have, that it is illegal, and that it is contextual.

Political discussions

Political discussions have been ongoing since time immemorial, but have not registered as a political activity because of the difficulty of measuring such a fluid, continuous and contextual action. Political discussions are a popular and regular activity among these respondents. However, not every political discussion is considered a political action: attempting to change the system or motivate others to take part in political action is construed as a basic political action, but not every political discussion has that root motivation – some are simply repeating news or substantiating information.

A political discussion is considered political activity if the person initiating it intends to use a political issue in order to change the opinions and views of others; in other words they are informing, motivating or persuading. If the discussion is simply the analysis of political news, or a description of a political scenario, then it is a political conversation rather than a political action. This distinction between political discussions and discussions about political issues is analysed further below.

Here are two examples of opposite views about political discussions. One states that discussions about political issues are neutral, and there is no agenda for change (Rashid); the other states that political discussions are an effective way to change people's views and to influence them to take action (Salman).

26. Rashid

They are a very useful tool, they are informal, they are friendly, it breaks down barriers, you don't have a certain agenda, it nurtures a relationship which is not necessarily based on a particular subject matter.

25. Salman

It's personal, genuine, effective having a one-to-one discussion, to spread an opinion and convince someone, you can't beat it.

Political discussions are not instrumental in motivation as much as they are expressive. Respondents state that political discussions are considered political actions; the motivations behind them include venting frustration, building an argument, expressing points of view, persuading to a cause and bringing attention to a topic. The respondents seem to be airing views, holding discussions and explaining political stances in order to gather others to a cause or a specific stance. Political discussions are the root form of political action – through discussions, respondents are persuading and motivating others to join their side and consequently to take further political action using other forms of engagement.

45. Hana

They can be political actions in the way of changing people's attitudes and I'm a great arguer, I have always, sort of, like, defending my point if I feel it needs defending, it's only worth discussing if you're ... if both sides are prepared to listen and change their attitudes.

3. Dalal

I guess people around me also influence my political views as well, and just having discussions with people, their point of view might change and my point of view might change the outcome.

30. Zayneb

We always have dinner table discussions ... (giggling) and they usually end up in, like, arguments sometimes. No, we have ... we have ... it's funny, because one of my brothers – well he's a lawyer so he loves playing devil's advocate – he just says really outrageous things ... he always makes me think of the other side of things (I mean the other point of view) ... you know it might not make me totally turn round, but it broadens your mind.

18. Tuqa

> I think it's great, like for example, at work we talk about it, I may not be on the winning end of an argument...

On the other hand, conversations about issues or news are popular, but seem to be differentiated from those 'political discussions' above which have other intentions apart from the analysis of information. These conversations on political topics are simply attempts to hold conversations with a political content, unlike the discussions noted above in which respondents attempt to influence, persuade or motivate a differing response or thought process.

43. Ilham

> Is it a political action? – no, it's just discussing issues, it's just like anything else what you'd talk over the table, I wouldn't say it was political action because you're just talking about things with your family...

11. Iman

> I don't think they are political, but it's important in shaping your political views. I have lots of conversations with my dad about what is happening in this country, what is happening in the Middle East, but that is family orientated.

Political discussions play a major part of everyday life for many people, yet because they are traditionally not considered to be a political action, this result is all the more revealing. Discussions are expressive: they allow the respondents to explore new ideas, to persuade and influence others and to coerce and manipulate others into further political activity. Political discussions are difficult to quantify because they are so convenient and frequent: they are held at dinner tables, in university lounges, in bedrooms and in workplaces. Political discussions clearly play an important role in political manoeuvring, in encouraging people to take action or to enhance any actions they do take. They are seen as a political activity by many people in the sample, even if they do not all agree with the conceptualisation of political activity: while some believe that it is construed as political action in some contexts, not all discussions about political issues are agreed to be political activities. However, there is a basic agreement that discussions are a political activity. They are popular for similar reasons to boycotting and voting – they are expressive, convenient and a public or group activity.

This analysis has been intriguing, but whether discussion is a political mode of participation is still unclear. While some discussions become political actions in certain contexts, the point at which they stop being political actions can be more difficult to pinpoint. It is clear that we should by no means limit what should and shouldn't be considered political activities. Rather we should place boundaries against which we can measure whether actions may be construed as political actions, instead of deciding in blanket terms whether actions are political modes of engagement or not. In the light of these findings, it may be seen that political discussions are very much a part of engaging in the political sphere for these young people.

Cartoons

The respondents argued that cartoons are political actions for the cartoonists who draw them, but for the viewers they are just information and amusement, though effective in forming opinions and judgements of the caricature. Cartoons intend to caricature political scenarios, people and institutions; their intended outcome is to inform, amuse and attach certain characteristics to those caricatured – the message in a political setting is politically informative.

2. Banan

Yes, you are satirising current affairs, and making a statement.

4. Emel

You are taking the mick out of the political bodies and establishment, they are saying a message, they are political action ...

8. Ghazal

I think that cartoons, especially in the kind of broadsheet newspapers, can have an enormous impact on the way that people think, on people's sense of humour, and also in really undermining otherwise quite important figures, I think that they're incredibly important political manifestations.

They are effective, influential and very popular among the group, but not one person mentions that by looking at satirical cartoons they are politically engaging. Cartoons, like graffiti, are an art. Unlike graffiti, cartooning is legal, and is very much enjoyed by the respondents. Then there are those who are influenced by the cartoons; their views and perceptions are moulded by the images. However, none of the respondents are cartoonists, and though the respondents gained information from the cartoons and find them amusing, none of them suggest that by seeing a cartoon they are conducting a political action.

31. Adam

No, cartoons are pretty satirical, I mean I'm an avid reader of *Private Eye* so it's a way of getting the message across more firmly I guess than from a graffiti perspective. Cartoons are a lot more institutional than graffiti. It does shape subconsciously the public's perception about a body, I think George Bush for instance, his lack of intellect it was captured... through a cartoon and there was some quite satirical works.

16. Mona

Oh yeah, I love cartoons! Humour is a good way of reaching to, like, a wider audience because you kind of stereotype (because you often use stereotypes) people can immediately recognise the character that we stereotype.

3. Dalal

Cartoons I think can be quite effective... I like Steve Bell, he's really funny.

The popularity of cartoons as a political activity on the part of the cartoonist is noted, but it is such a select number of people who have the skills and capability to develop iconic and humorous caricatures and images that it will always be a political activity for the few.

Conclusion

Traditional forms of political engagement follow a conventional format that has been popular over decades – including voting, campaigning and demonstrating. Owing to generational changes that occur, it is natural that newly formed activities may come to the forefront and become popular. Among a generation that has grown up with the globalisation of communication formats and the influence of mass media, this has inevitably influenced new possibilities of political action, which should be taken into consideration when measuring rates of and forms of political engagement; otherwise we are ignoring the possibilities of new forms of political engagement that are becoming far more popular, especially among the young.

8
Out of Favour and Other Avoided Activities

Understanding and appreciating the popularity of political activities is equally as important as exploring the reasons behind unpopular political activities. In order to recognise the relevance of their status as less popular forms of engagement and whether their unpopularity can be overcome, aided or encouraged, we must explore why they hold this status. There are two main reasons for the relative unpopularity of certain political activities: because they require resources (time, money, skills) or because they may be criminal offences (such as rioting, affray or violent disorder), including actions such as flag burning, burning cars and combative political action.

Unpopularity of political actions among the respondents lies in two camps. One group of political activities requires resources which the respondents are not able to provide. These include time commitments, financial expenditure and skill sets. The second group of political activities which are unpopular do not hold illegal statuses in and of themselves, but are usually offences under the Public Order Act 1986 – riots, violent disorder, affray and breach of the peace (including disorderly conduct, assault and threatening behaviour).

Letter writing and emails

Writing is one of the most direct ways in which people can highlight their views on a variety of issues. Whether it is to a local MP, a lobby group or media outlet, political pressure via writing email, letters or sending petitions is simple and direct. The development of internet communication makes writing as a form of pressure much easier. Networking sites help to gather more participants to add pressure; emails assist in the development of draft letters to be passed around; and search engines are useful in locating addresses, email addresses and other details of individuals and groups to be pressured. The internet has encouraged people simply to 'sign and send'.

Among the respondents, the few who do write or email letters about political issues consider it a better way of recording the argument than a verbal conversation, whereas the respondents who consider this method ineffective believe that there are other methods which are likely to get a better response. Very few of the respondents wrote letters as a form of political action; some of them see this from the other side (they are councillors or work for MPs) and so they see the action as inefficient. A slow and ineffectual response to written forms of political action leads respondents to take alternative action.

Writing letters is quite an individual activity, unless as part of a mass programme. It can be used to complain to or to request something from an MP or to petition local councillors, for example. However, it is usually very direct and personal. Quite a few of the younger people surveyed considered writing as a form of political action in the context of Amnesty International campaigns, which they took part in mainly within a school framework.

7. Farah

I always write letters...I think that writing letters is something that we should all do, perhaps people think that it's not going to have any effect because people are writing the same letter and just signing their name and maybe it won't make a difference but you know I do believe that it puts pressure on people and it's only by writing letters that you can get your voice heard and attending demonstrations and whatever, so I write a lot of angry letters.

20. Sana

It is a political action because you have to write and make your arguments, writing to councillors and MPs to anyone who received a service and write it down, it achieves more than a verbal conversation, it goes on record and someone has to respond to it...I fax my MP, not as much as I used to, I have written once or twice to the local paper, sometimes they don't get printed anyway.

Letter writing is not that popular because it is considered ineffective and slow, and there are other formats or methods that the respondents consider to be a better use of time and effort. They see letter writing as a pointless because correspondence is just thrown away (Noora, Tuqa) and also because, as an individual action, it is less effective than mass action (Iman).

8. Ghazal

I see letters as wholly ineffective, I don't see it as a credible political action.

17. Noora

Letter writing is not gonna do anything, throw it in the bin, or email, don't see any point in that.

18. Tuqa

I think they're less effective simply because I've seen the boxes of letters written by children who, you know, want to end poverty, and I don't think they get anywhere because we do just dump them at the end of the day, so I don't think anybody actually sits down and reads them, it's not the same, it's not going to have the same impact as, you know, chucking children's shoes at Downing Street so that they can see – there's a clear message, the media can get involved, they can see what's happening.

11. Iman

I do think it is political if you are writing to your MP or having your say, then yes. But I don't think it's effective because if one person does it, nobody is listening. If a million people are doing it, and flooding the gates with them, then it can be quite effective.

Written forms of political action are indeed seen as political actions, but are seen as ineffective among the group. They are considered ineffective compared with other direct actions. Writing is considered more time-consuming than other political activities, with less likelihood of success because of its individual nature.

Lobbying and campaigning

Lobbying, canvassing and campaigning are an integral part of the democratic process, from grass-roots leafleting to international private organisations and charities attempting to influence, persuade and cajole responses from interested parties. These forms of political participation usually require some form of dedication, interest in the issue and resources (time, finances, etc.).

> In particular, we must give due recognition to citizen involvement in a wide array of groups that seek to influence policy making. These groups may be formal or informal, local or national, overtly political or only intermittently engaged in such affairs. But collectively they represent a most important mechanism through which citizen preferences are made known to those who make decisions. Indeed, some argue that issue oriented 'preference groups'... are becoming an ever more important part of the whole process, challenging and possibly even partially supplanting the more traditional party based mechanisms of representation. In the present era of fast changing collectivist politics citizen participation through such groups plays a prominent part.
>
> (Parry et al., 1992: 40)

Lobbying and campaigning are not that popular among the group, but a few of them have participated in one or another, and those who do take part in lobbying and campaigning do it as part of a group or organisation. They take part because of their belief in a cause, for example to support those who are trying to get elected or to lobby for change in policy. Campaigning for political parties was not related to ethnicity or religion generally, though this could be disputed in the case of some of the respondents who campaign for the Respect Party in Birmingham on behalf of the Salma Yaqoob, or even for the Labour Party's Muslim MP Sadiq Khan. Those who were lobbying on behalf of organisations were lobbying on behalf of Muslim organisations,[1] and thus religious identity influenced their level of political activity.

Among the respondents, six have campaigned on electoral issues, usually on behalf of a political party. Two of them have campaigned on behalf of the Labour Party (Suhail, Adam), two on behalf of Respect (Yaman, Sana), Hassan on behalf of the Green Party and Mosab (who is a Labour supporter) to encourage higher voter turnout and improved information on candidate choice.

14. Mosab

> What I did at the last elections... local elections, we organised a list of campaign points. We did it in association with the Muslim Alliance and the Christian Churches. We did like a joint canvassing meeting,

you know like a 'please bear in mind these points when voting for a candidate'. During the last general election, we did platform issues as well.

20. Sana

Yes it is a political action... I support the Respect Party, I do a lot of canvassing for them, stand outside of polling stations and hand out leaflets and such... I do this outside of work, I think it will contribute to society, to contribute to make change you have to engage with the political process, to be smart with the system... on polling days I stand out and antagonise the Labour and Lib Dem supporters!

41. Suhail

I've been a member for six years now and I've been a strong supporter of Labour ever since I was 18... I'm actually a councillor in a ward called **** **** and **** ... canvassing, we do a lot of telephone canvassing, we do a lot of leafleting and I think the best way and my favourite way when I'm in the local elections is knocking on doors and speaking to people and face to face and understanding...

31. Adam

... I've been campaigning quite a lot but I would highlight a campaign that I've done for Sadiq Khan in Tooting, he's an MP for Labour, the fourth Muslim to be selected in the House of Commons... in terms of time it's usually two hours... two hours a week.

These respondents have used a variety of campaigning methods, including leafleting, stalls, door-to-door canvassing, phone calls and standing at polling stations antagonising other party campaigners. The wide variety of campaigning methods means that respondents need to have opportunities and a personality that suits the campaigning style. Campaigners usually need to be dedicated to a cause or passionate about an issue; they usually need to hold a set of helpful skills – whether in IT, organisation or confidence in social interaction. All six respondents who have campaigned are confident, outspoken and verbally expressive personalities. Campaigning may also be time-consuming, physically active and may require a financial cost. For these numerous reasons, the limited number of campaigners in the sample is explained by the demands of the job – and thus only the dedicated tend to follow.

[Campaigning] requires considerable social interaction with other people, some of it in a pleading or salesman like posture. This is especially true of canvassing from door to door or of making speeches. Evidence to be presented later shows that self-confidence and a feeling of social ease are important prerequisites to participation in the socially interactive phase of campaigning.

(Milbrath, 1965: 25)

Aside from campaigning on electoral issues, a few other respondents have lobbied on behalf of an organisation or cause. Though similar skills are usually needed in lobbying, the respondents mention that networking and knowing who to lobby are integral aspects of successful lobbying. The lobbyists also need not only to be dedicated to the cause, but also must be informed about the issues. While campaigning is usually most time-consuming just before an election, and thus an episodic activity, lobbying usually has a long-term strategy and pressure.

42. Sami

Lobbying, for the work I do, in trying to influence those people who are policy-makers, not so much politicians... mean it's important to lobby politicians, but mostly Civil Service, because politicians come and go, the Civil Service stays there... to influence the establishment, to indicate them and things.

So it can be said that campaigning and lobbying are unpopular political activities among these young British Muslims, because of the resources in terms of time commitment, financial expenditure and skills that are required.

Political donations and financial purchases

Both donating to political parties and buying particular items (e.g. fair-trade products) is seen as an expensive activity. Boycotting was seen in Chapter 7 to be popular among the respondents, because it meant that they chose alternative products to the item they would usually have chosen. The financial cost in that scenario was limited, mainly because of the wide variety of choice available in branding and marketed products. However, purchasing products is considered as more expensive than boycotting, because the products that are ethical or fair trade are not as cheap as the alternatives.

16. Mona

Sometimes we have to make compromises basically, and even though you might not agree with how bananas were plucked from the tree, you might have to buy them because, you know, that's the cheaper alternative and that's the one that you can afford, and you need bananas because they're good for your health.

42. Sami

If you can afford it, fantastic...fair trade – a fantastic idea – I wish Muslims were more involved in it, organic food and all this...Me? I think...it costs more money and I can't afford it, so, simple.

6. Bara

The problem with fair trade is that money's often an issue for people and people don't like to spend more money for the same product, so it's...I think in a way it's more difficult for people.

Donating to political parties was really unpopular among the group. This is unusual, because in many recent surveys donating to political parties tends to be popular. Pattie et al. (2004) found that donating to political parties was one of the most common political actions acknowledged by their sample. There may be numerous reasons why political donations are unpopular among the group – those sampled here are young people, so less financially affluent than wider society. Secondly, as mentioned in the voting section above, the respondents in this sample seem to be sceptical of political parties, and so making donations could be an unpopular activity as a result. Only one respondent donated to a political party, and even those who campaign for parties have not donated financially. Making financial donations is seen as a political action, though it is seen as intending to influence or gain favour from within rather than being a charitable donation:

10. Huma

Well yes, I gave money to Respect, and voted for Respect, and I gave them money because I agree with Respect, and I want them to go forward, and if the way is to give them money then so be it.

11. Iman

People who give money to political events or parties have an ulterior motive; it is political as you can sway opinions.

31. Adam

Again this is buying influence at the end of the day, I don't think we are in a day when the true desire to assist in a political party is out of a need to do it as opposed to safeguarding your interests or buying influence.

8. Ghazal

…I don't think I've ever donated to a political cause simply because I've never had enough confidence in any one political organisation to deem it worth sponsoring – I'd rather donate money to charity just because it makes me feel better.

Buying products as a form of political participation was generally greeted with lukewarm approval, but considered an expensive form of participation. Donating to political causes or parties was considered as only useful for those wishing to gain influence from within. Unless they personally believe in the values of the party, respondents do not donate to parties. They consider such monetary donations to be ineffective, and only useful to those wishing to curry favour within the party – preferring to ease their conscience by donating to charities.

Illegal status political activities

In the introduction to this chapter, I asked whether violent actions with political principles should be considered to be political actions. In the past, violent activities have been seen as outdated (Milbrath, 1965: 18; Verba and Nie, 1972; Verba et al., 1978). However, Britain has seen many violent protests, riots and bombings in the name of political causes, and so discussing these issues as potential political actions is crucial.

In Marsh's study (1977) on protest and political consciousness in Britain he asked many survey questions about political actions from petitions to property damage and violence. The survey included an aspect of 'protest potential', attempting to recognise the potential for participants to act on these potentials in a practical situation. The respondents in this research had not participated in violent political activity, but their responses regarding these actions (even though unpopular) are a reflection of their attitudes. The views of the respondents who are sympathetic or understanding towards certain violent political actions are indicative of some level of acceptance that these actions can be justified in certain situations.

The use of violent means as a method of political action is not seen favourably by the respondents. The varying actions have different levels of effectiveness, mostly in gaining media attention and venting frustration, rather than as a useful method for changing policy or direct representation. The overarching argument among respondents is that combative or military actions can be political actions under certain circumstances. They are effective in gaining media attention and, at times, in changing policy. These actions are also a last resort for people who cannot use other types of political actions to get a result.

Rioting, burning cars and vandalism were seen to be wrong, even if politically inspired. The few respondents who were sympathetic to such behaviour seemed to be able to identify with the roots of such problems. These actions were considered generally only to be effective in getting attention, but not in gaining sympathy for causes and not in changing much in terms of policy.

Flag burning is considered a political action and it is considered to be effective in venting frustrations, in highlighting views to the media and gaining attention for an issue, but not effective in changing policy. It has very negative connotations and is generally not condoned among the group. Few have done it. Getting arrested as a political action seems only to be seen as effective under specific circumstances – where media interest can gain the case a higher profile. In the majority of incidents, the respondents feel that getting arrested is useless, and more likely to be harmful in terms of a criminal record and so on.

All these forms of political activities were unpopular because of their indirectly illegal status: participants could be arrested under the Public Order Act 1986 for riots, violent disorder, affray and breach of the peace (including disorderly conduct, assault and threatening behaviour). For some respondents who identify with their religious identity, these activities are also viewed as being un-Islamic or prohibited to a certain degree, depending on the context or action.

22. Kamal/Munir/Noori

Okay, which ones [political action vignettes] are the most effective?

Using an AK47 and shooting a person.

Combative violence

This action was very difficult to discuss during the interviews, especially when attempting not to lead respondents but to extricate their views on a taboo subject. The photographic vignettes that were used as a research method helped to direct the discussion. Most respondents suggested that political violence in militant or combative terms was justifiable in certain circumstances, but there were a significant number who considered it completely indefensible.

45. Hana

Can be political, I think it comes down to the motivation. I mean, I'm not saying I think it's legitimate, but it can definitely be politically motivated, and can give a political message.

2. Banan

Political action... it is because it's to do with a political issue, I'm not saying it's legitimate but yes it is political action.

24. Wafa

I think it's... complicated really... I don't think it's a way forward, obviously I don't agree with it... I think it has an impact, and an effect – I'm not sure how you define it – effective, good-effective, bad-effective – but it has an effect.

22. Kamal/Munir/Noori

A terrorist attacking?

Yeh... it's a war...

Is it political?

Very political...

4. Emel

The guy with the gun... you'd think that was political given the circumstances of today's world, and yes he wants to achieve his objective in a way of doing it through violence... he wants to get through his message, and his message is political, and this is his way of doing it... it's oppositional, and I guess yes it is political, characterised as high politics.

44. Leyan

I understand it, but I think it's completely nuts... I think it can be effective and it depends on the cause... again it's a very shadowy debate, are we talking about resistance... violence is a very disgusting, I think we over-romanticise war and violence...but in certain circumstances it is unavoidable.

The research questions did not ask about suicide attacks or martyrdom operations specifically, or whether that is justified within Islam, but sensitive disclosures such as these could be mentioned if the respondents felt comfortable about discussing them while talking about combative violence. I showed respondents a photographic vignette of a masked man in camouflaged green army clothing and holding a gun, and asked about political violence as a wide term of reference. Many of the descriptions below highlight the fact that political combative violence is not a black and white issue.

Clearly, therefore, Muslims (and non-Muslims) can mean different things by jihad. Differences in interpretation are deeply rooted in Muslim history and reflect the diversity of Islamic thought.

(Ansari, 2005: 149)

References from the Quran were used by some respondents, mainly in order to refute the fact that violence was justified in Islam. Others used case studies in Islamic history to describe circumstances where violence may be justifiable. The context in which political violence was considered acceptable was mainly where people were defending land or being attacked. The issue here is of course complicated by the interpretation of Islamic sources, as discussed earlier in the book. Differing interpretations, not only in different eras but also depending on particular cases and aspects of jurisprudence, mean that opinions regarding the justification of political violence are complex. For example, there have been fatwas in recent years that have held that violence such as martyrdom is acceptable in Israel, because it is defending the Palestinian cause. On the other hand, fatwas have also held that martyrdom in states where Muslims reside peacefully (such as Europe) is forbidden – although you can find others that hold different views, which is how Al-Qaeda justifies its attacks on Western European targets.

There did not seem to be any link between Britishness and justification for violence. There were respondents in groups one and two such as Noora who argued that violence can be justified, and many in group three who identified themselves as British Muslims who also fell into this category. Alternatively, there were those in the fourth group, who identified themselves as mainly Muslim, who said that violence was not justified under any circumstances (Yahya, Jamila, Rashid). However, it may be that those who hold such extremist views were not sampled.

The most common response among the respondents was that political militant violence could be justified in certain contexts. These included defence of land or identity (Sana, Leyla, Mekki) or desperation when no other possible alternatives remain, especially when expressing grievances (Mekki, Farah, Samir, Noora).

20. Sana

It's used by both sides, we like to see the good and evil, always one right, one wrong, one freedom fighter, another's terrorist. It should be an option if they are defending the legitimate concerns of their country in defending their borders... I don't have a problem with Hezbollah or Hamas, it's legitimate, they have clear-cut political demands and they have tried to engage with the political process, but their demands have been rebuffed. What I don't agree with is when civilians are murdered for the sake of achieving a political goal.

15. Leyla

It's a hard one. It's hard coz I don't agree with violence at all, but when states carry out violence then that's all right? Then you should raise your arms against them too.

52. Mekki

People think that just because Palestinians or someone is fighting for their life, they don't have any other alternative, they only have these options, so for them it is a dire state of need, but we as Muslims, living in Britain especially in an open society, it is totally unjust, and Islam does not encourage or say that you should do these things, like kidnap other people or terrorism or arrest people, kill people, totally wrong.

7. Farah

Violence is a method used by people who think it is a last resort or perhaps it's the only resort they feel. I don't think it makes it correct and I don't think it makes it viable.

40. Samir

Violence is one means. It's a means of getting heard internationally, it is very effective... I think that's, in some ways it's the only way because people aren't going to get heard and it's what drives them to be violent, they're not getting heard, and for that, it's justified for me. You know, these people, it's a little voice, nobody listens to them getting their houses trampled over or bulldozed over, so these people go to extreme measures because they've got no hope of doing anything about it, so that makes it justifiable for me.

17. Noora

If it's your only way of making your statement, voice heard and that's all you have got. But I don't want people to die or anything. Never. But if it's all you have got, only opportunity you're left, only viable option, then take it if it's all you have got. It's the biggest way to get heard.

Most of the respondents used arguments similar to Bara. He argues that religiously and in certain contexts combative violence is permitted – though mostly prohibited. He argues that owing to the grievances that Palestinians are facing, they are justified in their political violence as a means of defence. On the other hand, though, terrorists who attack Western locations are not justified, because they are attacking rather than defending. The issue is complicated further by the fact that black to some is white to others; for some, groups such as Hamas and Hezbollah are terrorist organisations, while for others (Sana, above, for example), they are legitimate political parties. Bara refers to the popular phrase that one person's terrorist is another person's freedom fighter, while another respondent (Asif) mentions that political violence is used the world over, and the expectation that groups should not be using it as a moral high ground is hypocritical.

5. Asif

The Western states certainly have always used violence as a political means (usually violence as a political means)...it's not something that only these types of terrorists or whatever, these kind of, border organisations use, but it's something that's always gone on...the hypocrisy is something that I can get angry about (a lot) – the fact that...the whole kind of foreign policy issue – I mean if you look at the current war in Iraq – there's Bush and Blair, both up there, doing God's work.

6. Bara

Okay, if we're talking specifically about terrorism, Middle East, and the way that our media looks at it, it's important for everyone to understand why things are happening. I mean, no way am I saying it's right...killing people is not right...it says in the Quran – if you kill one person, it's like you've murdered the whole of mankind – that statement in the Quran shows how bad it is to do something which constitutes murder ...obviously there's a clause in between, and that's important, the clause is...unless they've caused mischief in the land...the saying goes that one person's terrorist is another person's freedom fighter...situations like the Palestinian issue where, every day, you get bulldozers coming into people's houses; you get people being killed for no reason, by Israelis, and you wonder 'well, do the Palestinians have any other choice? Is violence the right answer?' Well, if someone's coming and attacking your home you have no choice but to defend yourselves and, if by defending your-selves you go up to what is a legitimate border, then that's fine. I don't see a problem with that because you have no choice, but then when you look at something like September 11th, when you look at something like the London bombings...is it fair to go into that coun-try and then attack civilians? I wouldn't be able to justify that, I'd say 'no'...

More respondents were of the above view – that political violence in militant terms is acceptable under certain circumstances. However, there were a smaller group of respondents who argued that political violence is unacceptable in any circumstances. These respondents argue that reli-giously there is little justification for the use of violence, and secondly that political violence is ineffective, destructive and counter-productive. Some of the respondents agree that political violence gets results – usu-ally bringing different sides to the table but at the huge expense of innocent lives. Mona discusses at length her feelings that though cases such as Sinn Fein in Northern Ireland can eventually be successful, the years of destruction are not worth all that violence; there are always peaceful alternative methods that for some reason political groups are at times unwilling to accept.

16. Mona

Often other stakeholders, at the last resort, welcome people that use political violence and we can see that from the IRA and how...the British Parliament has...listened to Sinn Finn...so in terms of whether it's effective, I question it – well, look at what it actually does do, what we know it does – it kills a lot of people, some of them are combatants and some of them are not (innocent people die because of it and it's directly related to it)...So I've had debates where people have said that in some circumstances (most often friends have used examples from Kashmir and Palestine) people are in such a situation where they can't do anything but resort to violence to get their point across. I don't agree with that because it says that there is nothing else for us to do apart from become violent, and I don't agree with that. I think that there are always other options and you have to make those other options stronger, and you have to do it consciously.

57. Yahya

The holy Prophet said 'the real mujahid [one who fights for Islam] is the person who does jihad against his own *nafs* [soul] in the obedience of Allah (SWT). If he is strong and mighty and brave and goes to the battlefield, but if he's losing the battle with the *shaytan* [devil] and the inner self then there is no person weaker than him'...the current Muslim situation, and as simple as it may sound, but it's so effective, because this is the only ingredient that Muslims have lost...

12. Jamila

It's not a political action, it's a military action, and if these military armies didn't attack them, they wouldn't respond by suicide bombings. And I don't advocate military action for political change. Jihadis would advocate jihad and that would cause political change, I think political change comes through talking and exchange of ideas.

25. Salman

Islamically my view is that the Islamic texts show that violence in order to set up an Islamic political entity is prohibited in Islam. In addition to that, whether you have a state or no state, violence against civilians is prohibited, not much more to add to that, it's clear cut.

31. Adam

I mean historically in the 20th century any movement which were a great advocate for violence eventually come to the bargaining of the negotiating table so we have to learn from that and abstain from that.

3. Dalal

It really makes me so ashamed because it's not even like these guys are misinterpreting Islam, it's a complete contradiction and I just don't understand it, I can't get my head round where they got the justification from . . . it makes me really ashamed and sad that there's so much ignorance at the moment, and if people just picked up a good translation [of the Quran], or like a good book, then they would see that Islam isn't about that and know that's wrong . . .

Combative violence by some of the sample was considered justified as political action under certain circumstances; by others it was considered unjustified and was not considered political action but military activity. The semantics of the discussion are interesting yet inconclusive. What these responses do show, however, is that young British Muslims do not discuss combative violence with references to its illegality in terms of general or international law (like the rest of the subjects in this section), but with reference to Islamic law, morals and ethics; and this is the evidence for its unpopularity among the group.

Riots

When discussing rioting, burning cars and damaging property, respondent stances seem clearer than in the discussion on combative political violence. Rioting is more geographically localised and less influenced by foreign policy issues such as Iraq or Israel, tending to be more influenced by local issues, poverty and youth frustration. England saw some of its worst riots recently in August 2011, beginning in Tottenham, London and spreading to Birmingham and Manchester. The riots were sparked by the police shooting of Mark Duggan, and developing into rioting that included the looting of shops and offices, setting fire to business and homes, and vandalism. A report into this disturbance highlighted that it had little political relevance, but was an opportunity for young people to engage in mindless violence for their amusement, to loot and to respond to what was seen as police brutality (Morrell et al., 2011). Though these riots took place well after the fieldwork phases, the responses regarding rioting among the participants are reflected in wider public opinion – British people were unsympathetic and thought the riots were unjustified.

The majority of respondents did not agree with the use of methods such as riots as a form of political action. However, there were some sympathetic voices among the group, especially among those young Muslim men who reside in inner city areas such as Tower Hamlets, Birmingham and Bradford. They may be able to identify with the roots of such behaviour and the causes for such action. Some considered rioting, damage to property and so on as acceptable because the rioters are making a statement (Tower Hamlets' Umayr, Yunis and Zubair, and Birmingham's Bashir and Ali); they are attempting to gain government attention and to get their views across, usually regarding poverty and unemployment (Ali and Bashir from Birmingham). It is most certainly an expressive political action participated in by the few, but has an impact on more.

Do you not feel sorry for the person whose car is damaged?

46. Umayr

I do think it's wrong, but that person that done it is trying to get his point heard, bruver's taken major action!

47. Yunis

I watched on the TV about people who were protesting a few years ago about tax rises. For a few hours, it was a peaceful protest, they were making a statement. The mobs realised we are not getting through to them...so they thought let's heat it up a bit and get it interesting, so they started forcing their opinion on police officers, torching a whole building, they set the whole thing alight! That made a bigger statement than what they were doing for the first three hours! If the government paid some attention to the people doing some peaceful protest then the protestors wouldn't have to get to violence to get themselves [heard]...it's all to do with attention seeking, trying to show that look I'm doing this to make a stand for this reason, if you don't hear me, I'm going to take it to the extreme, make myself heard.

32. Ali

To be honest there are different scenarios [violence] those people that were doing it were doin' it [Bradford riots] 'cause they believed in it. They did it because they were really being affected. If you're really poor and you've got nothing and you're on the streets and the government is not being, looking after you, like our government looks after you. By doing this it's making your area more aware and by making your area more aware that increases public awareness and if it increases public awareness then the government is more likely to tackle that area and sort it out.

Flag burning

Flag burning is also another expressive and signalling political action: it is considered to be effective in venting frustrations, in gaining media and public attention for an issue, but not effective in changing any policy. It has very negative connotations and is not generally condoned among the group because of its illegal status. Though in fact flag burning in and of itself is not illegal in the UK, one may be arrested for flag burning in a public gathering for other reasons, such as breach of the peace or threatening behaviour. Few have participated in it.

17. Noora

Laughter ... I've done quite a bit of American flag burning in my past, I burnt the American flag on my desk and I support all flag burning really ...

What do you think it symbolises?

Well, I don't believe in nationality and borders and that's what a flag represents, in this country we're not allowed to fly a flag [you are allowed to fly any national flag, with some restrictions if you're advertising a business] – yet for the World Cup you are allowed. It supports segregation and doesn't support a community.

Was it only an American flag you burnt?

I've burnt an Israeli flag and a British flag ... (giggling)

Was it at demonstrations?

Just among me and my friends ... [laughter] well once I was at a festival and these punks had an upside-down American flag flying, and I was trying to set it on fire, but it wouldn't light! It would have been wicked if it had set alight and they were carrying it!

Whether participants agreed or disagreed with flag burning, they all acknowledged that flags are representations (nations, borders, etc.). They agreed that in terms of political policy change, flag burning is ineffective. However, as an expressive mechanism, whereby people send a message about their resentment, venting their anger and expressing their aggressive stance towards a state, flag burning is an effective political action. Flag burning is considered an emotive choice of action; symbolic; context driven; and a representation of feelings.

45. Hana

I think it shows a higher level of anger, resentment, so it can send a strong message, but again, it's open to be ignored by whoever is in power, and also it's likely to provoke strong reactions.

14. Mosab

It's just an emotional reaction … Yes, of course it is [political action], people are making a political statement, whether it's a method … strictly speaking it's not illegal, but whether it's a method I'd employ to make a political statement … no.

15. Leyla

I don't see why people should feel the need to burn flags to show how angry you are, but then in the context of say Iraq or Palestine where they don't have any other way to show their anger then perhaps that is a good way of doing it. But when I do see it I think what a waste of time.

26. Rashid

I think it's unnecessarily provocative. Intellectually it's wrong, because you're not against the people of America or Britain or whatever, you are against the policies of the government, or policy-makers, and to burn a flag represents burning their entire nation.

Nearly all the responses about flag burning acknowledge that because of the status of flags as a national symbol, and the offences for which individuals burning a flag could be arrested for (such as breach of the peace), as a political activity flag burning is unpopular. Many interviewees highlight that to offend a nation as a whole when responding to the actions of a few is unfair, and that as a political action flag burning is ineffective, offensive, wasteful, negative and pointless.

Getting arrested

Getting arrested as a political action seems only to be seen as effective under specific circumstances – where media interest can gain the case a higher profile. In the majority of incidents, the respondents feel that getting arrested is useless and more likely to be harmful in terms of a criminal record and so on. Getting arrested for a political issue is a purely symbolic action taken in order to draw attention to the case. Unsurprisingly, no one in the sample had been arrested for a political issue.

11. Iman

Yes, especially if you are campaigning, like something like Bloody Monday which happened in Ireland, people protesting, then they got shot. Now they would get arrested, people do make a political stand to get arrested. I read about this Christian woman who refused to pay her council tax and she got put in jail, it was her political stance.

29. Tufayl

...I know certain regimes where, yes, absolutely, carrying out a very forthright, provocative action like this can actually have a huge impact...Well I think some of the Muslim countries for example...we know of many stories of brothers who are in Uzbekistan for example, they're tortured (they're seriously tortured) but they have the courage, in a place like that, to come out after *Jummuah* [Friday prayers], make a speech, or distribute leaflets and in making that speech and then getting arrested, they're making a huge, huge impact...but in this country, in the UK, do I think that it's something that's very effective – I don't. I don't.

17. Noora

It's a good way to vent your frustration. You can get arrested, three of my friends got arrested at the G8, I didn't coz I was eating lunch at McDonalds! [laughter]

7. Farah

It can be, I mean you can't say it's not because look at Nelson Mandela for example, I mean him getting arrested was one of the things that brought so much attention to the issue that he was trying to fight.

Conclusion

Political participation in this day and age is in some respects an expressive aspect of people's lives. The political choices they make are in part influenced by their lifestyles, and the modes of participation they choose are influenced by their expressive abilities, skill set and networks. The least popular types of political action were those that demanded certain resources such as skill sets or financial flexibility, and violent activities which were likely to be offences for which you can be arrested, such as flag burning and damaging property.

So what have aggressive political actions to contribute to the arena of political engagement? All aggressive forms of political activity are expressive in nature, usually attempting to symbolically display the grievances that groups hold. Combative political violence as a political action is roughly condemned by most respondents, but in certain contexts it is considered to be justified. Riots also seem to have some justifiable reasons, such as high unemployment and poor conditions. However, rioting, flag burning and getting arrested are more unpopular among the group and more difficult to justify. The interviewees agree that most aggressive political activities are emotive, usually a way of venting frustration while gaining media attention. The message that is conveyed by the respondents in this research is that the illegal status of all these political activities dissuades people from participating in such activities.

According to survey research by the Pew Charitable Trust, it seems that British and other European Muslims tend to have higher rates of justifying suicide bombings in comparison with American Muslims:

> The Pew survey reveals that Muslim Americans are more moderate on questions pertaining to violence than other Muslims in Europe and across the Muslim world. The percentage of US Muslims who feel suicide bombing are justifiable and those who have favorable views of al Qaeda are remarkably low – especially when these percentages are compared to those for other Muslims in other countries. In Europe, 16 per cent of the Muslim population in France, 16 per cent of the population in Spain and 15 per cent of Britain's Muslim population felt suicide bombings are often or sometimes justified. Compared to the 8 per cent of US Muslims who felt so, European Muslims, then, are twice as likely to see suicide bombings are justifiable.
>
> (Jamal, 2010: 93–94)

Jamal argues that the reason for such variation between European Muslim and American Muslims is assimilation – that American Muslims are reflecting the same values of wider society because of socialisation in norms over time; and also the socio-economic success of American Muslims in comparison to other Western Muslims (Jamal, 2010). In addition to these arguments, there is a third possibility for the higher rates of denouncement of violence among American Muslims, and that is religious knowledge and education. The USA has a plethora of Western-educated Muslim scholars with widely held moderate views, and the American Muslim population is influenced by the enlightened discourse and religious interpretation this brings. Britain, I would argue, is not far behind, considering the shared language, but the lingual barriers across the rest of Europe may have a role to play in the lack of understanding and awareness among less-educated Muslims.

9
Concluding Words

This research has explored the role and context of identity in political engagement, and in these concluding comments I would like to reflect on the research findings and their greater bearing. In order to answer the question whether religious, national and ethnic identity influence the political engagement of young second-generation British Muslims, the research explored identity as perceived by the respondents themselves. The varied methodological approaches used to explore the concept of identity underlined the difficulties involved in expressing and defining identity. The fluidity of the concept over time and its context-dependent variance highlight that identity is by no means a given, and is subtly ever-changing. During the course of this book, the most pertinent references to identity from the respondents were with regard to religion and nationality. The focus on religion and religious identity from policy-makers and media outlets means that being Muslim is never far from the respondents' minds, and descriptively identifies many of these youths, whether because they wear hijab, sport beards or because their names are Mohammed or Aisha.

Being Muslim inevitably holds different values across the lives of these youngsters, as seen in Chapter 3: some hold religious obligations as necessary, others are willing to negotiate which practices they pursue, while others have a purely symbolic attitude towards being Muslim. The textual references, analysis, fatwas, scholarly guidance and cultural/historical practices all play varied roles in religious identity formation for these youngsters, and this is becoming ever more present in their lives because of the availability of information online, on television and in published media outlets.

It is clear that however little or however much Islam is relevant to the lives of these British Muslims, it is an identity which they explore and reflect on. As mentioned throughout this book, there has been increased pressure on Muslims since 9/11 – whether through media coverage, international political debates, local and national governmental schemes, the focus on integration, changes in laws banning hijabs, veils and minarets, regulations regarding security, and laws on preventing extremism – these have all focused heavily on Muslims, Islam and identity. Thus, as groups feel pressured, inspected and judged, it potentially breeds dissatisfaction, frustration, perceived inequality and double standards. Identity is a frail yet fluctuating phenomenon. As pressure increases, people seem to identify more: the use of religion in the political framework is a reflection of this trend – this is the power of identity politics. Because identity fluctuates, these opinions and views may not exist in 10 or 20 years, but currently religious identity is political identity for these young British Muslims.

> Two groups stand out for attracting more negative than positive feelings:[1] Muslims and (marginally) the deeply religious. A third of people give Muslims a cool rating, while under a quarter give them a warm one.
>
> (Voas and Ling, 2010: 78)

> Three key points emerge from this analysis. Firstly, some of the antipathy towards Muslims comes from people with a generalised dislike of anyone different. Secondly, a larger subset of the population – about a fifth – responds negatively only to Muslims. Finally, relatively few people feel unfavourable towards any other religious or ethnic group on its own... Some degree of generalised xenophobia is always likely to exist. Conceivably there is a spill-over effect, so that people who are worried about Muslims come to feel negatively about 'others' in general. In any case, the adverse reaction to religion in Britain and the United States towards Muslims deserves to be the focus of policy on social cohesion, because no other group elicits so much disquiet.
>
> (Voas and Ling, 2010: 80–81)

Alongside religious identity, British citizenship and Britishness are equally reference points which are relevant for some of these young British Muslims. Being British for the majority of respondents is a facet (or an identity) they do not question but feel is questioned by wider society. These respondents feel strongly that Britishness is all they know, that it is just as compatible with their religion as it is with other religions. For the few, Britishness is less relevant either because they identify with a wider concept of globalised individuals or because they identify with a narrower group of religious believers and no one else.

Despite the overwhelming number of respondents who identify themselves as being British, the majority of respondents feel under pressure to justify this identity, even though they know no other national or ethnic culture. These respondents were relatively passive about their ethnic identity. It may be that the relevance of religion and British nationality has superseded ethnic identification, leaving ethnicity dormant for the time being. Chapter 3 highlights that ethnic identity is becoming less relevant to the lives of these second-generation respondents. They pick and choose elements of ethnic practices which they feel are assets to their lives, and as generations pass these may be further filtered and distilled.

A focus on identity emphasises that social group identity is a reflection of surroundings, of environment and times (Tajfel and Turner, 1979; Tajfel, 1981; Turner et al., 1987; Hogg and Abrams, 1988). The importance of Islam and Britishness may be re-evaluated in years to come; it may become less or more important dependent on the social and political environment, on religious contextual sources and on social group dynamics. The very fact that ethnicity is passed on at birth, while religion and national identification can be chosen, redesigned and re-adopted in adulthood, is relevant to this discussion. These are choices young people make, which reflect their place, feelings, appearance and the decisions they take.

In order to understand if identity impacts political engagement, the motivation for political engagement was explored in Chapter 4. The connection between identity and political motivation is a factor that is symptomatic of respondent identification. That is, those respondents who felt very strongly about a facet of their group identity allowed it not only to be reflected in the political causes they chose to engage in or the political choices they made, but also allowed the identity to create boundaries around what it was acceptable/unacceptable to participate in (for instance, which causes to support). However, even among those respondents who are either symbolically Muslim or in whose lives Islam plays a peripheral role (typology groups one and two), religion accompanied post-material values as political motivation, mainly owing to socialisation and upbringing. Among identity groups three and four, religion was a crucial explanation for their political mobilisation and motivation.

The impact of the concept of ummah on the political motivation of young British Muslims cannot be sidelined either. Whether it is considered as an imagined group, or as an existing global brotherhood, the ummah has extensive implications for understanding political motivation. The notion of the ummah transcends national, ethnic and lingual boundaries, and this in itself means British Muslims can identify with others across the globe as part of their 'group', based on religious group identity. The ummah becomes more important to group affiliation when national identification is complicated by feelings of 'difference' from mainstream national group identity. Chapter 3 highlighted that at times the respondents have felt they have been required to justify their British identity and their British group belonging, which does not help them to feel welcome in their home country or feel as though they belong to any British national identity group.

Political motivation continues from Chapter 4 through to 6, where differences between the popular political activities in which respondents participated lay not in the level/availability of resources but in motivational distinctions. The difference between voting (as a political tool) and boycotting or demonstrating lies in differing motivation. These political activities are both convenient and expressive, but voting is motivated by civic duty, whereas boycotting, demonstrations and media formats were found to be influenced by the respondent's identity.

The later chapters focused on how young British Muslims are politically engaged and to what degree their engagements are focused on ethnic, national or religious issues. Are new modes of political activities becoming more prevalent? To a certain degree, newer forms of political activity have increased the likelihood of the political involvement of groups of people who may not have otherwise been attracted towards participation. Newer forms of political participation also encourage new voices and innovative and varied ways in which they may be heard. The popularity of boycotting, political discussions, new media formats and communication media suggests that newer modes of participation are useful and fashionable among the younger generations. The respondents effectively used forms of political participation that can overcome state borders; they are engaging in activities that can be conducted both in the private sphere as well as in a more public domain, and in activities that can be participated in as individuals or as part of a larger group action. The flexibility of these formats allows for many possibilities that the young Muslims feel appeal to them. It is also interesting that the most popular activities are relatively cost-free and easy to undertake – which is understandably an attraction for the young.

45. Hana

I'd have to say that how easy the action is comes quite high up; everyone's got a limited amount of time, haven't they?

These newer methods of engagement may still be viewed cautiously by political scientists; however, newer forms of engagement may become too popular to ignore. Today, political media and communication formats are still perceived as 'unorthodox', which was how protest movements were seen 40 years ago (Marsh, 1977; Muller, 1979); times change, as do circumstances, needs and methods of engagement. In half a century, we may find that these unusual forms have become normalised in the mindset of analysts, and that other 'unusual' methods have taken their place.

This book has clearly found that there is far more depth to political activities as perceived by the young respondents than is acknowledged in literature about political activities. Voting is popular, not only because as an action it is episodic and simple, but because the concept of voting as a civic duty is clearly a motivating factor in participation. The popularity of other unmonitored political activities such as boycotting, use of new media and communication formats is high. Though these activities are less likely to be monitored, many of them are personal choices and can be pursued in the peace of one's home without public or group observance.

What counts as political, it seems, can be a complex question. For those activities which are inherently political, such as voting, the question is not so important, but for those actions which are only political in certain circumstances, the answer is more problematic and context-dependent. However, it does highlight that what is considered 'political' varies, and that in itself is very important to acknowledge.

The varied forms of 'effectiveness' had a role to play in the choices the respondents made when participating in the political sphere. Effectiveness had a role in motivating these young people to choose one political action over another; however, effectiveness is relative – it does not necessarily mean policy change. For example, demonstrations are very popular among the group, but their effectiveness lies not in policy change, rather in expressive and signalling mechanisms such as showing support, media emphasis and signalling concerns to a wider audience;

whereas petitions were popular simply for their convenience, and other than that they were criticised as ineffective.

Financial resources seem to play a role in the political activities that respondents choose to engage in. Most political activities they chose were relatively costless. This may be related to the young age range or the fact that Muslim minorities come from some of the most deprived areas in the UK; however, in general, as mentioned before, the sample are relatively highly educated.

Although some have argued that society is becoming more individualistic and less group orientated, and that fewer people belong to organised groups and committees, this research highlights that although groups may not be organised in the traditional sense of a titled group with members and committees, people are still participating through collective action to express group concerns. Demonstrations and protests are organised usually by large-scale groups who motivate their members to attend, and many others who do not belong to the groups also join in. Boycotting, though an individual action, is still influenced by a 'collective' feeling: receiving emails from campaigning groups urging people to boycott and reading about mass boycotts makes the boycotting individual feel part of an invisible group. Media and communication formats are also strongly influenced by an invisible group mentality – forwarding the latest YouTube political message or an e-petition to your group of friends, a wide network of individuals who believe in or feel the same way about a political issue. Belonging to groups is no longer as formal as it was traditionally, but people still belong to informal or invisible groupings that follow the same ideology or belief and pursue the same political message:

> Participation in informal local groups, political consumerism, involvement in transnational advocacy networks, the regular signing and forwarding of email petitions, and the spontaneous organisation of protests and rallies are just a few examples of the growing importance of informal organisations, individualised action and network mobilization.
>
> (Stolle et al., 2005: 250)

It was also interesting to note how interlinked many of the political activities were. Many political issues usually demand action to be taken on several fronts. For a local case where a supermarket is to be built, political discussions may lead on to political lobbying and to the development of petitions, and those petitioners may then attend the demonstration or sign an online letter to be sent to the local MP. Very few political activities are stand-alone actions; usually they happen hand in hand with internet adverts, research and then campaigning and protesting. However, further research would be needed on this issue, exploring networks and resources.

The aim of this book was to find out what is considered to be a political activity by the young Muslim respondents, and which (if any) political activities are popular or unpopular. A few young Muslims, such as those in typology group four who view their identity as mainly Muslim, still voted, even though they may not necessarily identify strongly with being British; while young Muslims such as Ghazal (group two), though she perceives being Muslim as peripheral to her identification, engages in political activities that are 'Muslim based':

8. Ghazal

Yes... these were more international issues, mostly Muslim based.

Respondents from both group one and group two, who are likely to feel that Islam is symbolic and/or peripheral to their lives, may also be sceptical of voting and the electoral system – not because they feel less British, but because they are doubtful of the electoral system:

9. Hassan

Voting's a bit of a joke really. I mean, personally I think it's a joke because... although you've got it and you're part of the system... a country where everyone can vote... is a big thing I think and not everyone is registered to vote, so how far is it democratic?

Supporting Muslim causes and issues is obviously popular among the respondents; however, there are those (group three's Arwa, for example) who believe that going above and beyond Muslim issues is also very important:

1. Arwa

I don't know, people make such a big issue of being a Muslim these days... I would go to raise awareness on planet issues, or world issues, not just Islam and Muslims, it's not just identity related.

The research also underlines that though illegal activities vary in strength – from non-violent and non-obstructive actions through to extreme violence – most respondents who answered these questions drew a line at some point. They justify some violent activities, causes and scenarios, but not others. However, illegal political activities were popular and unpopular among different individuals, with support for or disapproval of violent political activities varying across the identity typology scale. Even if political activities are illegal, they are still considered to be political participation, and their status in the eyes of the law should not deter us from studying them or counting them in. There are many variations of illegal political activity – from non-violent and non-obstructive (e.g. not paying taxes, refusing military service), to blocking access (picketing, sit-ins, blocking traffic), to violence against property (slogan painting, breaking windows) and to violence against people (fights, death).

The illegal status of political activities and their justification, as mentioned earlier in the book, is not necessarily based on illegality in a state sense, but based on prohibition in an Islamic context. The respondents discussed illegal status activities and justification for such activities based on sharia law and hokum, which underlines that religion and political activities are intertwined in their minds.

The respondents repeatedly drew on religious symbols, language and law to motivate, encourage and continue political activity, as seen with reference to boycotting, demonstrations and the use of media and communication formats. The respondents choose to reflect their identity facets in the political activities they engage in and the political activities they choose to sideline. In Chapter 8, religion and religious obligation, laws and values were also linked to political engagement for many of the respondents. On numerous occasions, participants used religious text to condone or distance themselves from political actions. They used the Quran and sunnah as guidelines for judging the legality of some activities, such as combative violence. The participants discussed illegal political activities not only in a British legal sense, but also in an Islamic context (e.g. flag burning and rioting). They participate in certain political activities and support particular causes because of a sense of duty to their ummah. Other political activities are also governed by religious boundaries for some respondents (e.g. etiquette in demonstrations, gender mixing in public activities).

Further to the influence of religious identity on political engagement, the research also highlighted the importance of civic duty as a motivation for political engagement. It was clear that civic motivations come into play most keenly with regard to voting. The continuity of civic norms as a form of political motivation highlights that socialisation in a British civic context does influence the norms of political behaviour among the majority of young British Muslims. Even among typology group four, most of whom described their identity as mainly Muslim and who felt little emotive feeling for their nationality, voting was still an activity that some of the members took part in. This may mean that citizenship developed through socialisation and upbringing may be very measured, and though people do not realise they feel anything towards it (duty), they may feel that because they are given the opportunity (right) that this is encouragement enough to participate.

Interestingly, instrumental and resource-based theories found in mainstream literature about political participation (Leighley, 1990; Conway, 1991; Kenny, 1992; Leighley, 1995; Verba et al., 1993, 1995 for review of all studies) have played a limited role in the political participation of the respondents in this research. This does not mean that they are irrelevant to the political participation of other people and groups, but that in these cases, at this time, the respondents feel that their identity is more influential on their political participation.

This book has found that the popularity of new forms of political activity is a reflection of a change in wider society as well as a reflection of generational differences. Political discussions as a form of political activity, for example, as well as media and communication formats and boycotting, highlight the importance of unconventional methods of engagement that suit certain groups of people – especially youth. Developments in various forms of global communications impact on the types of political modes of engagement, which we have to acknowledge in order to understand why newer forms of political activity are preferred above other traditional methods. We must allow young people to express how they actively participate in order to appraise new forms of political action. Some are expressive and/or signalling political activities, which allow participants to convey messages, to vent frustrations, to display dissatisfaction and so forth. Also, we need to further explore how these modes impact on other forms of engagement – we need to explore the interconnectedness of political actions, especially with the wide usage of internet technology.

The emphasis is that we must go beyond the stereotypes of Muslims in the media and understand the undercurrents that exist. What the research has shown is that religious identity is important, less in some cases and more in others, but it is relevant in understanding the current political activities of young British Muslims. Muslims and Muslim views are by no means uniform, and this is reflected in their attitudes towards political activities.

The research did not find any experiences of what could be termed 'ethnic penalties' in the political sphere. It is true that in the UK we now have more minority ethnic and religious MPs in Parliament than ever before, but on the ground, cases still arise where minority groups are being penalised for self-expression and identity politics. A case in question (which unfortunately I was unable to explore further as it occurred after the fieldwork phase of this research was completed) was the arrest of demonstrators at a Pro-Gaza protest in London. Over 60 people (mostly youngsters) were arrested[2] and then sentenced for various acts of violent conduct. At one of the earlier sittings, Judge Jonathan Denniss, who sentenced most protestors to jail time, said he was sentencing these young protestors as 'examples' and as a 'deterrent'.[3] At a time when political participation is encouraged, especially for young people, these cases can be viewed as an extreme deterrent for the very people who should be more politically active. Whether these cases will result in less participation in demonstrations and public protests, or in increased distrust of public expressions of political views, is difficult to gauge at the moment, but would be interesting to monitor.

While race, ethnicity and political participation have been heavily linked in literature about migrant communities (Dawson, 1995; Saggar, 2000; Hechter, 2005), religion has until recently taken a back seat in the literature. In the introduction to the research, a quote from Tariq Modood asks: 'And yet all this leaves unanswered the question, why is it that ethnic (i.e. regional and national origins) and religious identities have come to be politically prominent among south Asians in Britain instead of other group identities, most notably, a colour-based identity?' (Modood, 2005: 158). The answer I believe lies in the responses from the respondents in this research.

First, as mentioned previously, the young British Muslims in this sample have experienced an intense spotlight on and scrutiny of their religious identity. The mixture of events that have exacerbated this occurrence include events such as 9/11, the 7/7 London bombings, the Iraq war, Afghanistan, the Israel/Palestine conflicts and a focus from policy-makers, think tanks, and government initiatives (such as the CONTEST strategy and PET, Preventing Extremism Together, working groups). Pressure from opinion polls and surveys[4] and the banning of religious clothing and other symbols in some European countries (hijabs, face coverings, minarets, etc.) has placed a constant spotlight on Muslims, and thus on Muslim identity. This can be and is perceived as a threat to identity and to belief, and thus the reaction from this cohort is to hold on to and tighten the link with their religious identity (see Chapter 3). The impact of religious group identity on even the most secular or non-practising of Muslims is apparent. The influence of religious identity on their political motivation is clear, and even its impact on the choices they make regarding political activity. As an individual, religious identity becomes more significant when threatened.

Second, as discussed in social identity theory, if a group experiences feelings of difference from the wider majority, they begin to identify more strongly with their group. This intensity of feeling is expressed with regards to the ummah. In a political environment where the group feel marginalised, group sympathy and identification becomes stronger (see Chapter 4) and develops into a politicised group identity.

This argument is reflected in symbolic interactionist theory. As discussed in Chapter 3, symbolic interactionists explore how people identify themselves and how they perceive their surroundings. Identity is constantly redefined and re-evaluated. Interactionists see humans as active participants in moulding and constructing their identity and how they perceive their surroundings (see Goffman, 1959; Blumer, 1969). At the moment, Muslims believe that wider society problematises being Muslim. These theories are very relevant in explaining why religion, over many other possible identity facets, has become the salient political identity.

I emphasise that religion has become the salient political identity because religion in other contexts is not as relevant. In the context of marriage, health and housing, for example, ethnicity may be far more important. However, specific to the political sphere, this research has highlighted that religious identity, and to a certain degree British national identity, explains the political motivation and participation of young British Muslims.

If we wish to see a positive change in the identity construction of British Muslims, to see a balance between being British and Muslim (which is the emphasis heard repeatedly in the media), this book suggests that overcoming negative stereotyping of Muslims is important. Labelling a religious group as problematic will eventually continue the cycle described in this research, and identity facets such as being British and Muslim may possibly become more polarised. Grievances over religio-political causes will only be overcome if these political grievances are ameliorated. If religious identity becomes less important, which other identity facet would supersede it? Are feelings of Britishness an area which will become more pertinent through the generations, or a matter of developing a person's rights and duties towards their nation state? If The American evidence from Portes and Rumbaut found that groups that experience 'extreme discrimination and derogation of their national origins are likely to embrace them ever more fiercely; those received more favourably shift to American identities with greater speed and less pain' (Portes and Rumbaut, 2001b: 187).

In another less politicised religious environment, the future of religious identity may follow in the footsteps of symbolic ethnicity. Just as we found in Chapter 3, among typology group one the development of a symbolic religious framework may become more prevalent as identification with the religious group weakens. Waters (1990) highlighted the role that symbolic ethnicity played in the life of many American white second- and third-generation migrants as they assimilated through the generations. Similarly, religious practice and identity may become 'optional' – some practices may be retained while others are sidelined.

Alternatively, similar to the experiences of African Americans, where politics and race are still inextricably linked (Dawson, 1995), Muslims may continue to choose religious group identity over other alternatives. Muslims may remain politically homogeneous to their religion even though within the group they are ethnically and socio-economically varied. Just as race was regarded as the uniting factor for African American politics before the 1960s, and is still significant today, religion may potentially continue to play an influencing role in the political participation of British Muslims – cutting across ethnic and class divisions. In fact, the literature on American Muslim political participation has found that African American Muslims have higher levels of political engagement than other American Muslims (Ayers and Hofstetter, 2008). This could be understood in a number of ways, but ultimately we could see the activism as a duality of race- and religious-based activism. Against a backdrop of African American activism, Muslim African Americans are choosing religious political activism together with the knowledge and awareness gained from race-based activism; thus race and religious politics are highly relevant in their lives.

The rampant debate currently spreading across Europe regarding multiculturalism and integration is highly relevant to the premise of this book. The research has repeatedly highlighted that identity is fluid and continually adapting. It is influenced by the wider society, our community or group and our own reflection of these varied elements. The research material has underlined the delicate balance most of these young British Muslims face when exploring who they are, as well as the motivations and decisions that follow. If society continues to question minorities on their beliefs and cultures, to question their civic belonging and criticise their stance on citizenship, then not only could this change the views of these participants, but the identities of generations to come.

This book has highlighted the nuanced differences in religious identification and practice found among Muslim populations. The perpetual assumption among the right-wing tabloid press as well as some think tanks and policy groups, that all Muslims have and hold the same values, choices and preferences, is incorrect, and I hope this research has drawn attention to this. The material from these interviews has provided rich analysis of both Muslim identity and political practices, but moreover it has underlined the diversity within and among religious minorities; these collective social identities are ever-relevant in today's more individualistic society as people search for meaning, reference and significance in their lives. To these young British Muslims I am greatly indebted, and I hope that I have done justice to the material they provided.

Appendix

Sampling frame

The non-probability sampling techniques were selected because of their suitability for the study and the absence of any sampling frame. The snowball sample began at a number of points, and interviewees were asked to recommend other possible respondents until a certain amount of material saturation was reached. At this point, purposive sampling began, as specifically missing cases were pursued that were significant for the research.

Participant recruitment

Recruitment of participants for this research occurred in numerous ways: emails to direct networks, contacting university societies (e.g. Pakistani society, Arab Society and Islamic Societies) in key active and multicultural universities as well as large mailing lists such as the City Circle in London and the National Muslim Events Listings. Written letters were posted including many A5 leaflets/posters to addresses from the Muslim Directory 2005–2006 including youth and community associations/clubs, as well as schools that included a sixth form with high numbers of Muslims students. The development of relationships with gatekeepers throughout the fieldwork period also assisted in the interviewing of respondents that were more difficult to recruit otherwise.

Sample

The sample included Muslims from a varied ethnic descent because British Muslims come from a number of different ethnic backgrounds. The majority of British Muslims come from an Asian background – mainly Pakistani, Bangladeshi, Indian and other Asian. Eleven per cent of Muslims were from a white ethnic group of white British origin and from another white background (Turkish, Cypriot, Arab and Eastern European). This research sample includes the largest groups – Pakistanis, Bangladeshis and Indians – as they are the largest Muslim minority ethnic groups, plus Arabs because, although they are the fourth largest group, few studies include them. It also includes English Muslims, converts and children of converts.

Respondent age ranges:

15 respondents aged 16–20
23 respondents aged 21–25
19 respondents aged 26–30
10 respondents aged 31–35

Geographical spread:

---

21 respondents from the North
(Blackburn, Bolton, Bradford, Burnley, Leeds, Manchester) (31%)

11 respondents from the Midlands
(Birmingham, Leicester) (16%)

35 respondents from the South
(London, Oxford) (53%).

Marital status:

---

14 respondents married
53 respondents single

Gender split:

---

38 male respondents
29 female respondents

Notes

1 Setting the Scene

1. There are 650 MPs in government and 4.8 per cent of British people are Muslims, of which eight are MPs, meaning only 1.2 per cent of MPs are Muslims.
2. Khalid Mahmood (Labour), Sadiq Khan (Labour), Anas Sarwar (Labour), Yasmin Qureshi (Labour), Rushanara Ali (Labour), Shabana Mahmood (Labour), Sajid Javid (Conservative) and Rehman Chishtie (Conservative).
3. Such as the Radical Middle Way (giving mainstream religious scholars a platform to speak, and touring) and MINAB (Mosques and Imams National Advisory Board).

2 Theorising Identity

1. Social Identity Theory (Tajfel and Turner, 1979; Tajfel, 1981; Turner et al., 1987; Hogg and Abrams, 1988) is a social psychological theory that sets out to explain group processes and intergroup relations. It is rooted in psychology. The arguments are based on categorisation (boundaries of norms, expectations) and self-enhancement (the in-group member prefers his/her own group and sees it in a positive light).
2. Identity Theory on the other hand has roots in Sociology (Stryker, 1968, 1980, 1987; McCall and Simmons, 1978; Burke, 1980; Stryker and Serpe, 1982). It is a microsociological theory that sets out to explain role-related behaviour. People take on a 'role' depending on group interaction or expectation.
3. Coined by Herbert Gans in his seminal work *Symbolic Ethnicity: The Future of Ethnic Groups and Cultures in America* (1979).
4. Portes and Zhou (1993) *Segmented Assimilation*; Portes and Rumbaut (2001a, 2001b) continued the segmented assimilation theme.
5. Consonant acculturation: parents and children adapt at the same pace, learning the second language and accepting cultural changes. They also have family resources and guidance, leading to upward assimilation. Dissonant acculturation: parents are left behind as children learn English quickly and pick up American culture. Conflict between parents' traditional values and fully acculturated youth occurs, with a decline in the authority of parents. Anticipated among human capital poor groups, who become concentrated geographically and socially in deprived areas. Selective acculturation: rapid economic advancement along with a deliberate attempt by the immigrant group to maintain their traditional ethnic values, norms and behaviour. Fluent bilingualism in second generation. Result is upward assimilation but bicultural.

6. Ogbu (1978, 2003) argued that when 'involuntary minorities' faced limitations in the employment sector, the younger generation developed an 'oppositional culture' to school achievement in response. His work attempts to explain racial or minority group differences in educational achievement. The lack of opportunities, barriers to employment, discrimination and structural inequalities faced by the older generation of the minority ethnic group affects the motivation for educational achievement among the younger age group. They develop an oppositional culture, resistant to educational achievement as a result.

7. Diaspora consciousness is usually specific to ethnic groups. However, there is contention among anthropologists as to whether religious groups constitute a diaspora, which Vertovec (1998) calls 'religious diaspora consciousness'. Cohen (Vertovec and Cohen, 1999) believes that Islam, like Christianity, does not hold a territorial homeland, and so cannot constitute a diaspora group. On the other hand, Vertovec (Vertovec and Cohen, 1999) considers Mecca, Rome and the Ganges as symbolic religious homelands, and thus religious groups may constitute a 'diaspora'. This would mean that the groups would have common global values.

8. The practice and example of the Prophet Muhammad.

9. For more detailed information regarding the theological differences within Islam, see Ramadan (2004).

10. The four schools of thought or of law/*fiqh* (called *madhhab*) are Hanafi, Hanbali, Shafii and Maliki. They are not sects. Similarities and differences can be found between them. Muslims usually follow the school that is geographically or regionally prevalent.

11. These customs and behaviour are not practised by all the respondents in each group, but are generalisations of group behaviour and preferences as perceived by the researcher.

12. These customs and behaviour are not practised by all the respondents in each group, but are generalisations of group behaviour and preferences as perceived by the researcher.

13. There are aspects of religious observances that are crucial in Islam such as prayer, fasting, Ramadan. Other aspects such as schooling, burials, cemeteries and education vary in importance depending on the Islamic interpretations. For further discussion, see Chapter 3 theory.

3 Identity Typology

1. Hajj is one pillar of five in Islam, attempted once in a lifetime (if the opportunity permits).

2. Symbolic interactionist thought suggests that identity is constructed based on interaction with others and the way in which others may define or categorise a person, which then influences their self-perception. See the work of Blumer (1969). Goffman (1956) also highlighted that when individuals come into contact with others they try to control the image they are presenting via signals and symbols of behaviour in order to guide the impression that is gained by others.

3. Labelling theory or social reaction theory was coined by sociologist Howard Becker (1963). The theory highlights the influence that negative labelling of minorities and those seen as different may have on behaviour. Individual behaviour may be influenced by the linguistics and terminology used to categorise them, and is associated with the self-fulfilling prophecy theory (Blumer, 1969).

4. Defined as 'hatred of Islam and therefore, to the fear and dislike of all Muslims' (Runnymede Trust, 1997), the practice of discriminating against Muslims by excluding them from economic, social and public life.

5. However, they did highlight conflicts between their ethnic practices and their nationality and religion; see ethnicity section above.

6. Available at: http://www.islamonline.net/servlet/Satellite?c=Article_C&pagename=Zone-English-Living_Shariah%2FLSELayout&cid=1248188089986

7. Such as Hizb ut Tahrir, to which both Jamila and Yara belong.

8. This has little to do with how religious or practising a person is.

9. More recently these include Guantanamo Bay, Abu Ghraib prison abuses in Iraq and so on.

10. Political Islam refers to the use of the religion as a means of overthrowing the dominant socio political systems and re-establishing an Islamic state. Groups such as Hizb ut Tahrir or the newly reincarnated organisation Islam4UK (aka Al Muhajirun) could be considered as following these aims.

11. Through either peaceful or violent means.

12. Second-generation ethnic minority youth reject mainstream values and norms by creating or joining subcultural movements that place a negative value on education and upward mobility.

13. See details on the four *fiqh* schools of thought/jurisprudence.

4 Impetus for Engagement

1. This chapter is focused on motivation, not mobilisation, such as social networks (Zipp and Smith, 1979; Ellison and Gay, 1989; Kenny, 1992; McClurg, 2003) and belonging to organisations such as churches and civic groups (McAdam, 1982; Morris, 1984; Harris, 1994; Verba et al., 1995).

2. This chapter will not cover actions they choose to engage in; that is covered in Chapter 5.

3. For a full analysis see Pattie et al. (2004).

4. Many researchers have propagated the view that class has become less influential to the political debate. Weakliem and Heath (1999) and Franklin et al. (1992) have argued that the size of the working class has declined because of the size of the manual labour force. However, the counter-argument is that though the link between class and parties has diminished, social class is still important and remains the most important social factor influencing voting patterns. There are similar claims from those who follow the Relative Deprivation argument; that however much a society becomes wealthier, unless this is equally distributed, the less wealthy will always call for economic redistribution. Thus, wealth inequality is unlikely to disappear altogether from political choices, but whether economic interests will be a salient issue for group behaviour is arguable.

5. See Whiteley and Seyd (2002).
6. Analysed 12 industrialised societies including USA, Canada, Mexico, Argentina, South Africa, Japan and other Eastern and Western European states.
7. Maslow's (1943, 1954) Hierarchy of Needs pyramid – survival, security, belonging and self-actualisation.
8. Relative deprivation coined by Sam Stouffer (1949) *The American Soldier.*
9. The root of Muslim beliefs in citizenship is the concept of *dar all ahd* (the domain of treaty); non-Muslim states are classified thus by scholars of Islamic political theory.
10. Inglehart (1971, 1977).
11. 'Soitary' incentives as explored by Rosenstone and Hansen (1993) (also called 'Selective' benefits by Pattie et al., 2004).
12. Differentiated between organisations belonged to and theological groups belonged to, such as Tabligh – I jammaat; deobandi.
13. Available at: http://www.iengage.org.uk/about-us
14. Available at: http://www.prc.org.uk

5   Political Participation

1. 2011 Census statistics show over 48 per cent of British Muslims are under the age of 25 (ONS, 2013a).
2. For an overview of the literature, see Brady, 1999; Van Deth, 2001.
3. Milbrath's (1965) distinctions of gladiatorial (e.g. campaigning), transitional (e.g. attending a rally) and spectator (e.g. voting) activities is one such division. A division into further groups was constructed by Verba and Nie (1972) and Verba et al. (1978), who split political activities into four different groups (voting, campaign activity, communal activity and contacting officials on personal matters). The division between conventional and unconventional activities was drawn up at around the same time by Barnes et al. (1979), who suggested that differences exist between conventional political participation (e.g. talking about politics and presence at political meetings or campaigning) and unconventional political behaviour (mainly protest activities).
4. Pictorial vignettes were used in the form of photographs in order to explore political actions. Numerous photographic images were randomly mixed together with the intention of extracting a response from the participants regarding that action. Respondents were asked whether they considered the act in the photograph to be a 'political action', why, and whether they have participated in a similar action. The reason behind the use of this method was essentially that verbal questioning was loaded and could be dangerously leading. In asking a participant 'Have you participated in flag burning' or 'What are your opinions on flag burning', the question in itself caused the respondent to be on guard, on the offensive; whereas a photograph of a group of men burning a flag presented a more neutral setting in which to express a viewpoint, the opinion regarding the action of flag burning being aimed at the group in the photograph.
5. Unlike research by O'Toole (2003), O'Toole et al. (2003) and O'Toole and Gale (2009), who found that some 'civic' activities such as belonging to community

groups were considered as political activities by young respondents in their research.

6. Further information, numbers, cities and dates concerning anti-Iraq war protests, available at: http://news.bbc.co.uk/1/hi/2875555.stm; or http://www.guardian.co.uk/world/2003/feb/17/politics.uk

7. Though unusually, Barnes et al. (1979) did consider reading about a political issue in a newspaper to be a political action.

8. Stolle et al. (2005) conducted a pilot survey among 1,015 Canadian, Belgian and Swedish students. Pattie et al. (2004) say that the evidence from their research suggests that political action nowadays is more individualistic than collective, because of the decline in traditional organised groups such as trade unions, and this has led to more individualist actions such as consumer politics (p. 79).

6 Politically Engaged and Ready for Action

1. The International Social Survey found that approximately 25 per cent of American, British and French respondents had politically boycotted and even more people had politically purchased products (Dalton, 2008: 50). Pattie et al. (2004) found that roughly a third of respondents had boycotted and 28 per cent had politically purchased products.

2. 'Starbucks the target of Arab boycott for its growing links to Israel' by Robert Fisk in Beirut, Friday, 14 June 2002. Available at: http://www.independent.co.uk/news/world/middle-east/starbucks-the-target-of-arab-boycott-for-its-growing-links-to-israel-749289.html

3. Available at: http://www.islamonline.net/servlet/Satellite?pagename=Islam-Online-English-Ask_Scholar%2FFatwaE%2   FFatwaEAskTheScholar&cid=1119503543874

4. Available at: http://www.islamonline.net/English/News/2002-11/14/article29.shtml

5. Available at: http://www.guardian.co.uk/world/2009/dec/10/guidance-label-ling-food-israeli-settlements

6. For a broad overview of protest politics see Dieter Rucht, chapter 38 in Dalton and Klingemann (2007).

7. Parry et al. (1992) state that two-thirds of those surveyed had signed a petition and over 40 per cent had petitioned more than once. Similar in other data (Dalton, 1988).

7 Borderline/Contextual Political Activities

1. Criminal Damage Act 1971 and The Anti-Social Behaviour Act 2003 means graffiti on public property is considered vandalism; anyone caught can be arrested and prosecuted.

8 Out of Favour and Other Avoided Activities

1. Such as Hizb ut Tahrir, Islamic Society of Britain, Al Khoi Foundation, FOSIS, etc.

9   Concluding Words

1. 2010 report results from the 2008 Social Attitudes Survey.
2. Available at: http://www.guardian.co.uk/uk/feedarticle/8777226
3. Available at: http://www.guardian.co.uk/theguardian/2010/mar/13/gaza-pro-testers-sent-prison
4. The latest results from the British Social Attitudes survey report highlight that only one-quarter of British people 'feel positive' about Muslims in Britain.

Bibliography

Abbas, T. (ed.) (2005) *Muslim Britain: Communities under pressure*. London and New York: Zed Books.

Adolino, J. (1998) 'Integration within the British political parties: Perceptions of ethnic minority councillors', in Saggar, S. (ed.) *Race and British electoral politics*. London: UCL Press.

Ahmed, A. and Donnon, H. (1994) *Islam, globalization and postmodernity*. London: Routledge.

Akhtar, P. (2005) '(Re)turn to religion and radical Islam', in Abbas, T. (ed.) *Muslim Britain: Communities under pressure*. London and New York: Zed Books.

Alba, R. (1981) The twilight of ethnicity among American Catholics of European ancestry. *Annals of the American Academy of Political and Social Science,* March: 86–97.

Alba, R. (2005) Bright vs. blurred boundaries: Second-generation assimilation and exclusion in France, Germany and the United States. *Ethnic and Racial Studies,* 28: 20–49.

Aleinikoff, T. and Rumbaut, R. (1998) Terms of belonging: Are models of membership self-fulfilling prophecies? *Georgetown Immigration Law Journal,* 13, 1: 1–24.

Allen, C. (2010a) *Islamophobia*. Farnham: Ashgate.

Allen, C. (2010b) Fear and loathing: The political discourse in relation to Muslims and Islam in the contemporary British setting. *Politics and Religion,* 4, 2: 221–236.

Allen, C. and Nielsen, J. (2002) *Summary report on Islamophobia in the EU after 11 September 2001*. EUMC.

Almond, G. and Verba, S. (1963) *The civic culture*. Princeton, NJ: Princeton University Press.

Ameli, S. and Merali, A. (2004) *Dual citizenship: British, Islamic or both? Obligation, recognition, respect and belonging*. London: Islamic Human Rights Commission.

Amnesty International (2012) *Choice and prejudice: Discrimination against Muslims in Europe*. Available at: http://www.amnesty.org/en/library/asset/EUR01/001/2012/en/85bd6054-5273-4765-9385-59e58078678e/eur010012012en.pdf

Anderson, B. (1991) *Imagined communities: Reflections on the origin and spread of nationalism*. London: Verso.

Anderson, B. (1998) *The spectre of comparisons: Nationalism, South East Asia and the world*. London: Verso.

Ansari, H. (2004) *The infidel within: The history of Muslims in Britain*. London: C Hurst.

Ansari, H. (2005) 'Attitudes to jihad, martyrdom and terrorism among British Muslims', in Abbas, T. (ed.) *Muslim Britain: Communities under pressure*. London and New York: Zed Books.

Anwar, M. (1979) *The myth of return: Pakistanis in Britain*. London: Heinemann.

Anwar, M. (1998) *Between cultures: Continuity and change in the lives of young Asians*. London: Routledge.

Anwar, M. (2001) The participation of ethnic minorities in British politics. *Journal of Ethnic and Migration Studies*, 27: 533–549.

Ayres, J. (1999) From the streets to the internet: The cyber-diffusion of contention. *Annals of American Academy of Political and Social Science*, 566: 132–143.

Ayers, J. and Hofstetter, R. (2008) American Muslim political participation following 9/11: Religious belief, political resources, social structures and political awareness. *Politics and Religion*, 1: 3–26.

Bagguley, P. and Hussain, Y. (2005) 'Flying the flag for England? Citizenship, religion and cultural identity among British Pakistani Muslims', in Abbas, T. (ed.) *Muslim Britain: Communities under pressure*. London and New York: Zed Books.

Barnes, S. H., Kaase, M., Allerbeck, K., Farah, B. G., Heunks, F., Inglehart, R., Jennings, M. K., Klingemann, H. D., Marsh, A. and Rosenmayr, L. (1979) *Political action: Mass participation in five Western democracies*. Beverly Hills, CA: Sage.

Barth, F. (1969) *Ethnic groups and boundaries: The social organization of culture difference*. London: Allen & Unwin.

Bawer, B. (2007) *While Europe slept: How radical Islam is destroying the West from within*. New York: Broadway Books.

Becker, H. (1963) *Outsiders*. New York: Free Press.

Berthoud, R. and Blekesaune, M. (2007) *Persistent employment disadvantage. Research*. Report No. 416, London: Department of Work and Pensions.

Bimber, B. (1998) The internet and political transformation: Populism, community and accelerated pluralism. *Polity*, 31: 133–146.

Bimber, B. (2003) *Information and American democracy: Technology in the evolution of political power*. New York: Cambridge University Press.

Bimber, B. and Davis, R. (2003) *The internet and U.S. elections*. New York: Oxford University Press.

Birdwell, J. and Littler, M. (2012) *Faithful citizens: Why those who do God, do good*. London: Demos.

Birt, J. (2005) 'Lobbying and marching: British Muslims and the State', in Abbas, T. (ed.) *Muslim Britain: Communities under pressure*. London and New York: Zed Books.

Blumer, H. (1962) 'Society as symbolic interaction', in A. M. Rose (ed.) *Human behaviour and social processes*. Boston: Houghton Mifflin.

Blumer, H. (1969) *Symbolic interactionism: Perspective and method*. Berkeley: University of California Press.

Bobo, L. and Gilliam, F. D. (1990) Race, sociopolitical participation, and Black empowerment. *American Political Science Review*, 84: 377–393.

Bové, J. and Dufour, F. (2001) *The world is not for sale: Farmers against junk food*. London: Verso.

Brady, H. (1999) 'Political participation', in Robinson, J., Shaver, P. and Wrightsman, L. (eds.) *Measures of political attitudes*. London and California: Academic Press.

Briggs, R., Fieschi, C. and Lownsbrough, H. (2006) *Bringing it home: Community-based approaches to counter-terrorism*. London: Demos.

Browne, A. (31 January 2006) Denmark faces international boycott over Muslim cartoons. *The Times*. Available at: http://www.timesonline.co.uk/tol/news/world/europe/article723266.ece

Burke, P. (1980) The self: Measurement requirements from an interactionist perspective. *Social Psychology Quarterly*, 43: 18–29.

Burke, P. and Stets, J. (2009) *Identity theory*. New York: OUP.

Cahalan, D. (1968) Correlates of respondent accuracy in the Denver validity survey. *Public Opinion Quarterly*, 32, 4: 607–621.

Caldwell, C. (2010) *Reflections on the revolution in Europe: Immigration, Islam and the West*. London: Penguin.

Cameron, D. (2011) *PM's speech at Munich security conference*. Available at: https://www.gov.uk/government/speeches/pms-speech-at-munich-security-conference

Castells, M. (1997) *The power of identity*. Oxford: Blackwell.

Choudhury, T. and Fenwick, H. (2011) The impact of counter-terrorism measures on Muslim communities. *International Review of Law, Computers & Technology*, 25, 3: 151–181.

CLG (2010) *Attitudes, values and perceptions: Muslims and the general population in 2007–2008*. London: Department for Communities and Local Government.

Conway, M. (1991) *Political participation in the United States*. Washington, DC: Congressional Quarterly Press.

Dalton, R. (1988) *Citizen politics in Western democracies: Public opinion and political parties in the United States, Great Britain, West Germany, and France*. Chatham: Chatham House.

Dalton, R. (1996) *Citizen politics: Public opinion and political parties in advanced Western democracies*. Chatham: Chatham House.

Dalton, R. (2002) *Citizen politics: Public opinion and participation in advanced industrial democracies*. Chatham: Chatham House.

Dalton, R. (2004) *Democratic challenges, democratic choices: The erosion of political support in advanced industrial democracies*. Oxford: Oxford University Press.

Dalton, R. (2008) *Citizen politics: Public opinion and political parties in advanced industrial democracies*. Washington, DC: CQ Press.

Dalton, R., Van Deth, J. and Klingemann, H. (2007) *Oxford handbook of political behaviour*. Oxford: Oxford University Press.

Dawson, M. (1995) *Behind the mule: Race and class in African-American politics*. Princeton, NJ: Princeton University Press.

de la Garza, R. (1992) *Latino voices: Mexican, Puerto Rican and Cuban perspectives on American politics*. Boulder: Westview.

Eickelman, D. and Piscatori, J. (1996) *Muslim politics*. Princeton, NJ: Princeton University Press.

Ellison, C. and Gay, D. (1989) Black political participation revisited: A test of compensatory, ethnic community and public arena models. *Social Science Quarterly*, 70: 101–119.

Esposito, J. and Voll, J. (1996) *Islam and democracy*. Oxford University Press.

Fieldhouse, E. and Cutts, D. (2006) *Voter engagement in British South Asian communities at the 2001 general election*. Joseph Rowntree Foundation Report.

Fieldhouse, E. and Cutts, D. (2007) *Electoral participation of South Asian communities in England and Wales*. New York: Joseph Rowntree Foundation.

Finch, J. (1987) The vignette technique in survey research. *Sociology*, 21: 105–114.

Foner, N. (1997) What's new about transnationalism? New York immigrants today and at the turn of the century. *Diaspora*, 6: 355–375.

Franklin, M., Mackie, T. and Valen, H. (1992) *Electoral change: Responses to evolving social and attitudinal structures in Western countries*. Cambridge: Cambridge University Press.

Friedman, M. (1985) Consumer boycotts in the United States, 1970–1980: Contemporary events in historical perspective. *Journal of Consumer Affairs*, 19, 1: 96–117.

Friedman, M. (1999) *Consumer boycotts: Effecting change through the marketplace and the media*. London and New York: Routledge.

Gallup coexist index (2009) *A global study of interfaith relations*. Washington: Gallup.

Gans, H. (1979) Symbolic ethnicity: The future of ethnic groups and cultures in America. *Ethnic and Racial Studies*, 2: 1–20.

Githens-Mazer, J. and Lambert, R. (2010) *Islamophobia and anti-Muslim hate crime: A London case study*. London: European Muslim Research Centre, University of Exeter.

Goffman, E. (1959) *The presentation of self in everyday life*. Edinburgh: University of Edinburgh.

Goodwin, M. (2013) *The roots of extremism: The English Defence League and the counter-jihad challenge*. Chatham House. Available at: http://www.chathamhouse.org/sites/default/files/public/Research/Europe/0313bp_goodwin.pdf

Gordon, M. (1964) *Assimilation in American life: The role of race, religion, and national origins*. New York: Oxford University Press.

Greeley, A. (1971) *Why can't they be like us? America's white ethnic groups*. New York: E.P. Dutton.

Greer, S. (2010) Anti-terrorist laws and the United Kingdom's 'Suspect Muslim Community': A reply to Pantazis and Pemberton. *British Journal of Criminology*, 50: 1171–1190.

Grossman, L. (1995) *The electronic republic: Reshaping democracy in America*. New York: Viking.

Gurr, T. R. (1970) *Why men rebel*. Princeton, NJ: Princeton University Press.

Hamid, S. (2007) 'Islamic political radicalism in Britain: The case of Hizb Ut Tahrir', in Abbas, T. (ed.) *Islamic political radicalism: A European perspective*. Edinburgh: Edinburgh University Press.

Hardin, R. (1982) *Collective action*. Baltimore: Resources of the Future.

Harris, F. (1994) Something within: Religion as a mobilizer of African American political activism. *Journal of Politics*, 1: 42–68.

Heath, A. (1985) *How Britain votes*. Oxford: Pergamon Press.

Heath, A. and Demireva, N. (2014) Has multiculturalism failed in Britain? *Ethnic and Racial Studies*, 37(1): 161–180.

Heath, A. and Roberts, J. (2008) *British identity: Its sources and possible implications for civic attitudes and behaviour*. Research Report for Lord Goldsmith's Citizenship Review. London: Ministry of Justice. Available at: http://www.justice.gov.uk/reviews/docs/british-identity.pdf

Heath, A. and Martin, J. (2013) Can religious affiliation explain 'ethnic' inequalities in the labour market? *Ethnic and Racial Studies*, 36(6): 1005–1027.

Heath, A., Fisher, S., Rosenblatt, G., Sanders, D. and Sobolewska, M. (2013) *The political integration of ethnic minorities in Britain*. Oxford: Oxford University Press.

Hechter, M. (2005) On the 2004 presidential election. *Daedalus*, 134, 2: 131–133.

Henn, M., Weinstein, M. and Wring, D. (1999) *Young people and citizenship: A study of opinion in Nottinghamshire*. Nottingham: Nottingham County Council.

Hickman, M. (2011) 'Suspect Communities'? Counter-terrorism policy, the press, and the impact on Irish and Muslim communities in Britain, A Report for Policy Makers and the General Public. Institute for the Study of European Transformations, London Metropolitan University (with L Thomas, S Silvestri and H Nickels).

Hogg, M. and Abrams, D. (1988) *Social identifications: A social psychology of intergroup relations and group processes*. London: Routledge.

Hogg, M., Terry, D. and White, K. (1995) A tale of two theories: A critical comparison of identity theory with social identity theory. *Social Psychology Quarterly*, 58, 4: 255–269.

Holpuch, A. (2012) Available at: http://www.guardian.co.uk/world/2012/sep/05/nypd-police-spying-muslim-ends. *The Guardian*.

Home Office Citizenship Survey (2001) Available at: http://rds.homeoffice.gov.uk/rds/pdfs2/hors270.pdf

Home Office Citizenship Survey (2003) Available at: http://rds.homeoffice.gov.uk/rds/pdfs04/hors289.pdf

Home Office (2009) *Pursue, prevent, protect and prepare: The United Kingdom's strategy for countering international terrorism*. London: Home Office.

Hussain, D. (2003) 'The holy grail of Muslims in Western Europe: Representation and their relationship with the state', in Esposito, J. and Burgat, F. (eds.) *Modernising Islam: Religion in the public sphere in the Middle East and Europe*. London: Hurst and Company.

Hussain, S. (2008) *Muslims on the map: A national survey of social trends in Britain*. London: Tauris Academic Studies.

Hutnik, N. (1985) Aspects of identity in multi-ethnic society. *New Community*, 12, 2: 298–309.

Inglehart, R. (1971) The silent revolution in post-industrial societies. *American Political Science Review*, 65: 991–1017.

Inglehart, R. (1977) *The silent revolution: Changing values and political styles among Western publics*. Princeton, NJ: Princeton University Press.

Inglehart, R. (1981) Postmaterialism in an environment of insecurity. *American Political Science Review*, 75: 880–900.

Inglehart, R. (1990) *Culture shift in advanced industrial society*. Princeton, NJ: Princeton University Press.

Inglehart, R. (1997) *Modernization and postmodernization: Cultural, economic and political change in 43 societies*. Princeton, NJ: Princeton University Press.

Jacobson, J. (1998) *Islam in transition: Religion and identity among British Pakistani youth*. London and New York: Routledge.

Jamal, A. (2005) The political participation and engagement of Muslim Americans: Mosque involvement and group consciousness. *American Politics Research*, 33: 521–544.

Jamal, A. (2010) 'Muslim Americans: Enriching or depleting American democracy?', in Wolfe, A. and Katznelson, I. (eds.) *Religion and democracy in the United States: danger or opportunity?* 89–113, Princeton and Woodstock: Princeton University Press.

Joseph, L. (2002) Facilitating word recognition and spelling using word boxes and word sort phonic procedures. *School Psychology Review*, 31, 1: 122–129.

Kasinitz, P., Mollenkopf, J. and Waters, M. (eds.) (2004) *Becoming New Yorkers: Ethnographies of the new second generation*. New York: Russell Sage Foundation.

Kasinitz, P., Mollenkopf, J., Holdaway, J. and Waters, M. (2008) *Inheriting the city: The children of immigrants come of age*. Cambridge: Harvard University Press & Russell Sage Foundation.

Kenny, C. (1992) Political participation and effects from the social environment. *American Journal of Political Science*, 36: 259–267.

Kibria, N. (2008) The 'New Islam' and Bangladeshi youth in Britain and the US. *Ethnic and Racial Studies*, 31, 2: 243–266.

Knudsen, K., Aggarwal, P. and Maamoun, A. (2008) The burden of identity: Responding to product boycotts in the Middle East. *Journal of Business & Economics Research*, 6, 11: 17–26.

Kundnani, A. (2009) *Spooked: How not to prevent violent extremism*. London: Institute of Race Relations.

Lane, R. (1959) *Political life: Why and how people get involved in politics*. New York: Free Press.

Leighley, J. (1990) Social interaction and contextual influences on political participation. *American Politics Quarterly*, 18: 459–475.

Leighley, J. (1995) Attitudes, opportunities and incentives: A field essay on political participation. *Political Research Quarterly*, 48: 181–209.

Levi, M. and Linton, A. (2003) Fair trade: A cup at a time? *Politics and Society*, 31, 3: 407–432.

Lewis, J., Mason, P. and Moore, K. (2011) 'Images of Islam in the UK: The representation of British Muslims in the national print news media 2000–2008', in Petley, J. and Richardson, R. (eds.) *Pointing the finger: Islam and Muslims and the British media*. London: Oneworld Publications.

Lewis, P. (2007) *Young, British and Muslim*. London: Continuum.

Lindley, J. (2002) Race or religions? The impact of religion on the employment and earnings of Britain's ethnic communities. *Journal of Ethnic and Migration Studies*, 28, 3: 427–442.

McAdam, D. (1982) *Political process and the development of Black insurgency, 1930–1970*. Chicago: University of Chicago Press.

McCall, G. and Simmons, J. (1978) *Identities and interactions*. New York: Free Press.

McClurg, S. (2003) Social networks and political participation: The role of social interaction in explaining political participation. *Political Research Quarterly*, 56, 4: 449–464.

Macdonald, M. (2011) British Muslims, memory and identity: Representations in British film and television documentary. *European Journal of Cultural Studies*, 14: 411.

McLoughlin, S. (1996) 'In the name of the ummah: Globalisation, "race" relations and Muslim identity politics in Bradford', in Shadid, W. and Kongisveld, P. (eds.) *Political participation and identities of Muslims in non Muslim states*. Kampen: Kok Pharos.

Macey, M. (2007a) 'Islamic political radicalism in Britain: Muslim men in Bradford', in Masood, E. (ed.) *British Muslim media guide*. British Council.

Macey, M. (2007b) 'Islamic political radicalism in Britain: Muslim men in Bradford', in Abbas, T. (ed.) *Islamic political radicalism: A European perspective.* Edinburgh: Edinburgh University Press.

Mandaville, P. (2001) *Transnational Muslim politics: Reimagining the umma.* London: Routledge.

Marsh, A. (1977) *Protest and political consciousness.* California and London: Sage.

Marsh, A., Barnes, S. and Kaase, M. (1979) *Political action: Mass participation in five Western democracies.* Beverly Hills and London: Sage.

Marsh, D., O'Toole, T. and Jones, S. (2007) *Young people and politics in the UK: Apathy or alienation?* Basingstoke: Palgrave Macmillan.

Maslow, A. (1954) *Motivation and personality.* New York: Harper and Row.

Maslow, A. H. (1943) A theory of human motivation. *Psychological Review,* 50, 4: 370–396.

Masood, E. (2006) *British Muslims: Media guide.* British Council.

Maxwell, R. (2006) Muslims, South Asians and the British mainstream: A national identity crisis? *West European Politics,* 29, 4: 736–756.

Mead, G. (1934) *Mind, self and society.* Chicago: University of Chicago Press.

Micheletti, M. (2003) *Political virtue and shopping: Individuals, consumerism and collective action.* New York: Palgrave.

Micheletti, M. (2006) Blogging: A new people's movement? *Net Pulse,* 10, 19, Oct 19. Available at: http://www.politicsonline.com/netpulse/soundoff.asp?issue_id=10.19. Accessed 23 November 2009.

Micheletti, M. and Stolle, D. (2006) The market as an arena for transnational politics. *Youth Activism,* published on 7 June 2006, Available at: http://ya.ssrc.org/transnational/Micheletti_Stolle/

Micheletti, M., Follesdal, A. and Stolle, D. (eds.) (2003) *Politics, products and markets: Exploring political consumerism past and present.* New Brunswick, NJ: Transaction Press.

Miller, A., Gurin, P., Gurin, G. and Malanchuk, O. (1981) Group consciousness and political participation. *American Journal of Political Science,* 25: 494–511.

Milbrath, L. W. (1965) *Political participation: How and why do people get involved in politics?* Chicago: Rand McNally & Company.

Mirza, M., Senthilkumaran, A. and Zein, J. (2007) *Living apart together: British Muslims and the paradox of multiculturalism.* London: Policy Exchange.

Modood, T. (1990) British Asian Muslims and the Rushdie affair. *Political Quarterly,* April–June: 152.

Modood, T. (2005) *Multicultural politics: Racism, ethnicity and Muslims in Britain.* Edinburgh: Edinburgh University Press.

Modood, T. and Berthoud, R. (eds.) (1997) *Ethnic minorities in Britain: Diversity and disadvantage.* London: Policy Studies Institute.

Moore, K., Mason, P. and Lewis, J. (2008) *Images of Islam in the UK: The representation of British Muslims in the national print news media 2000–2008.* Cardiff: Cardiff School of Journalism, Media and Cultural Studies.

Morey, P. and Yaqin, A. (2011) *Framing Muslims: Stereotyping and representation after 9/11.* Harvard University Press.

Morrell, G., Scott, S., McNeish, D. and Webster, S. (2011) *The August riots in England: Understanding the involvement of young people.* London: NatCen prepared for the Cabinet Office.

Morris, A. (1984) *The origins of the civil rights movement.* New York: Free Press.

Mueller-Rommel, F. (1989) *New politics in Western Europe: The rise and success of green parties and alternative lists.* Boulder: Westview Press.

Muller, E. (1979) *Aggressive political participation.* Princeton, NJ: Princeton University Press.

Mythen, G., Walklate, S. and Khan, F. (2009) I'm a Muslim, but I'm not a terrorist: Victimization, risky identities and the performance of safety. *British Journal of Criminology,* 49: 736–754.

Nickels, H., Thomas, L., Hickman, M. and Silvestri, S. (2010) *A comparative study of the representations of 'suspect' communities in multi-ethnic Britain and the impact on Irish communities and Muslim communities – Mapping newspaper content.* Institute for the Study of European Transformations working paper. London: London Metropolitan University.

Nielsen, J. (1988) 'Muslims in Britain and local authority responses', in Gerholm, T. and Lithman, G. (eds.) *The new Islamic presence in Western Europe.* London: Mansell Publishing Ltd.

Norris, P. (2002) *Democratic phoenix: Reinventing political activism.* Cambridge: Cambridge University Press.

Novak, M. (1978) *The rise of the unmeltable ethnics: Politics and culture in the seventies.* New York: Macmillan.

Oates, S., Owen, D. and Gibson, R. (2006) *The internet and politics: Citizens, voters and activists.* Oxon and New York: Routledge.

Oborne, P. and Jones, J. (2008) *Muslims under siege: Alienating vulnerable communities.* Democratic audit, Human rights centre, University of Essex.

Ogbu, J. (1978) *Minority education and caste: The American system in cross-cultural perspective.* New York: Academic Press.

Ogbu, J. (2003) *Black American students in an affluent suburb: A study of academic disengagement.* Lawrence Erlbaum Associates. New York: Academic Press.

Office of National Statistics (2001) Available at: http://www.statistics.gov.uk/default.asp

Olsen, M. (1970) Social and political participation of blacks. *American Sociological Review,* 35: 682–697.

ONS/Office of National Statistics (2013a) Available at: http://www.ons.gov.uk

ONS (2013b) Available at: http://www.ons.gov.uk/ons/dcp171776_310454.pdf

Open Society Institute (2009) *Muslims in Europe: A report on 11 EU cities.* New York.

Opp, K. D. (1990) Postmaterialism, collective action and political protest. *American Journal of Political Science,* 34: 212–235.

O'Toole, T. (2003) Engaging with young people's conceptions of the political. *Children's Geographies,* 1, 1: 71–90.

O'Toole, T. and Gale, R. (2009) 'Young people and faith activism: British Muslim youth, globalisation and the umma', in Dinham, A., Furbey, R. and Lowndes, V. (eds.) *Faith in the public realm: Controversies, policies and practices.* Bristol: Policy Press.

O'Toole, T., Lister, M., Marsh, D., Jones, S. and McDonough, A. (2003) Tuning in or left out? Participation and non participation among young people. *Contemporary Politics,* 9, 1: 45–61.

Pantazis, C. and Pemberton, S. (2009) From the 'old' to the 'new' suspect community: examining the impacts of recent UK counter-terrorist legislation. *British Journal of Criminology,* 49: 646–666.

Pantazis, C. and Pemberton, S. (2011) Restating the case for the 'suspect community': A reply to Greer. *British Journal of Criminology*, 51, 6: 1054–1062.

Park, R. and Burgess, E. (1921) *Introduction to the science of sociology*. Chicago: University of Chicago Press.

Park, R., McKenzie, R. and Burgess, E. (1925) *The city: Suggestions for the study of human nature in the urban environment*. Chicago: University of Chicago Press.

Parry, G., Moyser, G. and Day, N. (1992) *Political participation and democracy in Britain*. Cambridge: Cambridge University Press.

Pattie, C., Seyd, P. and Whiteley, P. (2004) *Citizenship in Britain: Values and democracy*. Cambridge: Cambridge University Press.

Peach, C. (2005) 'Muslims in the UK', in Abbas, T. (ed.) *Muslim Britain: Communities under pressure*. London and New York: Zed Books.

Pew Report (2012) Rising tide of restrictions on religion. Pew Research Center's Forum on Religion & Public Life. Available at: http://www.pewforum.org/uploadedFiles/Topics/Issues/Government/RisingTideofRestrictions-fullreport.pdf

Phillips, M. (2006) *Londonistan: How Britain created a terror state within*. London: Gibson Square Books Ltd.

Poole, E. (2002) *Reporting Islam: Media representations of British Muslims*. London: I.B.Tauris.

Poole, E. and Richardson (2006) *Muslims and the news media*. I.B.Tauris.

Portes, A. and Rumbaut, R. (2001a) *Ethnicities: Children of immigrants in America*. California: University of California Press.

Portes, A. and Rumbaut, R. (2001b) *Legacies: The story of the immigrant second generation*. Berkeley: University of California Press; New York: Russell Sage Foundation.

Portes, A. and Rumbaut, R. (2006) *Immigrant America: A portrait*. Berkeley: University of California Press. 3rd Edition.

Portes, A. and Zhou, M. (1993) The new second generation: Segmented assimilation and its variants. *Annals of the American Academy of Political and Social Science*, November, 530: 74–96.

Purdam, K. (1996) 'Settler political participation: Muslim local councillors', in Shadid, W. and Konigsveld, P. (eds.) *Political participation and identities of Muslims in non Muslim states*. Kampen: Kok Pharos.

Putnam, R. (2000) *Bowling alone: The collapse and revival of American community*. New York: Simon and Schuster.

Putnam, R. (1993) *Making democracy work: Civic traditions in modern Italy*. Princeton, NJ: Princeton University Press.

Ramadan, T. (2004) *Western Muslims and the future of Islam*. Oxford: Oxford University Press.

Read, J. G. (2008) Muslims in America. *Contexts*, Fall: 39–43.

Richardson, J. (2004) *(Mis)Representing Islam: The racism and rhetoric of British broadsheet newspapers*. Amsterdam: John Benjamins.

Roots, C. (1991) The greening of British politics? *International Journal of Urban and Regional Research*, 15: 287–301.

Rosenstone, S. and Hansen, J. M. (1993) *Mobilization, participation and democracy in America*. New York: Macmillan.

Rubin, H. and Rubin, I. (2005) *Qualitative interviewing: The art of hearing data*. Thousand Oaks, CA: Sage.

Rucht, D. (2007) 'The spread of protest politics', in Dalton, R. and Klingemann, H. (eds.) *The Oxford Handbook of Political Behaviour*. Oxford: Oxford University Press.

Rucht, D. and Ohlemacher, T. (2002) 'Protest event data: Collection, uses and perspectives', in Eyerman, R. and Diani, M. (eds.) *Studying collective action*. California: Sage.

Rumbaut, R. (2008) Reaping what you sow: Immigration, youth and reactive ethnicity. *Applied Development Science*, 12, 2: 108–111.

Runcimon, W. G. (1966) *Relative deprivation and social justice*. London: Routledge and Kegan Paul.

Runnymede Trust (1997) *Islamophobia: A challenge for us all*. London: The Runnymede Trust.

Saeed, A., Blain, N. and Forbes, D. (1999) New ethnic and national questions in Scotland: Post-British identities among Glasgow-Pakistani teenagers. *Ethnic and Racial Studies*, 22, 5: 821–844.

Saggar, S. (1998) *The general election 1997: Ethnic minorities and electoral politics*. London: Commission for Racial Equality.

Saggar, S. (2000) *Electoral representation: Electoral politics and ethnic pluralism in Britain*. Manchester: Manchester University Press.

Samad, Y. (1992) Book burning and race relations: Political mobilisation of Bradford Muslims. *New Community*, 18, 4: 507–519.

Samad, Y. (1996) 'The politics of Islamic identity among Bangladeshis and Pakistanis in Britain', in Ranger, T., Samad, Y. and Stuart, O. (eds.) *Culture, identity and politics*. Avebury: Ashgate Publishing Ltd.

Sapiro, V. (1983) *The political integration of women: Roles, socialization, and politics*. Urbana: University of Illinois Press.

Sarwar, G. (1991) *British Muslims and schools: Proposals for progress*. London: Muslims Educational Trust.

Saunders, D. (2012) *The myth of the Muslim tide: Do immigrants threaten the west?* New York: Vintage Books.

Sayyid, S. (2003) 'Muslims in Britain: Towards a political agenda', in Seddon, M. S., Hussain, D. and Malik, N. (eds.) *British Muslims: Loyalty and belonging*. Markfield: The Islamic Foundation; London: The Citizen Organising Foundation.

Seidman, G. (2003) Monitoring multinationals: Lessons from the anti apartheid era. *Politics and Society*, 32, 3: 381–406.

Sellick, P. and Oxford Centre for Islamic Studies (2004) *Muslim housing experiences: A research report for the housing corporation*. London: Housing Corporation.

Shaheen, J. (2003) Reel bad Arabs: How Hollywood vilifies a people. *Annals of the American Academy of Political and Social Science*, 588: 171–193.

Shaw, A. (1988) *A Pakistani community in Oxford*. Oxford: Blackwell.

Shingles, R. (1981) Black consciousness and political participation: The missing link. *The American Political Science Review*, 75: 76–91.

Simon, B. and Klandermans, B. (2001) Politicised collective identity: A social psychological analysis. *American Psychologist*, 56: 319–331.

Simpson, L., Purdam, K., Tajar, A., Fieldhouse, E., Gavalas, V., Tranmer, M., Pritchard, J. and Dorling, D. (2006) *Ethnic minority populations and the labour market: An analysis of the 1991 and 2001 census*. Department for Work and Pension, Research Report no. 333.

Skocpol, T. and Fiorina, M. (eds.) (1999) *Civic engagement in American democracy*. Washington, DC: Brookings Institution.

Sobolewska, M. and Ali, S. (2012) Who speaks for Muslims? The role of the press in the creation and reporting of Muslim public opinion polls in the aftermath of London bombings in July 2005. *Ethnicities*, 0, 0, 1–21.

Spalek, B. (2007) 'Disconnection and exclusion: Pathways to radicalisation?', in Abbas, T. (ed.) *Islamic political radicalism: A European perspective*. Edinburgh: Edinburgh University Press.

Spalek, B. (2010) Community policing, trust, and Muslim communities in relation to 'New Terrorism'. *Politics & Policy*, 38, 4: 789–815.

Spalek, B. and Lambert, B. (2007) Muslim communities under surveillance. *Criminal Justice Matters*, 68, 1: 12–13.

Spalek, B. and McDonald, L. (2010) Terror crime prevention: Constructing Muslim practices and beliefs as 'anti-social' and 'extreme' through CONTEST 2. *Social Policy and Society*, 9, 1: 123–132.

Stets, J. and Burke, P. (2000) Identity theory and social identity theory. *Social Psychology Quarterly*, 63, 3: 224–237.

Stolle, D. and Hooghe, M. (2004) 'Consumers as political participants? Shifts in political action repertoires in Western societies', in Micheletti, M., Follesdal, A. and Stolle, D. (eds.) *Politics, products and markets: Exploring political consumerism past and present*. New Jersey: Transaction Press.

Stolle, D., Hooghe, M. and Micheletti, M. (2005) Politics in the supermarket: Political consumerism as a form of political participation. *International Political Science Review*, 26, 3: 245–269.

Stouffer, S. (1949) *The American soldier*. Princeton, NJ: Princeton University Press.

Stryker, S. (1968) Identity salience and role performance: The importance of symbolic interaction theory for family research. *Journal of Marriage and the Family*, 3: 558–564.

Stryker, S. (1980) *Symbolic interactionism: A social structural version*. Menlo Park: Benjamin Cummings.

Stryker, S. (1987) 'Identity theory: Developments and extensions', in Yarkley, K. and Honess, T. (eds.) *Self and Identity*. New York: Wiley.

Stryker, S. and Serpe, R. (1982) 'Commitment, identity salience and role behaviour', in Ickes, W. and Knowles, E. S. (eds.) *Personality, roles and social behaviour*. New York: Springer-Verlag.

Tajfel, H. (1981) *Human groups and social categories*. Cambridge: Cambridge University Press.

Tajfel, H. and Turner, J. C. (1979) 'An integrative theory of intergroup relations', in Austin, W. G. and Worchel, S. (eds.) *Social psychology of ingroup relations*. Monterey: Brooks-Cole.

Tate, K. (1991) Black political participation in 1984 and 1988 presidential elections. *American Political Science Review*, 85: 1159–1176.

Teske, N. (1997) *Political activists in America. The identity construction model of political participation*. Cambridge: Cambridge University Press.

Topf, R. (1995) 'Beyond electoral participation', in Klingemann, H. and Fuchs, D. (eds.) *Citizens and the state*. Oxford: Oxford University Press.

Toynbee, P. (23 October 1997) In defence of Islamophobia; religion and the state. *The Independent* (London). Excerpt available at: http://hurryupharry.org/2011/01/21/warsi-attacks-polly-toynbee-praises-milne/

Tullock, G. (1971) The paradox of revolution. *Public Choice*, 11: 89–99.

Turner, J. C., Hogg, M. A., Oakes, P. J., Reicher, S. D. and Wetherell, M. S. (1987) *Rediscovering the social group: A self categorization theory*. Oxford and New York: Blackwell.

Van Deth, J. (2001) *Studying political participation: Towards a theory of everything?* Introductory paper prepared for delivery at the Joint Sessions of Workshops of the European Consortium for Political Research. Available at: http://www.essex.ac.uk/ECPR/events/jointsessions/paperarchive/grenoble/ws3/deth.pdf.

Verba, S., Nie, N. and Kim, J. (1978) *Participation and political equality: A seven-nation comparison*. Cambridge: Cambridge University Press.

Verba, S. and Nie, N. H. (1972) *Participation in America*. New York: Harper & Row.

Verba, S., Schlozman, K. and Brady, H. (1995) *Voice and equality: Civic voluntarism in American politics*. Cambridge: Harvard University Press.

Verba, S., Schlozman, K. L., Brady, H. and Nie, N. (1993) Race, ethnicity and political resources. *British Journal of Political Science*, 23: 453–497.

Verkaik, (2009) *Exclusive: How MI5 blackmails British Muslims. The Independent*: Available at: http://www.independent.co.uk/news/uk/home-news/exclusive-how-mi5-blackmails-british-muslims-1688618.html.

Vertovec, S. (1998) *Muslim European youth: Reproducing ethnicity, religion, culture*. Aldershot: Ashgate.

Vertovec, S. and Cohen, R. (1999) *Migration, diasporas, and transnationalism*. Cheltenham: Elgar.

Voas, D. and Ling, R. (2010) 'Religion in Britain and the United States', in Park, A., Curtice, J., Thomson, K., Phillips, M., Clery, E. and Butt, S. (eds.) *British social attitudes: The 26th report*. London: Sage.

Warikoo, N. (2008) 'Cosmopolitan ethnicity: Second-generation Indo-Caribbean identities', in Kasinitz, P., Mollenkopf, J., Holdaway, J. and Waters, M. (eds.) *Inheriting the city: The children of immigrants come of age*. Cambridge: Harvard University Press & Russell Sage Foundation.

Waters, M. (1990) *Ethnic options: Choosing identities in America*. California and London: University of California Press.

Waters, M. (1999) *Black identities: West Indian immigrant dreams and American realities*. New York: Russell Sage Foundation; London: Harvard University Press.

Weakliem, D. and Heath, A. (1999) 'The secret life of class voting: Britain, France and the United States since the 1930s', in Evans, G. (ed.) *The end of class politics? Class voting in comparative context*. Oxford: Oxford University Press.

Weber, M. (1978) *Economy and society*. Berkeley: University of California Press.

Werbner, P. (1994) 'Diaspora and millennium: British Pakistani global–local fabulations of the Gulf War', in Ahmed, A. and Donnan, H. (eds.) *Islam, globalization, and postmodernity*. London: Routledge.

Werbner, P. (2000) Divided loyalties, empowered citizenship? Muslims in Britain. *Citizenship Studies*, 4, 3: 307–324.

Werbner, P. (2002) *Imagined diasporas among Manchester Muslims*. Oxford: James Currey.

White, C., Bruce, S. and Richie, J. (2000) *Young people's politics: Political interest and engagement amongst 14–24 year olds*. New York: York Publishing Services.

Whiteley, P. and Seyd, P. (2002) *High-intensity participation: The dynamics of party activism in Britain*. Michigan: University of Michigan Press.

Wind-Cowie, M. and Gregory, T. (2011) *A place for pride*. London: Demos.

Wirth, L. (1928) *The ghetto*. Chicago: University of Chicago Press.
Wirth, L. (1941) Morale and minority groups. *The American Journal of Sociology*, 47, 3: 415–433.
Wood, R. (1995) *Faith in action: Religion, race and the future of democracy*. PhD dissertation, University of California at Berkeley.
Ziller, R. and Lewis, D. (1981) Orientations: self, social, and environmental perception through auto-photography. *Personality and Social Psychology Bulletin, 7*, 2: 338–343.
Zipp, J. and Smith, J. (1979) The structure of electoral political participation. *American Journal of Sociology*, 85: 167–177.
Zusman, M., Knox, D. and Gardner, T. (2009) *The social context view of sociology*. Carolina Academic Press.

Website Links

http://www.islamonline.net/servlet/Satellite?c=Article_C&pagename=Zone-English-Living_Shariah%2FLSELayout&cid=1248188089986
http://news.bbc.co.uk/1/hi/2875555.stm
http://www.guardian.co.uk/world/2003/feb/17/politics.uk
Blogging: A new people's movement? by Michele Micheletti, 10, 19, 19 October 2006. Available at: http://www.politicsonline.com/netpulse/soundoff.asp?issue_id=10.19
Starbucks the target of Arab boycott for its growing links to Israel by Robert Fisk in Beirut, Friday, 14 June 2002. Available at: http://www.independent.co.uk/news/world/middle-east/starbucks-the-target-of-arab-boycott-for-its-growing-links-to-israel-749289.html
http://www.islamonline.net/servlet/Satellite?pagename=IslamOnline-English-Ask_Scholar%2FFatwaE%2 FFatwaEAskTheScholar&cid=1119503543874
http://www.islamonline.net/English/News/2002-11/14/article29.shtml

Index

Printed and bound by CPI Group (UK) Ltd, Croydon, CR0 4YY